MW01255829

THE KEYSTONE OF MORMONISM

THE KEYSTONE OF MORMONISM

ARZA EVANS

KEYSTONE BOOKS INC.

First edition
Printed in The United States of America

Published by: Keystone Books Inc.
P.O. Box 910717
St. George, Utah, 84791

Distributed by: BookMasters, Inc.
30 Amberwood Parkway
Ashland, Ohio 44805
419-281-1802
Fax: 419-281-6883
(Toll free 1-800-247-6553)

Publisher's Cataloging-in-Publication
(Provided by Quality Books, Inc.)

Evans, Arza.
The keystone of Mormonism / Arza Evans.
p. cm.
Includes bibliographical references and index.
LCCN 2003090773
ISBN 0-9728813-0-1

1. Book of Mormon--Evidences, authority, etc.
2. Book of Mormon--Criticism, interpretation, etc.
3. Church of Jesus Christ of Latter-day Saints--Doctrines.
4. Mormon Church--Doctrines. I. Title.

BX8627.E79 2003 289.3 22
QBI03-200217

TO:

NANCY RIGDON

SARAH PRATT

MARTHA BROTHERTON

JOSEPH SMITH, JR. 1805-1844

NOTE: All of the pictures in this book are used by permission of the Utah State Historical Society (all rights reserved) unless otherwise attributed.

CONTENTS

ILLUSTRATIONS

INTRODUCTION

> Do not be angry with me
> if I tell you the truth.
> - Socrates

This is a book that questions the authenticity of *The Book of Mormon* and the honesty of Joseph Smith, the founder of Mormonism. It is important that readers understand my qualifications and also my motivation to spend thousands of hours over a period of twenty years doing the difficult, often painful, and sometimes heartbreaking research necessary to write this book. The unusual nature of this book requires me to introduce myself.

The Author

I was born in a small copper-mining town in Southern Arizona during the great depression of the 1930s. I was named after Apostle Arza Alonzo Hinckley, uncle of L.D.S. Church President Gordon B. Hinckley. Both of my parents were members of polygamist families from the Mormon Colonies in Mexico. When the Mexican Civil War forced them to flee for their lives back across the border into Arizona, they lost almost everything. But one thing they had in abundance was religion.

My parents have always taken religion very seriously. My father left his new bride of a few days in order to go on a two year Church mission to Florida. (Please note: The term "Church," when capitalized, refers specifically to the Church of Jesus Christ of Latter-Day Saints.)

My father has served on stake presidencies, given thousands of patriarchal blessings, and served many years as a temple worker. He has also worked closely with L.D.S. Church President Spencer W. Kimball and other General Authorities on special assignments. We have had General Authorities in our home on several occasions. I think it would be safe to say that my father has done his very best to dedicate not only his own life but also the lives of his children and grandchildren to the Church. My mother has also held important Church callings and has been equally devoted to Mormonism.

As a very young child, I was told many stories about angels, Joseph Smith, gold plates, and pioneers. Some of my earliest memories include family prayer (both night and morning), singing a Mormon hymn before morning prayer, and fasting for two meals the first Sunday of every month. We paid tithing, fast offerings, and other Church contributions. We went to Church three or four times each week. This included Sacrament meetings, Priesthood and Relief Society meetings, Sunday School, Primary, M.I.A., firesides, and conferences. Sometimes it seemed that we were always in some kind of Church meeting.

I was taught who and what to pray for. I was told stories about members of our family who had suffered great hardships and persecution because of their loyalty to Mormonism. I was taught that our Church was the only Church on earth that had any priesthood authority to perform baptisms or any other ordinances acceptable to God and necessary for salvation or exaltation in the celestial kingdom.

We often made the long pilgrimage from Southern Arizona to Salt Lake City to attend general conference. We considered it a rare privilege to sit or even stand for hours in the crowded Tabernacle listening to Church leaders who were speaking for God. When I was eleven years old, my family moved to Murray, Utah, where we could be near a temple and closer to the center of the Church.

I was taught as a small child that the most important thing for any person to do in this life was to gain a "testimony" of Mormonism and then remain faithful to it forever. The worst sin that a person could commit wasn't lying, stealing, adultery, or even killing. It was **apostasy**! Other sins could be repented of and forgiven. *The Doctrine And Covenants*, clearly teaches that there will be no forgiveness in this life nor in the next for a man who receives the Melchizedek (higher) priesthood and then changes his mind and turns against Mormonism.[1] Apparently, conversion to Mormonism is supposed to be a one-way street.

My parents did, in fact, **belong** to the Church. It owned them, and they owned me. I trusted completely in the wisdom and honesty of my parents. It never occurred to me that they could be wrong or even partly wrong or misled. I was quite sure that any negative feelings or thoughts that I might have about the Church were only because I was young, immature, ignorant, weak, or perhaps even tempted by the Devil.

Church Authorities were doing the thinking for my parents who, in turn, were doing my thinking for me. I was never encouraged to do my own thinking nor to seek my own identity. Any of my thoughts or feelings that did not fit into the Church mold were irrelevant or, perhaps, even worse, a sign of rebelliousness or apostasy. I had very little confidence in my own mind or in my own feelings. The important thing was to think and feel the way I was supposed to think and feel. I grew up thoroughly programmed with Mormonism.

I was very active in the Church. I dropped out of college, sold my car, and used my entire savings in order to go on a two year Church mission to the Chicago area where I helped convert many people to Mormonism. It was a tough mission. I had my life threatened several times and came home with stomach ulcers. But I felt fortunate because I knew of others who had been sent to foreign missions who came home with diseases that most American doctors had never seen before. I served in several ward bishoprics, worked in an L.D.S. Temple, worked on welfare farms, and "magnified my callings" in many Church positions.

I learned some things in my academic work that could have caused me to ask some serious questions about Mormonism. But I had been so effectively programmed during my formative years that I simply rejected anything that somehow got as far as my **Mormon thought filter**.

I was eventually able to become a college professor while still switching off my critical thinking skills when it came to religion. This is not unusual. I know many L.D.S. scholars who are able to do this. They are not open-minded philosophers seeking truth. They already have the truth and are able to rationalize anything that comes into conflict with Mormonism.

I was about forty years old before I began to seriously question my Mormon indoctrination and programming. It is very ironic how this happened. I had decided to strengthen my faith and testimony by making a serious study of the foundations of Church history. With the honest intent of increasing my knowledge and my testimony of Mormonism, I spent thousands of hours doing research into Church history.

I read the seven volume *History of the Church* by Joseph Smith. Then I read the six volume *Comprehensive History of the Church* by B.H. Roberts. I read most of the twenty six volume *Journal of Discourses* containing the sermons of early Church leaders. Then I read books about the lives and teachings of Joseph Smith, Brigham Young, Heber C. Kimball, Orson Pratt, John Taylor, and other Church leaders. I also read *The Book of Mormon* for the tenth time.

The result of all this research was just the opposite of what I expected. As I read, I saw a great deal of deception, meanness, lust for power, and even criminal activity. I saw glaring contradictions and inconsistencies in Church doctrine. I began to realize that the "Church history" I had been taught in Sunday School and seminary was mostly sanitized, faith-promoting propaganda. This new perspective came mostly from reading Church publications, not from non-Mormon or anti-Mormon sources. I didn't start reading these until much later.

For the first time in my life I began to have serious doubts about the divine origin and mission of my Church. This was a very frightening experience for me! I did my best to hide my doubts from my family. I became a "**closet doubter**." For several years I continued my Church activity while denying even to myself the validity of what I was learning. Dreams die hard!

I didn't want to believe what I was finding out. It was too frightening and painful. It was pushing me out of my comfort zone and threatening my very identity. I desperately wanted to believe in the divine origin and destiny of the Church. It was comforting to believe in a loving Heavenly Father who is concerned enough with human affairs to communicate with this world through a series of latter-day prophets beginning with Joseph Smith. This gave me a warm and secure feeling.

It made me feel important and special to believe that despite the billions of people and thousands of religions on this earth, I was one of the few favored with the true religion and the divine authority to perform ordinances, give blessings, and even speak in the name of God. It gave my life a sense of purpose to be part of an organization that was working with God to save humanity.

Believing also gave me a sense of identity, a feeling of belonging. It created a common bond between me and my family. As a believer, I enjoyed the smiles, handshakes, and friendship of an entire community of believers. As a doubter, I would be isolated and alienated. The social pressure to believe -- or at least pretend to believe -- was almost overwhelming.

During these years as a closet doubter, the one thing that I couldn't bring myself to doubt or explain away, the last pillar of my faith, was *The Book of Mormon.* Then, however, as I began, for the first time in my life, to apply my critical thinking skills to this book, I could see overwhelming scientific evidence against its authenticity. This broke my heart. I felt profoundly betrayed by those I had trusted the most. I became torn between what I now sensed as the truth and my fear of what would happen to me if I told the truth. Would I lose my marriage, my job, and my friends? How would my children react? Would this destroy my aged parents and anger my brothers and my sister? Would I be excommunicated?

I was facing the greatest dilemma and trauma of my life. I was learning that religious freedom in America may be true for a community of believers but it may **not** be true for an individual within that group unless he or she is willing to pay a very high price.

After living several years as a closet doubter, I finally became inactive in the Church and started expressing a few of my doubts. My parents were upset and heartbroken. My brother informed me that I was possessed of a "lying spirit." I was not allowed to see my children married in an L.D.S. temple nor help bless my grandchildren. This hurt me very deeply. I became an embarrassment to my family. The pressure to deny all that I had learned and go back into the closet was almost overwhelming. But living a lie was too painful. I just couldn't go back.

Nearly every time I started to ask questions about Church history or doctrine, people immediately began to defend the Church by pointing out how much good it does. They didn't seem to understand that I wasn't questioning the fact that the L.D.S. Church does a lot of good in the world. It helps the poor, provides members with hope in an afterlife and faith in God, provides close social relationships and support groups, performs marriages, conducts funerals, teaches high moral values, provides activities for young people, helps people stay away from smoking, drinking, and drugs, and promotes a strong work ethic.

But these qualities do **not** make all of its claims and doctrines "true." Other churches perform many of these same functions. Of course, in fairness, despite the good that churches do, it is a fact that organized religion has also done a great amount of harm and left many casualties in this world. Perhaps more people have been persecuted, tortured, and killed in the name of God than for any other reason. And even now, ardent Moslems, Christians, Jews, and other religious fanatics are killing each other by the thousands in the name of God. Those men who flew airliners into The World Trade Center buildings in New York City are considered sacred martyrs in much of the Moslem world.

With the exception of two or three other college professors, I found very little understanding or sympathy for the struggle that I was having. I found myself increasingly isolated, alienated and unable to communicate with others. There does not seem to be any community or support group for doubters.

About this time, a close friend and colleague ask me to write down some of the things that I had found in my research. He wanted to show them to his mother who was very upset and heartbroken over his inactivity in the Church. Every time he went home for a visit she begged him to go back to Church, start paying his tithing, put his regulation garments back on, and start going to the temple again so that her entire family could be together in the celestial kingdom. She couldn't understand why her son no longer believed the indoctrination that she had so carefully given him.

I empathized with my friend's dilemma because my mother, even on her deathbed, made this very same request of me. I found this extremely painful. She wasn't asking for my time, my money, or my love which I would have willingly given. She was asking for my honor and integrity. I just couldn't do it. She was asking too much.

I'm sure that neither of these faithful Mormon mothers realized the pain that they were causing for their sons. These women had been programmed to act this way out of love for their children. They didn't realize that they were being used to control their families and to promote Church power.

At first, I started writing down a few things that I had learned, and then a few more, and then it seemed like a floodgate opened. My Mormon thought filter had developed some major leaks. Many things came into my mind that were new to me, things that I had never thought about before.

Soon, I was no longer writing for my friend or his mother, but for myself. For the first time in my life, I was beginning to discover who I was. I even started to believe that maybe it was all right to have my own thoughts and feelings even if they were unorthodox.

After many years of pretending, trying to please others, self deception, and playing the game, I found that honesty and self respect were good for my mental health. I also began to believe that writing a book might be a good way to communicate with my family and friends. Also, I thought, perhaps there are other men and women who, like my friend, would like to have something to help them articulate their questions and doubts. Many people have neither the time nor the resources to do their own research.

Priorities In Life

I have written this book for men and women who like to do their own thinking. However, when a person stands to lose her job, her marriage, and her friends, she may begin to believe that the price of truth is just too high. After all, why should a person be willing to sacrifice everything on the altar of truth? And should truth always take priority over other important values such as kindness, family unity, and social relationships? I have struggled with this dilemma for many years. It has not been an easy decision to make, but I have come to believe that truth is very, very important.

Ironically, the basic Mormon assumption that every man and every woman should be willing to sacrifice everything for the truth or else face eternal damnation helped me to make this difficult decision. Converts to Mormonism are expected to turn their backs on their former churches and also on their families and friends if necessary. If we accept this "truth over all" assumption, however, it only makes sense that a person should be willing to follow truth out of Mormonism as well as into Mormonism, if that is where it leads.

Even though truth sometimes comes at a very high price, it can also bring great rewards and compensations. There can be great exhilaration and excitement in being set free from one's programming and spiritual slavery. It is exciting to be able to consider something honestly without first asking whether it goes along with Mormonism. It becomes easier to respect others, especially those from other religious, cultural, and ethnic backgrounds when a person no longer sees them as misguided outsiders in need of conversion.

It also feels great to abandon the heavy burden of guilt created by the unreasonable expectations of Mormonism. An L.D.S.

person is expected to attend numerous Church meetings, pay tithing and other obligations, keep the word of wisdom, have and support a family, hold family home evenings and family prayer, go home teaching, do genealogy, attend the temple, do missionary work, accept all Church "callings," send children on missions, fast one day each month, and store a year's supply of food.

The list goes on and on and on. There are so many rules, duties, and responsibilities in Mormonism that it is almost impossible for any L.D.S. man or woman to escape feelings of unworthiness, guilt, and even depression. Very few Church members can live up to all of this.

But are all of these rules and requirements really part of the Gospel of Jesus Christ or are they a matter of Church power and security? I don't think Jesus taught all of these things. These requirements are not true Christianity. Perhaps it is easier to exploit and manipulate a person who has been indoctrinated, made to feel guilty, and then kept too busy for serious research and contemplation. It feels great to be set free from this burden of guilt!

It is also a welcome relief to no longer feel obligated to explain away or rationalize some of the teachings and behavior of Joseph Smith, Brigham Young, John Taylor and other Church leaders. On many occasions they contradicted themselves, other Church authorities, and even the Bible. They also broke many state and federal laws, and did a number of other things that were clearly immoral according to widely accepted standards of Christianity. Many examples of such teachings and behavior are well documented within the chapters of this book.

My Book Title

Joseph Smith, with characteristic arrogance, described his *Book of Mormon* as " . . . the most correct of any book on earth, and the keystone of our religion. . . [2]." He also made the critical importance of his book very clear when he said, "Take away *The Book of Mormon* and the revelations and where is our religion? We have none . . . [3]."

L.D.S. Church President Ezra Taft Benson said, "*The Book of Mormon* is the keystone of our religion. . . . Just as the arch crumbles if the keystone is removed, so does the Church stand or fall with the truthfulness of *The Book of Mormon*. . . . If it can be discredited, The Prophet Joseph Smith goes with it and so does the claim to priesthood keys, and revelation, and the restored Church. . . . Yes, my beloved brothers and sisters, *The Book of Mormon* is the keystone of our doctrine."[4]

B.H. Roberts' book, *The New Witness For God* says:

> While the coming forth of *The Book of Mormon* is but an incident in God's great work of the last days, . . . still the incident of its coming forth and the book are facts of such importance that the whole work of God may be said in a manner to stand or fall with them. That is to say, if the origin of *The Book of Mormon* could be proved to be other than set forth by Joseph Smith; if the book itself could be proved to be other than it claims to be, . . . then the Church of Jesus Christ of Latter-Day Saints, and its messages and doctrines, which in some respects may be said to have risen out of *The Book of Mormon*, must fall; for if that book is other than it claims to be; if its origin is other than that ascribed to it by Joseph Smith, then Joseph Smith says that which is untrue: he is a false prophet of false prophets; and all he taught and all his claims to inspiration and divine authority, are not only vain but wicked; and all that he did as a religious teacher is not only useless, but mischievous beyond human comprehending.[5]

The Challenge

Apostle Orson Pratt wrote a small book, *Divine Authenticity of The Book of Mormon*, that was widely used by early Church missionaries. This book contains the following challenge:

> **The nature of *The Book of Mormon* is such, that if true, no one can possibly be saved and reject it; if false, no one can possibly be saved and receive it.**

> **Therefore, every soul in all the world is equally interested in ascertaining its truth or falsity. . . . If after a rigid examination, it be found an imposition, it should be extensively published as such; the evidence and arguments on which the imposture was detected, should be clearly and logically stated, that those who have been sincerely yet unfortunately deceived may perceive the nature of the deception and be reclaimed, and that those who continue to publish the delusion, may be silenced.**

Since Joseph Smith, Ezra Taft Benson, B.H. Roberts, Orson Pratt, and other Church leaders are willing to stake the legitimacy of Mormonism upon the authenticity of *The Book of Mormon*, then a deep, concentrated, and scientific study of this book seems to be worth whatever time and effort it may take. I have taken these men up on this challenge in the following chapters.

Dedication Of This Book

I have dedicated this book to Nancy Rigdon, Sarah Pratt, and Martha Brotherton. These three honest, strong-willed, and virtuous women of Nauvoo, Illinois resisted the advances of Joseph Smith and Brigham Young. They refused to accept both polygamy and Smith's oath of secrecy. Smith required this oath because polygamy was against the law in Illinois and in most other states.

Both Mormon and non-Mormon historians have documented as many as fifty women who were married to Joseph Smith. Many of these women were still married to living husbands and several were just teenage girls.[6] Apparently the youngest of these teenagers was Helen Mar Kimball, the fourteen year old daughter of Apostle Heber C. Kimball. In front of her parents, Smith promised Helen, "If you will take this step, it will ensure your eternal salvation and exaltation and that . . . of your father's household and all of your kindred."[7] Thirty eight years later, Helen wrote in her autobiography, "I willingly gave myself to purchase so glorious a reward."[8]

Nancy Rigdon was the attractive and spirited nineteen year old daughter of Sidney Rigdon, First Counselor to Smith. But unlike

Helen Kimball, Nancy rejected Smith's prophetic promises and then refused to take an oath of secrecy about his attempt to seduce her. In other words, she refused to go along with Smith's standard operating procedure.

Nancy first started to cry, but when she saw that this did not alter Smith's intentions, she became frightened and angry. She threatened to scream until the whole town came to her rescue.[9]

After her traumatic encounter with Smith, Nancy went home and told her family everything. The next day a messenger brought Nancy a letter from Smith which included the following paragraph:

> Whatever God requires is right, no matter what it is, although we may not see the reason thereof until long after the events transpire. If we seek first the kingdom of God, all good things will be added. So with Solomon: first he asked wisdom, and God gave it him, and with it every desire of his heart; even things, which might be considered abominable to all who understand the order of Heaven only in part, but which in reality were right because God sanctioned them by special revelation.[10]

Apparently, Smith was saying that Solomon's hundreds of wives and concubines were a gift from God despite the fact that in his own *Book of Mormon*, Smith had quoted God as saying, "Behold, David and Solomon truly had many wives and concubines, which thing was abominable before me . . ."[11] This is but one example indicating that consistency was **not** important to Smith. Another example is that over a period of years, Smith recorded several very different accounts of his first vision in a grove of trees.[12] In one, he saw only an angel. In another, he saw only Jesus. In still another, he saw both the Father and the Son.

Smith's letter to Nancy provides an insight into his remarkable powers of rationalization and manipulation. If a person accepted Smith's assumption that "Whatever God requires is right, no matter what it is," along with the second assumption that Smith knew the mind and will of God and was speaking for God, then

Smith would indeed have unlimited power. **He would be a God unto his people!** If any man or woman didn't do whatever Smith asked them to do, even if considered immoral or illegal, they would be going against God at the jeopardy of their eternal souls!

As a matter of fact, on April 6, 1830, the day he organized his Church, Smith claimed to have just such a revelation directing Church members to consider his words as coming from God, thus making Smith a God unto his people:

> **. . . thou shalt give heed unto all his words and commandments which he shall give unto you . . . For his word ye shall receive as if from mine own mouth, in all patience and faith. (D.& C. 21:4,5)**

When Nancy's father and other family members learned of Nancy's experience and read Smith's letter they were furious. They sent for Smith at once. At first Smith denied the entire incident, but when confronted by Nancy and the letter, he admitted everything (that he had been lying when he denied the incident) but claimed that he was merely testing Nancy's virtue.[13]

This ploy was also part of Smith's standard procedure when caught in a lie. For example, after Zion's Camp, Smith's private army, failed to establish Zion in Missouri as promised by revelation, Smith said that the real purpose of this entire operation was **not** to redeem Zion as clearly stated in his revelation but to test the loyalty of his followers.[14]

Sarah Pratt, the wife of Apostle Orson Pratt, claimed that while her husband was away on a Church mission in England, Smith came to her home and said:

> "Sister Pratt, the Lord has given you to me as one of my spiritual wives. I have the blessings of Jacob granted me, as God granted holy men of old; and as I have long looked upon you with favor, and an earnest desire of connubial bliss, I hope you will not repulse or deny me."[15]

Never mind that Jesus said, "But I say unto you, That whosoever looketh on a woman to lust after her hath committed adultery with her already in his heart."[16] If Smith's "earnest desire for connubial bliss" with Orson Pratt's wife, Sarah, does not constitute adultery of the heart, then what does?

Sarah refused to allow Smith to stand proxy in the bedroom for her absent husband and also refused to be sworn to his oath of secrecy.

Several months later when her husband came home, Sarah told him everything. Smith denied having anything to do with Sarah. When Pratt chose to believe his wife, Smith accused Sarah of lying and Orson of apostasy. He excommunicated them both.

After apparently having a nervous breakdown and even contemplating suicide, a repentant and broken spirited Orson Pratt was re-baptized and even reinstated into Smith's Quorum of Twelve Apostles.[17] But Pratt lost his seniority in that quorum to Brigham Young who then became first in line to succeed Smith as the second President of the Church. Orson paid a high price for believing his wife and questioning Smith's honesty and supreme authority. But Pratt had learned his lesson about authoritarian government. After that, he became an obedient soldier for Smith and later for Brigham Young.

In 1842, Martha Brotherton, an attractive and high spirited eighteen year old convert from England came to Nauvoo anxious to meet the Prophet and join the saints in Zion. Her utopian dreams and her idealism were soon to be shattered. Brigham Young went to Joseph and asked for Martha. Martha was soon called to meet with Smith and Young. She felt greatly honored to be singled out for special attention by these two great men. But why were they taking such a special interest in her? Martha's account is as follows:

> Brigham Young said, "Brother Joseph has had a revelation from God that it is lawful and right for a man to have two wives. . . . if you will accept of me, I will take you straight to the celestial kingdom, and if you will have me in this world, I will have you in that which

> is to come, and brother Joseph will marry us here today, and you can go home this evening, and your parents will not know anything about it."
>
> When I declined this offer, Joseph Smith said, "He is the best man in the world, except me. If you will accept Brigham you shall be blessed. God shall bless you, and my blessing shall rest upon you . . . and if you don't like it in a month or two, come to me, and I will make you free again; and if he turns you off, I will take you on."[18]

This incident speaks volumes. Smith and later Young, in his Great Basin Kingdom, believed that they **owned** all Mormon women and could give them to any man or take them away as they pleased, as a reward for faithful service or punishment for apostasy. This policy is well documented in some of the later chapters of this book.

Smith and Young wanted Martha to join their world of secret oaths and deception. They encouraged her to deceive her own parents. They tried to put Martha into a position where she would be forced to lie in order to keep her oath of secrecy about polygamy. She would also have been forced to lie, later on, about her pregnancy and the fact that Brigham Young was the father of her child. "What a tangled web we weave, when first we practice to deceive" !

Martha refused to be coerced and intimidated even by these two powerful men. Eighteen year old Martha, tearfully asked for permission to go home. She not only told her parents everything but wrote down the entire episode while it was still fresh on her mind.

After telling others in Nauvoo about this incident, Martha and her disillusioned parents took a steamboat to St. Louis where Martha published her account in a St. Louis newspaper.[19] This caused such a scandal that in the next Church conference, Joseph and Hyrum stood up and denied that any Church leaders had more than one wife. Martha was called a liar, an apostate, and a harlot. Smith had control of both the pulpit and the media in Nauvoo. He could destroy the reputation of anyone who went against him, and he often used this power.[20]

By now, quite a few men and women in Nauvoo knew that polygamy was a fact of life among the Mormons and that Church leaders who denied this were lying. But almost everyone honored their oaths of secrecy, kept silent, and became accessories to the lies of their leaders.

Unfortunately for the Church, Martha also wrote letters back home to England telling her friends about what had happened to her in Nauvoo. This caused serious problems for Apostle Parley Pratt and other missionaries in England.

Church leaders acted quickly. The August 1842 edition of *The Millennial Star*, a Mormon Church newspaper, edited and published by Apostle Pratt for the saints in England contained the following editorial under the general title "Apostasy."

> Among the most conspicuous of these apostates, we would notice a young female who emigrated from Manchester in September last, and after conducting herself in a manner unworthy the character of one professing godliness, at length conceived the plan of gaining friend-ship and extraordinary notoriety with the world, or rather with the enemies of truth, by striking a blow at the character of some of its worthiest champions. She well knew that this would be received as a sweet morsel by her old friends, the Methodists, and other enemies of the Saints. She accordingly selected President J. Smith and Elder B. Young for her victims, and wrote to England that these men had been trying to seduce her, by making her believe that God had given a revelation that men might have two wives; by these disreputable means she thought to overthrow the Saints here, or at least bring a storm of persecution on them and prevent others from joining them; but in this thing she was completely deceived by Satan. . . .
>
> But, for the information of those who may be assailed by those foolish tales about two wives, we would say that no such principle ever existed among the Latter-Day Saints, and never will; this is well known to all who are acquainted with our books and actions. *The*

> *Book of Mormon, Doctrine and Covenants*; and also our periodicals are very strict and explicit on that subject, indeed far more so than the Bible.[21]

Apostle Pratt was lying. The young female from Manchester (Martha Brotherton) was telling the truth. Smith had taught the Apostles, including Pratt, "the principle" in 1841, a year before Pratt published this deceptive editorial.[22] By August of 1842 when this "apostate" wrote to her friends and relatives in Manchester, Joseph Smith, Brigham Young, and other Church leaders were living polygamy just as Martha claimed they were. But very few Church members would take the word of an obscure eighteen year old girl against that of such distinguished and powerful men.

I am honored to dedicate this book to these three honest, courageous, and virtuous women who stood firm for their convictions even under overwhelming pressures. Someday, I hope to meet Nancy Rigdon, Sarah Pratt, and Martha Brotherton. I would like to congratulate these three “apostate” women in person.

The Power Of Mormonism

I honestly believe that The Church of Jesus Christ of Latter-Day Saints is so large, powerful, and wealthy that it may be impossible for anyone or anything to even slow it down. I believe that most of the dynamic power of Mormonism comes from its strong appeal to **human nature**. It offers security and certainty in a frightening universe of ambivalence, uncertainty, and apparent randomness. It gives people a meaningful life, a chance to be part of a great movement destined to change the world.

Mormonism makes people feel chosen and special. It provides identity and community. A Church member can travel all over America and also in many foreign countries and find almost instant bonding and friendship with other Church members who share their world view.

Mormonism’s appeal to human nature also includes strong family bonds. The L.D.S. Church tells its members, and anyone else who will listen, that "families can be together forever." But they claim that these eternal family relationships can only happen through the exclusive priesthood authority of the L.D.S. Church! Mormons have a monopoly on this sealing power. Catholic, Methodist, Baptist, Jewish, Moslem, Buddhist, and Hindu marriages and family relationships are over when a person dies unless that person accepts Mormonism in the next world. And even then, they may have to stay single and separate for thousands of years until someone on Earth finds their records, does their genealogy, and has them sealed in a Mormon Temple. It seems to me, that in order to sanction this Mormon doctrine, God would have to be very unjust.

The L.D.S. Church offers many economic advantages for its members. It provides contacts for salesmen and businessmen. It provides clients for dentists, doctors, lawyers, and other professional people. It provides jobs for thousands of faithful recommend holders in Church offices, at B.Y.U., teaching seminary and institute classes, and in all kinds of other employment. It also provides financial help for members in need of welfare assistance.

The economic, emotional, spiritual, psychological, and sociological appeal of Mormonism is very powerful, indeed. But all of these benefits do **not** make its doctrine nor the claims that it makes about exclusive priesthood authority true.

Smith's Book

Now that I have introduced myself and my book, I would like to make a very brief introduction to *The Book of Mormon* itself for the benefit of readers not familiar with this controversial publication.

The original *Book of Mormon* was a 588 page book self-published by Joseph Smith in Palmyra, New York, in 1830. Smith listed himself as the author but claimed to have translated his book from reformed Egyptian hieroglyphics engraved upon some gold plates that he found buried in a hill near his home.

Smith's book is primarily the history of two Israelite families who were warned by the Lord to leave Jerusalem about 600 B.C. They were instructed by the Lord how to build a ship and how to sail to their "promised land" (America). Once there, they divided into two groups, the Nephites (nee-fights), followers of Nephi, and the

Lamanites (lay-mon-ites), followers of Laman. Nephi and his followers were favored of the Lord, while Laman and his rebellious followers were cursed by the Lord with a dark skin.

There was hatred and constant warfare between these two groups, eventually ending with the extermination of the Nephites about 400 A.D. This explains why Columbus found only dark skinned Native Americans when he came to the New World about eleven hundred years later. This is why Latter-Day Saints have always referred to Native Americans as "Lamanites."

During this one thousand year history, the Nephites were favored with prophets who received revelations, visions, and direct communication with God. This divine communication even included a visit by the resurrected Jesus Christ who came to America, blessed the people, and organized His church.

Nephite prophets recorded many of their experiences on gold plates which were hidden away in a hill near the home of Joseph Smith in Palmyra, New York. Thus, Latter-Day Saints consider their *Book of Mormon* to be a sacred scripture superior to the Bible since it was not translated by a group of men, possibly arguing with each other, but by a true prophet through the gift and power of God.

Since its publication in 1830, *The Book of Mormon* has gone through many revisions and editions. Millions of copies of this book have been sold or given away by Church members and missionaries all over the world.

The Fallacy Of Feelings

Unfortunately, many people believe that they can always discern truth from error and good from evil by how they feel when they hear or read something. But it is only human nature to feel bad or even become angry when one's long cherished beliefs are challenged. However, that does not mean that the new ideas are wrong or from an evil source. Sometimes a person becomes all excited and feels good about something that will later prove to bring great sadness and pain. **Feelings are not always a reliable way to make judgements.** I sincerely hope that my readers will be open minded and rely more upon reason than upon feelings.

A Personal Comment

Before continuing, perhaps I should reassure readers that I have no desire to self-destruct, offend God, or lose my soul. I am just a person who is trying to find the truth, tell the truth, and document my sources of information. I have no hidden agenda or ulterior motives. I see no possibility of becoming rich or famous. In fact, just the opposite seems evident. I have already paid a very high price for my work and expect to pay a great deal more.

When some of my relatives and friends have found out about my book questioning the authenticity of *The Book of Mormon* and the honesty of Joseph Smith, almost all of them have strongly advised against writing or publishing it. These friends and relatives are well meaning. They are concerned about what might happen to me and, in some cases, to them. I hope that nothing bad happens to any of them since I, alone, am responsible for the contents of this book. I have even typed and retyped every word of it, myself. However, I would like to express my gratitude to those few who have given me valuable suggestions and much needed encouragement. But to mention their names may cause some of them trouble in their professional careers and also serious problems with their families.

And finally, this book is intended to help any Church member who has become disillusioned with Mormonism. You are not alone. Thousands of other intelligent people share your questions and doubts and also your feelings of betrayal and entrapment.

Disclaimer

Before we begin chapter one, perhaps L.D.S. readers should be warned that once a person has been exposed to new ideas and a new perspective, it is not easy to ever go back and become the same person again. I now cordially invite readers to come with me on a very important and exciting journey, a search for the truth about the authenticity of *The Book of Mormon* and the honesty of Joseph Smith. We will begin our adventure with *Book of Mormon* claims about the law of Moses and Christianity. Welcome aboard.

Arza Evans

Chapter 1

THE LAW OF MOSES AND CHRISTIANITY

> And ye shall know the truth,
> and the truth shall set you free.
> - Jesus Christ

The Book of Mormon begins with Lehi, a Hebrew Prophet, leaving an unrepentant Jerusalem about 600 B.C. After escaping into the wilderness, Lehi sent his four sons on a dangerous mission back to Jerusalem in order to obtain some brass plates in the possession of an evil tyrant, Laban. Lehi explained to his sons that these plates were extremely important because they contained his genealogy, the record of the Jews, and the law of Moses.[1]

After two attempts by the young men, including a large bribe, failed to secure the plates, Nephi, one of Lehi's sons, was commanded by an angel to kill Laban because, "It is better that one man should perish than that a nation should dwindle and perish in unbelief."[2] Nephi then explains why the angel commanded him to kill Laban:

> And now, when I, Nephi had heard these words, I remembered the words of the Lord which he spake unto me in the wilderness, saying that: inasmuch as thy seed shall keep my commandments, they shall prosper in the land of promise. Yea, and I also thought that they could not keep the commandments of the Lord according to the law of Moses, save they should have the law. And I also knew that the law was engraven

> upon the plates of brass. . . . Therefore I did obey the voice of the Spirit, and took Laban by the hair of the head and smote off his head with his own sword.[3]

After killing Laban, Nephi and his brothers took Laban's plates, his sword, and also Laban's servant, Zoram, down to their father's camp by the Red Sea.

The Law Of Moses Ignored

Despite the danger and difficulty in obtaining these plates and the burden of carrying them across one of the world's most dangerous deserts and even across an ocean, Lehi and his descendants didn't seem to care about the law of Moses. Although claiming to be "strictly" living this law, they largely ignored it.[4] For example, there is no record of anyone ever observing the Passover. It isn't even mentioned in *The Book of Mormon*. The Feast of the Tabernacles isn't mentioned either. There is nothing said about scapegoats, sabbatical years, jubilees, thank offerings, tabernacles, unleavened bread, ephods, usury, purification, circumcision, idolatry, witchcraft, sorcery, or unclean animals.

It seems strange that Joseph Smith would claim that his Nephites were strictly living the law of Moses while at the same time ignoring nearly all of the customs and rituals that were so important to Moses and the Israelites.

Another problem in Smith's book is that the Nephites and Lamanites were from the tribe of Joseph.[5] But where were the Levites who alone were given the authority by the Lord and by Moses to function in the priests' office?

Polygamy Condemned

Another serious problem in Smith's book is that the Mosaic law accepted polygamy and even commanded it in a few cases. For example, if a man died leaving no children, his brother, even if already married, was commanded to take his brother's widow and raise up children unto his dead brother.[6]

Moses, himself, had at least two wives.[7] And yet, *Book of Mormon* prophets condemned polygamy on five different occasions.[8] They made **no exceptions**, even when great civil wars left thousands of widows alone in the world. Once again, Smith and his *Book of Mormon* prophets are clearly in conflict with the Bible and the law of Moses.

No Circumcision

A major concern for the descendants of Abraham, Isaac, and Jacob has always been the covenant of circumcision. The law of Moses was very strict about this ordinance. It was also the cause of considerable controversy for the Apostle Paul and his "gentile" converts to Christianity. However, circumcision is never even mentioned in *The Book of Mormon.* And yet, Nephi informs us that his people "did observe to keep the judgments and the statutes and commandments of the Lord in all things according to the law of Moses."[9]

Isn't it reasonable for a person to ask why a group of Israelites who migrated to America about 600 B.C. had so little concern for their own religion and culture? And why did these people claim to be strictly living the law of Moses while at the same time ignoring it? Perhaps Nephi didn't need to kill Laban to get the brass plates after all! The answer to all of these contradictions seems obvious. Smith made some very serious mistakes when writing his book.

Christianity In Ancient America

The Book of Mormon describes the coming of the resurrected Christ to ancient America.[10] It explains how Jesus taught His gospel and organized His church in the New World. Almost all of the Nephites and Lamanites eventually became converted to Christianity.

This is a very heartwarming and faith promoting story, but it contradicts the findings of archaeologists, anthropologists and historians. Scientists have not been able to find evidence of anything even remotely resembling Christianity in ancient America. The religions of these people included all sorts of gods, spirits, rituals, magical incantations, spells, tributes, and even human sacrifices.

They had gods of the underworld, rain, thunder, wind, earth, harvest, sun, puberty, fertility, sickness, and death. Hallucinogens made from peyote cactus, mescal beans, mushrooms, the sophora bush, and a large variety of other psychotropic plants found in the tropical flora were an important part of the ancient American spiritual experience.[11]

Perhaps the most important god of the Mayas was the Jaguar. Paintings, tapestries, and statues of the Jaguar have been found all over Central America. Another god, the Jester, was the special patron of royalty. Gods of the underworld were greatly feared. The Mayas were also deeply involved in ancestor worship. Mayan mythology, like Greek mythology, was filled with a pantheon of different gods.[12]

Aztec worship included the twin gods Quetzalcoatl (plumed serpent) and Tezcatlipoca (smoking mirror). These gods demanded the sacrifice of human blood and still beating hearts in exchange for light, warmth, corn, and other foods. Huitzilopochtli, the Aztec god of the sun and war required the sacrifice of captured enemy warriors.[13] Some of these religious traditions existed in the Americas long before the Christian era and yet no mention of them is made in *The Book of Mormon.* Apparently Smith didn't know anything about them.

A Christian Calendar

The Book of Mormon also claims that once the sign was given for the birth of Christ, ancient Americans began to reckon their time the same as Christians living in the Old World.[14] Events were depicted as happening a certain amount of time before or after the birth of Christ. Although ancient Americans developed some very complex and accurate calendars, the birth of Christ did not influence the time-keeping of the Aztecs, Mayans, Incas, Toltecs or any other ancient American civilization.

Overwhelming scientific evidence refutes *Book of Mormon* claims that ancient Americans were Israelites who became converted to Christianity. And there is absolutely no evidence that ancient American calendars had anything to do with the birth of Christ. The findings of archaeologists, anthropologists, geologists, and historians clearly refute the story telling of Joseph Smith.

Chapter 2

TALL TALES, A FANTASY WORLD

> Truth is such a precious commodity, let's keep its use to a minimum.
>
> - Mark Twain

Many of the stories in *The Book of Mormon* are far-fetched and fantastic. Nephi starts out by saying that he is writing the history of his people in "the language of the Egyptians."[1] This is very strange, indeed. The Israelites considered Hebrew to be sacred, the language of God. It would have been unthinkable for an Israelite to write sacred scriptures in the obscene language of Egyptian idol worshipers as claimed by Smith.

Sacred Hieroglyphics ?

Nephi told his brothers that one of the reasons that they needed to obtain the brass plates of Laban was "that we may preserve unto our children the language of our fathers."[2] If the brass plates were inscribed in Hebrew, then why didn't Nephi continue this tradition by writing his family record in Hebrew, his own language and that of his fathers, instead of "reformed Egyptian" as claimed by Smith.[3]

The entire cultural orientation of the Egyptians was so different from the Israelites that it would have been impossible for Nephi to express many aspects of the complex Hebrew culture and the law of Moses in the hieroglyphic (picture) language of the Egyptians. Why would Nephi set out to do the unthinkable and the impossible, write his sacred record in a pagan language?

Amazing Travelers

Nephi said that his family left Jerusalem with their "tents and provisions" and traveled into the wilderness for three days. They camped by the Red Sea right next to a river flowing into the sea. Lehi named this river after his oldest son, Laman.[4] But there is no such river, and they couldn't possibly have traveled the 170 miles from Jerusalem to the Red Sea **in just three days**. I have hiked in this area. It includes the Grand Canyon of the Middle East and some of the most rugged and desolate terrain in the entire world. It would have been very difficult for Lehi's family to travel more than just a few miles a day even without carrying their heavy "tents and provisions." And yet, Smith has these men, women, and children traveling almost sixty miles a day! This is incredible.

Imaginary Geography

The Gulf of Aqaba on the Red Sea is one of the oldest inhabited areas on earth. If there had been a river flowing into the Red Sea at this point, there would probably have been a major city located there, just as there was where the Tigris and Euphrates Rivers flowed into the Persian Gulf. The River Laman has never existed except in the fertile imagination of Joseph Smith.

A Fantastic Murder

Another part of *The Book of Mormon* that is not easy to believe is the killing of Laban incident.[5] Do powerful and paranoid tyrants like Laban go wandering around at night in the dark streets of Jerusalem alone, without their bodyguards? And how did Nephi keep from getting blood all over himself and Laban's clothing when he ". . . took Laban by the hair of his head, and smote off his head with his own sword."[6] Perhaps Nephi took Laban's clothes off first, but there remains the problem of cleaning things up before approaching Laban's most trusted servant, Zoram, while wearing the dead man's clothing.

And how could this have happened without any witnesses? Where did everybody go? And is it likely that Laban's clothing would have fit Nephi? Were they the same size and stature despite differences in age and lifestyle? And how did Nephi disguise his face and his voice well enough to fool Zoram, one of Laban's closest and most trusted servants? And does it make sense that Zoram would switch his loyalty from Laban to the assassin, Nephi, in a matter of minutes? The entire incident is implausible and ridiculous, a product of Smith's boundless imagination.

Dangerous Desert Travel

Taking their tents, provisions, and seeds of every kind, Lehi's family crossed the "River Laban" and continued along the east coast of the Red Sea. Lehi then turned east, apparently crossing about 400 miles of arid mountain ranges and almost 1000 miles of the great Rub al Khali Desert of Saudi Arabia, over which even the most desert-wise Bedouins are reluctant to travel.

There is no mention of camels or horses. How did Lehi and his family carry their heavy tents, their brass ball, Laban's brass plates, and enough food, water, and other provisions to last them the "eight years" they would spend in this desert?[7] Did they carry all of their provisions on their backs? And why did they spend eight years in a dangerous desert that anyone else would have avoided or else tried to cross as quickly as possible?

Nephi said that his people lived upon raw meat during this period of time.[8] But where did they get raw meat? *The Book of Mormon* makes the great Rub al Khali Desert of Saudi Arabia sound like a game preserve. A desert-wise Bedouin would find Nephi's desert crossing story ridiculous, even laughable.

A Magical Ball

The story about the "ball of curious workmanship . . . of fine brass" is not easy to believe either. This magic ball just appeared out of nowhere in front of Lehi's tent one morning to the great astonishment of Lehi and his family. This ball or "director" had two spindles which "pointed whither we should go into the wilderness."

This magic ball was also capable of intelligent communication through written messages which changed from time to time.[9]

Where in all of the scriptures do we read of such a thing as this? Did Moses have a magic ball to guide him in the wilderness? Do prophets of God gaze into crystal balls, or does this sound more like Gypsy fortune tellers, glass lookers, and other practitioners of the occult?

Is it just a coincidence that both Mormon and non-Mormon historians have documented the fact that Joseph Smith was a practitioner of the occult? Court records indicate that Smith was arrested and convicted as a "glass looker" in New York in 1826."[10]

Nephi's Steel Bow

Next we read that Lehi's family nearly starved to death in the wilderness when Nephi broke his steel bow.[11] This brings up several important questions such as where did Nephi get a bow made out of "fine steel" in 600 B.C.? At this time, iron was a rather new development in human history, and only primitive methods of carbonation into steel had been developed.[12]

Spring steel, the kind necessary to make a bow, requires complex technology that would not be introduced for several centuries. It is very difficult to make steel that combines the properties of strength and flexibility. And even if Nephi could have somehow come up with a steel bow, why didn't his father and his brothers have steel bows too? Why was Nephi the only one who had one? And if Nephi left Jerusalem with a steel bow about 600 B. C., why doesn't the Bible say anything about steel bows at that time? It seems that Nephi was the only person in the entire world who had a bow made out of "fine steel."

Bountiful

Then another incredible thing happened to Lehi and his family. They found themselves in a land with "much fruit" and "wild honey." Lehi named this place "Bountiful."[13] Strangely, this fertile area on the Persian Gulf, just south of Babylonia, the cradle of civilization, was uninhabited! Why hadn't anyone ever discovered this remarkable Garden of Eden? Bountiful also happened to have iron ore, coal, tar, timber, and all of the other things that Nephi would need to make tools and construct a ship that could sail half way around the world.[14]

Amazing Builders

After arriving in their promised land (America), Nephi, Sam, Zoram, Joseph, and Jacob (five men):

> . . . did build a temple and did construct it after the manner of the temple of Solomon save it were not built of so many precious things; for they were not to be found upon the land, wherefore, it could not be built like unto Solomon's temple. But the manner of construction was like unto the temple of Solomon; and the workmanship thereof was exceeding fine.[15]

When Nephi wrote these words, he had been gone from Jerusalem about thirty years.[16] Since Lehi's family had "sojourned" eight years in the wilderness and had taken a few years to build their ship and travel half way around the world, they had been in the promised land less than twenty years. Already, Nephi and his small band of followers had buried their father Lehi, fought with the Lamanites, moved to a new location, built new homes, planted and harvested crops, mined and smelted ore, made tools, made many swords "after the manner of Laban's," inscribed their history on two sets of plates, took care of the needs of their families, and, in their spare time, built a temple "like unto the Temple of Solomon."[17]

The Bible informs us that Solomon contracted with Hyrum of Tyre and his expert masons to build his temple. It took over 150,000 laborers and 3,300 skilled supervisors seven years to complete this project.[18] And yet, Joseph Smith expects us to be gullible enough to believe that five men did the job in their spare time in less than twenty years!

An Unbelievable Disappearance Act

Still another incredible incident takes place when the Nephite King Limhi and thousands of his followers got their Lamanite guards drunk and then gathered together all of their "flocks and herds" and their "gold and silver" in one night and escaped through Lamanite territory so rapidly that their Lamanite pursuers, who were **not** hampered with women, children, flocks, herds, and other possessions, were unable to catch them.

The Lamanites couldn't find any trace of this large Nephite migration. Thousands of people along with their flocks and herds just disappeared without leaving any tracks! And then to make matters worse, the stupid, bungling, Lamanites couldn't even follow their own tracks back home. They got lost in the wilderness![19]

Successful Seducers

Next, we are asked to believe Smith's story about 24 young and beautiful Lamanite maidens who were kidnapped by the lecherous Nephite priests of King Noah. These young, unprotected girls were just out in the wilderness dancing and having some fun when they were kidnapped and forced into sexual relationships with their abductors. And yet, despite the fact that they had been taught an "eternal hatred" for the Nephites, these young girls forgot about their ethnic hatred, forgot their parents, forgot their boyfriends back home, forgot about being kidnapped and raped, and fell in love with their captors!

When their parents finally found them, these Lamanite girls expressed great love for their Nephite kidnappers and convinced their parents to accept their new sons-in-law. The Lamanite leaders then somehow forgot centuries of racial and ethnic hatred and put these Nephite kidnappers and rapists into positions of great power and authority in their Lamanite government. They also appointed them teachers throughout the land, to teach all of their children the culture and values of the hated Nephites![20]

Nephite Superman

Another tall tale in Smith's *Book of Mormon* is about Ammon, one of the sons of King Mosiah, who refused the kingdom in order to become a missionary to the Lamanites. After becoming a servant to the Lamanite king, Lamoni, Ammon single-handedly cut off the arms of a large number of thieves who had come to steal the king's livestock. Then Ammon took care of the king's horses and chariots. (Never mind that scientists tell us that early Americans did not have horses, wheels, or chariots).

King Lamoni began to think that Ammon was some kind of god. Both Lamoni and his wife then went into a trance, became converted while in the trance, and then proceeded to convert a large number of their fellow Lamanites to Ammon's religion.[21] Joseph Smith was a great believer in visions, dreams, trances, and mass conversions.

An Indestructible Army

Another far-fetched story relates to the "Sons of Helaman." It is not easy to believe that two thousand young men could engage in hand-to-hand combat against battle-hardened Lamanite warriors over a long period of time without losing a single man![22] When has this ever happened before even among God's chosen people in the Bible? This is not real history. It's simply one more fictional superman story coming from Smith's imagination.

Amazing Submarines

Another story in *The Book of Mormon* that insults the reader's intelligence is the episode of the Jaredites. Jared, his brother and their twenty-two friends, along with their wives and children, were saved by the Lord from having their language confounded at the time of the Great Tower of Babel (about 2000 B.C.).

The brother of Jared prayed unto the Lord and was commanded to build eight small submarines and to collect flocks and herds, male and female of every kind, and prepare for an ocean voyage to the promised land (America).[23] The Lord then said to the brother of Jared:

> What will ye that I should do that ye may have light in your vessels. For behold, ye cannot have windows for they shall be dashed in pieces; neither shall ye take fire with you for ye shall not go by the light of fire.[24]

It is ludicrous to suggest that the Lord would even bring up the possibility of building a fire inside of an airtight submarine! The comment about glass windows which could be “dashed in pieces” also shows the ignorance of the author. This incident supposedly took place almost 2000 years before the Romans finally developed small pieces of flat glass and almost 3,700 years before clear, flat, window glass that could be “dashed in pieces” was developed![25]

Smith claims that the Lord eventually solved the submarine lighting problem by touching sixteen stones (two for each vessel) causing the stones to glow brightly enough to light the submarines.

Joseph Smith's description of the eight submarines built by the Jaredites includes the following:

> And they were small, and they were light upon the water, even like unto the lightness of a fowl upon the water. And they were built after a manner that they were exceedingly tight, even that they would hold water like unto a dish; and the bottom thereof was tight like unto a dish; and the sides were tight like unto a dish; and the ends were peaked; and the top thereof was tight like unto a dish; and the length thereof was the length of a tree; and the door thereof when it was shut, was tight like unto a dish.[26]

Even though these vessels were light upon the water, they were at times submerged "as a whale" and often "buried in the depths of the sea." It seems strange that some light, air-tight vessels could sink down into the depths of the sea or that if they were heavy enough to sink, they could then rise to the surface of the ocean again. These strange Jaredite submarines didn't need strong steel hulls, compressors, pumps, valves, or even a dependable air supply.

The story goes on to say that the Jaredites gathered together their "flocks and herds, male and female of every kind" and then somehow loaded them into their submarines for the long journey to the promised land. But how could they have taken flocks and herds when a single cow eats about one half of a bale of hay and drinks about ten gallons of water each day. When multiplied by the 344 days that the Jaredites were at sea, this would amount to about six tons of hay and over 3000 gallons of fresh water for **just one cow**!

This much loose hay and fresh water couldn't possibly have been loaded onto one of these "small" vessels. And yet the Jaredites did not take just one or even two animals of "every kind" but "flocks" and "herds." They also took swarms of bees and even an aquarium of fish![27]

It is not clear what the reference to male and female animals of "every kind" means, but later in his book Joseph Smith refers to **elephants** as being very useful to the Jaredites.[28] Just imagine the food and water they would have needed for their elephants! And how did they get elephants and herds of other animals through a small "stoppable" hole and into their submarines?

And besides all of these animals, the Jaredites had to have enough room on their eight "small" vessels for twenty-two men along with their wives and children. This could have amounted to over one hundred people along with the food, fresh water, and other provisions they would have needed for 344 days at sea![29]

A Death Trap

It would have been very difficult if not impossible to cook anything or to take a bath on one of these small submarines. And what about human and animal needs for sunlight and fresh air? There was a small stoppable hole in the top and also in the bottom of each vessel, but these stoppable holes were often of no use because they were "many times buried in the depth of the sea."

How could anyone survive being cooped up in one of these air-tight underwater stockyards for 344 days? And what about the filth and stench from animal and human excrement? **Even one day in such an environment would have been intolerable and probably fatal**!

These Jaredite "barges" had no sails and were under the water much of the time. And yet, they were driven by "fierce winds." These "fierce winds" somehow managed to blow the Jaredites half way around the world and to keep all eight barges **together** for almost an entire year!

A sea captain would not believe this nonsense. Smith's story about airtight wind powered submarines, glowing stones, underwater stockyards, and promised lands is ridiculous. It is **not** authentic history. How can true believers blame doubters for asking serious questions about such fantastic tales?

Steel Swords In 1900 B.C.

Adding to the incredibility of the Jaredite story is what happened after they arrived in their "promised land." Shule, a Jaredite prince made swords of steel for all of those who would follow him. He used these steel swords to take the kingdom away from his brother, Corihor.[30]

The problem is that all of this happened about 1900 B.C., some 700 years before the earliest record of iron smelting took place in the Old World![31] How did Shule come to have steel in 1900 B.C. when nobody else would have any for about 1000 years? And why has no one ever found the remains of a steel sword or any kind of iron in the ruins of ancient America? Did all of their iron and steel just disappear? Scientists tell us that early Americans did not have any iron or steel. (see chapter 7)

Civil Genocide

After several centuries of civil wars among the Jaredites, Smith says that a battle of complete extermination took place on the hill Ramah. This war continued until only two mighty men (Shiz and Coriantumr) were left to fight. Coriantumr killed Shiz and became the lone survivor out of millions of people! When has this ever happened before in world history?

A similar story of the complete extermination of the Nephites several centuries later and on **that very same hill** is not easy to believe either. And what were all of the Nephites doing upon the Hill Ramah (Cumorah), in Western New York, conveniently right next door to young Joseph Smith's house and thousands of miles from Central America where supposedly they had built their great cities? Does any of this make sense?

Great Natural Disasters

Another part of *The Book of Mormon* that is not easy to believe is the account in 3 Nephi about the great earthquakes and other natural disasters that took place at the time of the crucifixion of Christ. This account says, "And thus the face of the whole earth became deformed . . . there was thick darkness upon the land . . . for the space of three days."[32]

Where is the geological evidence that great changes took place in the American landscape as recently as 2,000 years ago? And where is the historical evidence of three days of darkness?

Could these three days of darkness have been confined to the New World, or wouldn't this much volcanic dust, or whatever caused the darkness, have darkened the entire earth? Also, if the entire earth had become deformed, as Smith claims, wouldn't this have been an event important enough for comment by Old World prophets and historians?

Three of the gospels mention darkness from the sixth until the ninth hour at the time of the crucifixion. Matthew mentions an earthquake, but there is no record of the destruction of cities, or "deformity" of the entire earth, nor of three days of darkness. Where is the historical or archeological evidence supporting Smith's claims?

God's Conquistadors

Nephi further informs us that no one will come to America unless brought here by the hand of God.[33] Cortez and other European conquistadors came to the New World and gave the natives a simple choice: conversion to their version of "Christianity" or death. After killing a large number of Native Americans, these "missionaries" firmly established the Roman Catholic Church in Mexico and South America. Today, over one half of the world's Roman Catholics live in North and South America.

Did God bring Cortez and other conquistadors over to the Americas to plunder, rape, kill, and force native Americans to accept their version of Christianity? Did the Lord bring the Italian Mafia to

His promised land? Was the hand of God behind the cruel slave trade that brought millions of Africans to America against their will?

The discovery of the New World by the "gentiles" as prophesied in 1 Nephi chapter 13 pertains almost entirely to Columbus and to the original British Colonies. Other important explorers, conquerors, and colonizers are completely ignored. For example, the Spanish explored and colonized Mexico, Central and South America, Cuba, Florida, and California. The French explored and colonized most of Canada and the large area covered by the drainage into the Ohio, Missouri, and Mississippi Rivers. This included territory all the way from Canada down to New Orleans.

The Portuguese colonized the Amazon drainage area and the east coast of South America. Russia colonized Alaska and the west coast of Canada. Why is all of this ignored by *Book of Mormon* prophesies about the colonization of America? Obviously, Smith's book reflected his ignorance about American history.

Piety - Prosperity Theory

Another part of *The Book of Mormon* that is difficult to believe is Smith's piety-prosperity theory. This theme is repeated over and over again throughout the entire book. This doctrine states that those who are righteous will "prosper in the land" and become wealthy, and those who do not obey the commandments of God will not only be cut off spiritually but will also become economic failures.[34]

This piety-prosperity theory sharply contradicts the Biblical view that evil powers are in control of this world and its wealth, and that only dramatic intervention from God can alter the normal situation where the wicked prosper and the righteous suffer.

In fact, a major theme of the Book of Job is to demonstrate the absurdity of Job's "friends" who believed that Job must have sinned or else he would not have lost his flocks, herds, land, family, and health. *The Book of Mormon* clearly contradicts the Bible regarding the relationship between righteousness and wealth. Neither Jesus nor his apostles had great material wealth.

Smith's piety-prosperity theory also runs counter to reality and world history. Babylon, Egypt, Rome, the Chinese Dynasties, and other major civilizations known for their tyranny, corruption, and sin have also been the most powerful, wealthy, and enduring. Some of them lasted for many centuries. "Righteous" societies have been short-lived and difficult to find in world history. Again, Smith's ignorance about world history becomes obvious.

Smith's piety-prosperity theme sounds more like Calvinism, wishful thinking, Yankee optimism, utopian dreaming, and dime store novel morality where the good guys always get the bad guys. It may be romantic and heart warming, but it is **not** reality nor serious history. But many people love to hear heartwarming stories and faith promoting myths. Joseph Smith was a very shrewd observer of human nature.

Fantasy Vs. Reality

Smith was not a scientist. His mind was not bound by scientific principles or even by reality. His only limitation was his own imagination. His world was supernatural and mystical. It included visions and dreams, steel bows, magic balls, submarines lighted by glowing stones, an army of young supermen, battles of complete extermination, seduction of beautiful maidens, slippery treasures, mass conversions, and gold plates.

Joseph's mother, Lucy, was fascinated by his remarkable imagination. In her book about Joseph, she recalls a common occurrence in their home:

> During our evening conversations, Joseph would occasionally give us some of the most amusing recitals that could be imagined. He would describe the ancient inhabitants of this continent, their dress, their mode of traveling, and animals upon which they rode; their cities, their buildings, with every particular; their mode of warfare; and also their religious worship. This he would do with as much ease . . . as if he had spent his whole life with them.[35]

Lucy's book also explains that this storytelling started when Joseph was only six years old, several years before any angels or gold plates came into his life. Perhaps he didn't even need gold plates to write his book. Joseph's family enjoyed his imaginary world and encouraged his storytelling. After all, the real world of the Smith family was quite painful at that time.

But escape from reality by entering a fantasy world can become addictive. **Enthusiasm** for any political or religious ideology or even for the selling of some product **is contagious**. And when reality begins to set in, a person can get a "fix" by going to another church meeting, political gathering, or sales convention.

L.D.S. Church members spend many hours in "testimony meetings" reassuring each other that *The Book of Mormon* is true, that Joseph Smith was a true prophet, and that Mormonism is the only church on earth today with any priesthood authority recognized of God. Church members have a very strong need to believe all of this. Otherwise they have wasted a lot of money paying tithing and other contributions. They have also wasted a lot of time serving in Church “callings”, going on missions, and teaching other people, including their own children and grandchildren, things that are not true. **This desire to believe in Mormonism can be overpowering. It just has to be true**. But the minute a person acquires an intense need to believe something, she loses her objectivity and her critical thinking skills. She is no longer truly rational.

The Con-Man

Smith seemed to have a cynical (or perhaps realistic) opinion about human nature. Maybe most people **are** gullible and naive. After all, thousands of people seemed to enjoy his fantasy world. They were (and still are) fascinated by his tall tales, incredible stories, and pretended revelations. **But if Smith had been an honest man and a person who really loved people, he would not have taken advantage of their trusting nature and played the con-man on such a massive scale.**

Chapter 3

BEWARE OF FALSE PROPHETS

> In every generation there has to be some fool who will speak the truth as he sees it.
>
> - Boris Pasternak

The basic assumption underlying Mormonism is that Joseph Smith was a true prophet of God. And, if a person accepts this, then it follows that his *Book of Mormon* prophets are also true prophets and not just fictional characters. Church members spend a great amount of time reassuring each other that these basic assumptions are true. But do Smith and his *Book of Mormon* prophets pass the test? Do they qualify as true prophets?

A Test For Prophets

Jesus warned us, "And many false prophets shall rise, and shall deceive many."[1] But how can a person know a false prophet? The Bible provides us with a simple test:

> But the prophet which shall presume to speak in my name, which I have not commanded him to speak . . . even that prophet shall die. And if thou say in thine heart, How shall we know the word which the Lord has not spoken? When a prophet speaketh in the name of the Lord, if the thing follow not nor come to pass, that is the thing which the Lord has not spoken, but the prophet has spoken presumptuously: thou shalt not be afraid of him.[2]

The Bible prescribes the death penalty for false prophets and commands us to not be afraid of them. Is Smith a true prophet or a false prophet? And should we be afraid of him?

The July 1833 edition of an early Mormon newspaper, *The Evening and the Morning Star*, contained a feature article by Smith entitled, "Beware of False Prophets." This article included a statement almost identical to the Biblical test for prophets:

> When, therefore any man, no matter who or how high his standing may be, utters or publishes anything which proves to be untrue, he is a false prophet.[3]

In this newspaper editorial, Smith agreed with the examination for prophets as prescribed in the Bible. But what happens if we apply this test to Joseph Smith himself? Have any of the predictions that he made through his *Book of Mormon* prophets and also through his own published revelations actually happened?

The true test of Smith's prophetic powers involves his predictions of events that were supposed to happen **after** the publication of his *Book of Mormon* in 1830. Prophecies given by Nephi and other *Book of Mormon* prophets about historical events such as the destruction of Jerusalem, the coming of Christ and His virgin birth, the twelve apostles, the discovery of America, the Revolutionary War, the coming forth of *The Book of Mormon*, and other events out of the past could easily have been put into a book by almost anyone living in 1830.

But what about future events, things that are supposed to take place after 1830? What kind of "track record" do Smith and his *Book of Mormon* prophets have when it comes to future events?

Joseph Smith Fails The Test For True Prophets.

Nephi (Smith) predicted that other books in addition to *The Book of Mormon* would soon miraculously come forth and convince the gentiles, the Native Americans, and the Jews that Jesus is the Christ.[4] Where are these books? The sealed portion of *The Book of Mormon* is supposed to be brought forth and be read from the housetops.[5] This hasn't happened either.

Nephi also prophesied that three scriptures would come together in the last days. This would include the record of the Jews (the Bible), the record of the Nephites (*The Book of Mormon*), and the records of the lost Ten Tribes of Israel who are up in the "north countries" on this earth.[6] Where are these lost tribes and where is their record?

Nephi also predicted that the "great and abominable church" would soon cause all nations of the earth to gather together to fight against the Latter-Day Saints. A great division of people would take place. The wrath of God would then be poured out upon the enemies of God until they were destroyed by fire while the saints would enjoy the protection of God and also have great power and glory.[7]

Nephi also prophesied that a great destruction would take place in America after *The Book of Mormon* came forth. This would include earthquakes, thunder, storms, and devouring fire.[8] **Not a single one of these *Book of Mormon* prophesies has come true** !

But let us continue with Smith's failed prophesies. Next, we read that the entire House of Israel, including the lost tribes, will gather together "unto the land of their possession."[9] The remnants (Native Americans) will eventually become converted to Mormonism and become a "white and delightsome" people.[10] This has now been changed to "pure and delightsome" in later editions of *The Book of Mormon*, but early Church leaders understood that Native Americans would become "white and delightsome."[11]

Another prophecy concerning these remnants is that they would be converted to the gospel in the last days and then serve as an instrument of destruction in the hand of God used to destroy the gentiles in America. The remnants are to "tread them down and tear them into pieces like a young lion." This event is predicted in **five** separate places in *The Book of Mormon.*[12] All of this seems very strange because the Native Americans are to do all of this violence **after** they are converted to the gospel of love and peace. Obviously, this prophesy has never happened.

Book of Mormon prophets also predicted that the cities of the gentiles who would not accept the gospel (Mormonism) would be wiped out. Their strongholds would be thrown down and their chariots destroyed.[13] Is this policy, accept the gospel or be wiped out, typical of the teachings of Jesus, the advocate of love and free agency, or does it sound more like the policy of Cortez in Mexico or perhaps even a doctrine of Satan?

The restoration of the lost tribes of Israel along with their sacred scripture is a myth. How could the Ten Tribes exist somewhere in the "north countries" as a distinct group when our entire planet has been explored and mapped? Native Americans have **not** been converted to Mormonism and then become violent enough to tread down the gentiles, and tear them into pieces. And where is this "great and abominable church" that is supposed to gather all of the nations in the world together into one group to fight against the Mormons? **All of this is part of Smith's fantasy world, a serious departure from reality.** I challenge anyone to find one single *Book of Mormon* prophesy that was supposed to take place after the publication of Smith's book in 1830 that has come to pass.

True believers argue that these things can still be fulfilled at some time in the future. But how long are we supposed to wait? Many of Smith's prophecies had a time limit that has long since passed. Should a reasonable and prudent person dedicate his own life and the lives of his children and grandchildren to the reality of these unfulfilled prophesies? I don't believe that it is fair or reasonable for an active Church member to judge or condemn a friend or relative who sincerely doubts all of this.

Smith also made many other "Thus saith the Lord" prophesies in Church conferences and also in his *Doctrine and Covenants*. For example, in 1833 he prophesied:

> And now I am prepared to say by the authority of Jesus Christ, that not many years shall pass away before the United States shall present a scene of bloodshed as has not parallel in the history of our nation; pestilence, hail, famine, and earthquake shall sweep the wicked of this generation from off the face of the land, to open and prepare the way for the return of the lost tribes of Israel

> from the north country. The people of the Lord, those who have complied with the requirements of the new covenant, have already commenced gathering together to Zion, which is in the state of Missouri; therefore I declare unto you the warning which the Lord has commanded to declare unto this generation, remembering that the eyes of my Maker are upon me, and that I am accountable for every word I say. . . . flee unto Zion, before the over-flowing scourge overtake you, for there are now living upon the earth whose eyes shall not be closed in death until they see all of these things which I have spoken, fulfilled.[14]

This prophecy was given in 1833. Where are Smith's listeners who believed they would live to see all of these things happen? They have all been dead for a long, long time. The ten tribes have **not** returned; the wicked of Smith's generation were **not** swept off the face of the land by pestilence; those who didn't flee to Zion (Missouri) were **not** overtaken by an overflowing scourge. Smith's prophecy had a time limit**. None of these events happened**.

The bitter irony is that hundreds of those who heeded Smith's advice, who came out of "Babylon" and fled to Zion before the wrath of God destroyed the wicked, died in religious battles in Missouri, or of malaria in Nauvoo, or else on the plains of Nebraska and Wyoming of cholera, scurvy, or exposure while struggling to migrate west. But most of those who ignored Smith's prophesies and warnings died at home of old age!

When Mormons in Missouri ran into trouble with their neighbors, Smith came to their rescue with another revelation instructing members in Kirtland to form an army (Zion's Camp) under the command of Smith. They were promised a military victory in Missouri and also and that the Lord Himself would fight their battles and destroy their enemies.[15] Nothing was to stand in the way of God's plans for establishing Zion, restoring the Lost Ten Tribes, and bringing about the second coming of Jesus Christ in "this generation."[16]

A small army of believers was formed. Smith's private army marched all the way from Ohio to Western Missouri. But when Smith found armed opposition, he abandoned the whole project explaining his decision with another revelation claiming that Church members had not lived worthy of the Lord's intervention. Therefore, the Lord was not going to fight their battles, as promised, but was giving members of Zion's camp a trial of their faith to see if they would be willing to fight and perhaps even die in order to establish Zion, Smith's mythical utopia.

Soon after Joseph Smith returned from the Zion's Camp fiasco, he left Kirtland on a mission to the Eastern States. While in Salem, Massachusetts, Smith had a revelation intended to help him out of his serious financial trouble:

> I The Lord . . . have much treasure in this city for you . . . And it shall come to pass in due time that I will give this city into your hands; that you shall have power over it, . . . and its wealth pertaining to gold and silver shall be yours.[17]

Here is another of Smith's failed prophesies. Neither Salem nor its silver and gold ever came into Smith's power in due time or any other time. This nonsense is still canonized in section 111 of the L.D.S. *Doctrine and Covenants.*

In 1835, Smith prophesied that the second coming would take place by the year 1891.[18] In 1844, Smith prophesied that many people of his generation would not taste of death until after the second coming of Christ.[19] All of those who believed him are dead.

The list of Smith's failed prophesies goes on and on and on. But perhaps we should look at just one more because it is often used by Church members to prove Smith's prophetic powers. This is Smith's famous Civil War prophecy contained in section 87 of *The Doctrine and Covenants*:

> Verily, thus saith the Lord concerning the wars that will shortly come to pass, beginning at the rebellion of

> South Carolina, which will eventually terminate in the death and misery of many souls. And the time will come that war will be poured out upon all nations, beginning at this place. . . . And it shall come to pass, after many days, slaves shall rise up against their masters, who shall be marshaled and disciplined for war. And it shall come to pass also that the remnants who are left in the land will marshal themselves, and become exceedingly angry, and shall vex the gentiles with a sore vexation . . . and with famine and plague, and earthquake, and the thunder of heaven, and the fierce and vivid lightning also, shall the inhabitants of the earth be made to feel the wrath, and the indignation, and the chastening hand of an Almighty God, until the consumption decreed hath made an end of all nations.[20]

This prophesy is full of false predictions. The Civil War was **not** "poured out upon all nations." Nor did it result in "an end of all nations." Very few slaves fought in this war. Nor did many "rise up against their masters." Most of the slaves who did fight tried to help their "masters" defeat the Yankees.

The remnants (Native Americans) did not have a significant role in the Civil War. Nor were there devastating natural disasters such as famines, plagues, and earthquakes as predicted by Smith. None of these things actually happened.

Smith's prophesy was not unusual. Many people were predicting a civil war in America in 1832. British textile companies were even stockpiling cotton because they expected their supplies from the Southern States to be cut off.

In November of 1832, just one month **before** Smith made his prophecy, South Carolina declared itself a sovereign state and an independent nation.[21] Almost any person who read the newspapers could have predicted a war between the North and the South and picked South Carolina as the instigator.

Brigham Young Also Fails The Test.

Tabernacle sermons in the early 1860s indicate that Brigham Young and other Church leaders in the Utah Territory had complete faith in Smith's Civil War prophesy. They expected famines, plagues, earthquakes, and general destruction. They also expected America's Civil War to expand into a world war that would result in the end of all governments including that of The United States as prophesied by Smith. After the "chastening hand of the Almighty God" had destroyed the wicked, the rightful government (Mormon Priesthood Leaders) would assert their legitimate authority, take over the world, establish the kingdom of God upon the earth, and usher in the Millennium.

In 1861, Brigham Young told a congregation of Church members meeting in Salt Lake City:

> How is the Lord going to empty the earth? . . . President Lincoln called out soldiers for three months and was going to wipe out the blot of secession from the escutcheon of the American Republic. . . . Do they know what they are doing? No; but they have began to cleanse the earth and prepare the way for the return of the Latter-Day Saints to the center Stake of Zion. . . . When I left the State of Missouri, I had a deed for five pieces of as good land as any in the State, and I expect to go back to it. . . . Will we return and receive an inheritance there? Many of the saints will return to Missouri, and there receive an inheritance. . . . The abolitionists would set free the Negroes at the expense of the lives of their masters; they would let the Negroes loose to massacre every white person. . . . Will it be over in six months or in three years? No, . . . it will spread and continue until the land is emptied.[22]

Brigham Young also made a number of other prophesies that were faithfully recorded in the *Journal of Discourses*. His other predictions were no better than the one just quoted. They didn't happen either.

We have given Joseph Smith and Brigham Young the Biblical test for true prophets. They have both failed to predict future events. I don't understand why millions of people still revere them as true prophets of God.

Chapter 4

CONTRADICTORY DOCTRINE

> Human beings never welcome the news that something they have long cherished is untrue. They almost always reply to that news by reviling the promulgator.
>
> \- H.L. Mencken

Some of the doctrine taught by *Book of Mormon* prophets clearly contradicts that which is now taught in the L.D.S. Church. One example of this is disagreement over the nature of the trinity. The prophet Abinadi said:

> I would that you should understand that God himself shall come down among the children of men, and shall redeem his people. And because he dwelleth in the flesh he shall be called the Son of God and having subjected the flesh to the will of the Father, being the Father and the Son. The Father, because he was conceived by the power of God; and the Son because of the flesh; thus becoming the Father and the Son and they are one God, yea, the Eternal Father of heaven and earth.[1]

The following dialogue between Amulek, another of Smith's prophets, and Zeezrom confirms Abinadi's statement that the Father and the Son are one and the same person:

> Zeezrom said: "Is there more than one God"? And he answered, "No." . . . Now Zeezrom saith again unto him: "Is the Son of God the very Eternal Father?" Amulek saith unto him: "Yea, he is the very Eternal Father of Heaven and Earth, and all things which in them are, he is the beginning and the end, the first and the last."[2]

About 2000 B.C., the pre-mortal Jesus, speaking with the brother of Jared, another *Book of Mormon* prophet, supposedly said:

> I am the Father and the Son. . . . And never have I showed myself unto man whom I have created, for never has man believed in me as thou hast.[3]

This statement not only teaches that the Father and the Son are the same person, it contradicts other L.D.S. scriptures claiming that God appeared unto prophets long before the brother of Jared.[4]

Many Gods

These *Book of Mormon* scriptures clearly contradict Smith's claim that the Father and the Son are two separate persons and also his later revelations that there are many gods and that **L.D.S. men and women can become gods and goddesses themselves** through a process called "eternal progression."

Heaven And Hell Vs. Three Degrees Of Glory

The Book of Mormon creates another conflict for Latter-Day Saints when it teaches the traditional heaven-hell dichotomy and says nothing about degrees of glory.[5] Hell is described as "a lake of fire and brimstone whose flame ascendeth up forever and ever and has no end."[6] It is also referred to as, "that lake of fire and brimstone which is endless torment"[7] and a "great pit."[8] The righteous go to heaven; the sinners go to hell. This traditional view of heaven and hell is repeated over and over again in *The Book of Mormon*. **The L.D.S. Church no longer teaches this doctrine.**

Only two years after publishing his book, Smith decided that there were three degrees of glory, the celestial (heaven), the terrestrial (middle kingdom), and the telestial (hell).

Instead of fire and brimstone, a great pit, awful chains, endless torment, and eternal damnation, he informs us that he has been shown in vision where liars, murderers, whoremongers, and other serious sinners go. Smith says, "These are they who are thrust down to hell." He then describes the "glory" of the telestial kingdom: "And thus we saw, in heavenly vision, the glory of the telestial which surpasses all understanding . . . "[9] Contrary to *Book of Mormon* prophets, even murderers, liars, and whoremongers will go to a kingdom of "glory" beyond human comprehension.

Postmortem Repentance

The Book of Mormon teaches that a person has only this life in which to accept or reject the gospel and that endless punishment and damnation are the "**final**" state of the wicked.[10] And yet the L.D.S. Church today performs baptisms, endowments, marriages, and other ordinances for millions of people including serious sinners and those who have rejected the gospel in this life but who later may have a change of heart and accept it in the next world.

Confusion About The Resurrection

Another doctrinal problem contained in *The Book of Mormon* relates to the resurrection. The prophet Alma clearly taught that all of those who came to earth, both good and evil, before the time of Jesus would take part in the **first** resurrection. Those coming to earth after Jesus, both good and evil, would not be resurrected until the second resurrection.[11] According to Alma, the determining factor is **when** a person lived, not **how** he lived.

Smith's book containing his revelations, *The Doctrine and Covenants,* clearly contradicts this. It teaches that whether a person comes forth in the first resurrection or the second depends on how righteous he or she has been in this life.[12] Apparently, Smith changed his mind about the resurrection too.

Polygamy Condemned And Also Justified

The early Mormon practice of polygamy also runs counter to *Book of Mormon* teachings. *Book of Mormon* prophets condemned polygamy on five separate occasions. (Jacob 1:15; Jacob 2:23-28; Jacob 3:5; Mosiah 11:1,2; and Ether 10:5). No exceptions were made even when major wars created large numbers of widows and orphans.

The *Book of Mormon* prophet, Jacob, condemned David and Solomon for having "many" wives and concubines. Nothing is said about how David obtained Uriah's wife nor of Solomon's pagan wives. David and Solomon are specifically criticized for having "many" wives.[13]

And yet, only a few years later, Joseph Smith had a revelation that justified not only the many wives of David and Solomon but also their concubines![14] Brigham Young said that true servants of the Lord have always practiced polygamy and that neither a man nor a woman could be exalted without living this "principle."[15]

Young, following the example of his file leader, saw no need to be consistent. He clearly contradicted Smith's *Book of Mormon* prophets. If Young is correct, the Nephite people and their prophets will be denied exaltation because they were not polygamists. Who is right about polygamy, Smith and Young who lived it and praised it or the *Book of Mormon* prophets who condemned it ?

And how can Smith expect anyone to believe that the Lord would give His blessing to a cruel situation where one man (Solomon) had 700 wives and 300 concubines![16] Almost all of these unfortunate women were deprived of a loving and intimate relationship. They were also denied a home and family. They were housed together like a stable of horses for the use and convenience of their chauvinistic lord and master.

Any relationship that took place between Solomon and his harem (or Smith and his harem) was not one of love and intimacy between equals but a patronizing situation where the man had all of the power and the women were weak and vulnerable. They had to submit to the whims of their shared husband and hide their true feelings or else face rejection and punishment.

What kind of sadistic mind set does it take for a man to practice or even justify this pathetic degradation of women? Is this the sort of life-style that a loving and kind Heavenly Father has in mind for His daughters?

The Book of Mormon rightly calls these things an "abomination" unto the Lord.[17] But Smith, Young, and other Church leaders contradicted this and defended this degrading practice.

Racism

Another doctrine clearly taught in *The Book of Mormon* that has become an embarrassment and has been officially discarded by the L.D.S Church is racism. Smith and other early Church leaders openly taught that black people were cursed of God and should not be ordained to the priesthood nor allowed inside of L.D.S. temples.[18] Smith considered skin color an indication of righteousness.

The terms "fair and beautiful," "white and delightsome," and "dark and loathsome" are used by Smith over and over again in his *Book of Mormon*. For example, he informs us that Mary, the mother of Jesus, was:

> ". . . exceedingly fair and white . . . a virgin, most beautiful and fair above all other virgins.[19]

Smith gives us a description of the gentiles who will discover America: ". . . I beheld that they were white, and exceedingly fair like unto my people before they were slain."[20] Smith then goes on to explain how his Lamanites came to have dark skin:

> And he had caused a cursing to come upon them, yea, even a sore cursing, because of their iniquity. For behold, they had hardened their hearts against him, that they had become like unto flint; wherefore, as they were white, and exceeding fair and delightsome, that they might not be enticing unto my people the Lord God did cause a skin of blackness to come upon them.[21]

It is quite clear that Nephi (Smith) considered dark skin repulsive and white skin "delightsome."

Later, in Smith's story, when the Lamanites became converted to Christianity, an amazing thing happened to their skin pigmentation:

> And their curse was taken from them, and their skin became white like unto the Nephites; And their young men and their daughters became exceeding fair, and they were numbered among the Nephites, and were called Nephites.[22]

But then as the Lamanites went back to their old sinful ways, God again cursed them with a dark skin. Nephite prophets, however, held out hope that future generations of Lamanites in the latter days would get their white skin back and become a "white and delightsome people" if they accepted the gospel.[23]

Later in Smith's book, Jacob, one of the Nephite prophets, threatens his people with a darker skin than the Lamanites:

> O my brethren, I fear that unless ye shall repent of your sins that their skins will be whiter than yours, when ye shall be brought with them before the throne of God.[24]

Thus, according to Smith, light skin is an indication of favor with God, and nonwhite people will be in big trouble when they are brought before the throne of God on judgment day!

Smith's racism was echoed by his alter-ego, Brigham Young:

> Shall I tell you the law of God in regard to the African race? If the white man who belongs to the chosen seed mixes his blood with the seed of Cain, the penalty under the law of God is death on the spot. This will always be so. [25]

As a young child growing up in the Church, I was taught by my parents and also by Church leaders that black people were disobedient in their premortal lives and that they came into this world under a curse. They were not to hold the priesthood nor enjoy the blessings of temple ordinances.

The Church had been organized more than 150 years before God changed His mind and supposedly gave L.D.S. Church President Spencer W. Kimball a revelation rejecting the racist doctrines of early Church leaders. But how does the L.D.S. Church get pigmentocracy out of *The Book of Mormon* and out of the minds and hearts of its membership?

Secret Societies

Another contradiction between *Book of Mormon* doctrine and the present day L.D.S. Church has to do with secret societies. The Anti-Masons were a very important social and political group in 1830 when *The Book of Mormon* was published. Condemnation of secret societies along with their secret signs, tokens, handclasps, and passwords is one of the major themes repeated over and over again in *The Book of Mormon*. It claims that Satan himself introduced these things to Cain, thus tempting him to become a murderer.[26]

Secret societies were known to the Jaredites and also among the Nephites. A secret criminal society, the Gadianton Robbers, almost destroyed the Nephite civilization. *The Book of Mormon* warns Americans that a similar organization will exist in the latter-days that, if not stopped, will prove the destruction of The United States.[27]

The September 2, 1828 issue of *The Palmyra Freeman*, a newspaper published in Joseph Smith's hometown, contained the following:

> Almost two years ago a free citizen was taken violently from the protection of the laws, carried one hundred and fifty miles, confined in a magazine, and deliberately murdered. This was done by a "secret society" to vindicate its "secret laws" . . . We cannot contemplate the overwhelming power of free Masonry, without trembling for the safety of our country. Freemasonry must be put down or freedom must be banished from her last abode.[28]

Martin Harris, the man Joseph Smith was trying to persuade into paying for publication of his *Book of Mormon*, belonged to the Wayne County Anti-Masonic Convention.[29] Perhaps Smith reasoned that his often-repeated *Book of Mormon* theme against secret societies would encourage Harris to finance his book and also help Smith sell his book to the anti-Masonic crowd.

It is interesting to note that the widow of William Morgan, the Mason who was murdered for exposing Masonic secrets, later became one of Joseph Smith's plural wives![30] Morgan's expose included the following:

> Master returns to his seat . . . and gets a lambskin or white apron, presents it to the candidate, and observes, Brother, I now present you with a lambskin or white apron: it is . . . the badge of a Mason.[31]

Referring to the Gadianton Robbers, a secret society in ancient America, *The Book of Mormon* says:

> And it came to pass that they did come to battle; . . . and they were girded after the manner of the robbers; and they had a lambskin about their loins . . .[32].

One of the most prominent New York Masons, a person who was involved in the Morgan murder was a man named Giddins.[33] In *The Book of Mormon* we discover the following:

> And behold I am Giddianhi, and I am Governor of this secret society of Gadianton; which society, and the works thereof, I know to be good; and they are of ancient date, and they have been handed down unto us.[34]

Are the obvious similarities between the names Giddins, Giddianhi, and Gadianton only a coincidence? Smith claimed that after being introduced to these same secrets by Satan, Cain became known as "Master Mahan."[35] Is the similarity between "Master Mahan" and "Master Mason" also a coincidence?

A few years later, after all of this Anti-Masonic furor had gone away, apparently, Smith changed his mind about secret societies. Smith not only joined the Masons but introduced secret oaths, handclasps, passwords, signs, and tokens as part of his new temple ceremony. Again, we see Smith's contradictions and inconsistencies.

Important Doctrine Is Missing From *The Book of Mormon.*

The Book of Mormon is also an embarrassment and a problem for modern Latter-Day Saints because of the things that it does **not** teach. This includes some of the most important doctrines in the Church today. For example, there is not a single word that even hints at baptism for the dead, temple ordinances, or eternal marriage. Why are such important things left out of a book that supposedly contains the "fullness of the gospel of Jesus Christ"?[36] And what does the word "fullness" mean anyway? If it means total or complete, then what need is there for the new doctrine and rituals adopted by the Church since the publication of this book in 1830?

Joseph Smith Ridicules Eternal Marriage.

Perhaps these new things not found in "the fullness of the gospel," are not even necessary. For example, Joseph Smith publicly ridiculed the doctrine of eternal marriage on several occasions.[37] He also explained why it is impossible for any marriage to be eternal. Smith held up his ring and challenged anyone to find the beginning of it or the end. Then he said, "That which has a beginning must have an end."[38] Thus, according to Smith, **marriage cannot be eternal** whether performed in the temple or anywhere else. Since every marriage has a beginning date, it must also have an end! And this is Joseph Smith talking!

Brigham Young Denies The Importance Of Eternal Marriage.

Brigham Young also ridiculed eternal marriage. Only four years before he died, Young, who had been President of the L.D.S. Church for twenty six years, told an L.D.S. congregation:

> **I do not know that I shall have a wife or child in the resurrection. I have never had any thoughts or reflections upon this, or cared the first thing about it.[39]**

Was Young telling the truth or was he lying? Either possibility creates a serious dilemma for Mormons who consider temple (eternal) marriage to be one of the most sacred aspects of their religion. And yet, their own Church president and Prophet said that he cared nothing about whether he would have any wives or children in the resurrection!

Jesus Denies Eternal Marriage.

The scriptures do not teach eternal marriage nor do they say that a person can do anything to help save his dead relatives. When the Sadducees asked Jesus about marriage in heaven, Jesus answered, "Ye do err, not knowing the scriptures. . . ."[40] Where in all of the scriptures did the Sadducees read such a thing? Which of the prophets taught eternal marriage? Jesus knew that eternal marriage was **not** scriptural. Jesus said to the Sadducees:

> The children of this world marry, and are given in marriage: But they which shall be accounted worthy to obtain that world, and the resurrection from the dead, neither marry, nor are given in marriage.[41]

Jesus was also critical of the pride the Jews took in their genealogy:

> And think not to say within yourselves, we have Abraham to our father: for I say unto you, that God is able of these stones to raise up children unto Abraham.[42]

Paul Criticizes Genealogy.

The Apostle Paul also had a very negative opinion of genealogy:

> But avoid foolish questions, and genealogies, and contentions, and strivings about the law; for they are unprofitable and vain.[43]

> Neither give heed to fables and endless genealogies which minister questions rather than godly edifying . . .[44].

And yet, genealogy and temple work are considered some of the most sacred obligations of L.D.S. Church members today.

Baptism For The Dead Is Not Christian Doctrine.

Joseph Smith quoted the Apostle Paul in order to defend his new doctrine of baptizing Church members for their dead ancestors. But there is no evidence that Jesus, Paul, nor any of the other apostles ever taught or practiced this ordinance. Why has such an important teaching been left out of the Bible?

It is true that in order to support his faith in the resurrection, Paul referred to some other people who were baptizing for their dead:

> Else what shall they do which are baptized for the dead if the dead rise not at all? Why then are they baptized for the dead?[45]

Paul did not say, "Why then are **we** baptized for **our** dead"? Obviously, he was talking about other people.

Is it reasonable that Jesus would support a principle which discriminates against the poor masses of humanity, the billions of poor and illiterate people who have lived and died and have never been able to keep records? Baptism for the dead favors the rich who have kept their genealogy in order to inherit property or social position. Does this "save the rich" program sound like something Jesus would favor?

Also, is it logical that a person who lived thousands of years ago should depend upon someone living today for his or her salvation? This doctrine of doing genealogy and then doing vicarious baptisms, priesthood ordinations, endowments, and marriages for people who have been dead hundreds or even thousands of years is not scriptural nor is it reasonable.

Confused Doctrine

Shouldn't a person at least question the fact that *The Book of Mormon* teaches things that contradict present day Church doctrine about the Trinity, heaven and hell, the resurrection, polygamy, and racism? And why doesn't a book that contains the "fullness of the everlasting gospel" say anything about genealogy, temple endowments, eternal marriage, and baptism for the dead?

Where does a person look for true Mormon doctrine anyway? Should a person look to *The Book of Mormon* or to Church leaders who often contradict their own scriptures?

Chapter 5

FICTITIOUS TRANSLATIONS

> Morally, a philosopher who uses his professional competence for anything except a disinterested search for truth is guilty of a kind of treachery.
>
> - Bertrand Russell

Several of Joseph Smith's closest associates claim that he didn't even use gold plates when "translating" *The Book of Mormon*. He simply used a "seer stone" which he placed in his hat! Martin Harris, a close friend of Smith who mortgaged his farm in order to pay for printing the first edition of *The Book of Mormon,* said:

> The prophet possessed a seer stone, by which he was enabled to translate as well as from the Urim and Thummim, and for convenience he used the seer stone. . . . By aid of the seer stone, sentences would appear and were read by the Prophet and written by Oliver, and when finished he would say, "written," and if correctly written that sentence would disappear and another appear in its place. But if not written correctly, it remained until corrected so that the translation was just as it was engraven on the plates, precisely in the language then used.[1]

David Whitmer, one of the three witnesses to *The Book of Mormon*, published the following statement in 1887:

> I will now give you a description of the manner which *The Book of Mormon* was translated. Joseph Smith would put the seer stone into a hat, and put his face in the hat, drawing it closely around his face to exclude the light; and in the darkness a spiritual light would shine. A piece of something resembling parchment would appear, and on that appeared writing. One character at a time would appear, and under it was the interpretation in English. Brother Joseph would read off the English to Oliver Cowdery, who was his principal scribe, and when it was written down and repeated to Brother Joseph to see if it was correct, then it would disappear and another character with the interpretation would appear. Thus *The Book of Mormon* was translated by the gift and power of God, not by any power of man.[2]

David Whitmer also claimed that Smith used this amazing stone-in-his-hat method for receiving many of his other revelations:

> Joseph looked into the hat in which he placed a stone, and received a revelation that some of the brethren should go to Toronto, Canada, and that they would sell the copy-right of *The Book of Mormon*. Hirum Page and Oliver Cowdery went on this mission, but they failed entirely to sell the copy-right, returning home without any money. Joseph was at my father's house when they returned. I was there also, and am an eyewitness to these facts. Jacob Whitmer and John Whitmer were also present when Hiram Page and Oliver Cowdery returned from Canada. Well, we were all in great trouble; and we asked Joseph how it was that he had received a revelation from the Lord and the brethren had utterly failed in their undertaking. Joseph did not know how it was, so he inquired of the Lord about it, and behold the following revelation came through the stone: "Some revelations are of God; some revelations are of man; and some revelations are of the devil."[3]

This incredible incident, reported by David Whitmer, creates many questions and doubts. It implies that Smith did **not** receive the Toronto revelation from the Lord but either made it up himself or else received it from Satan! It also suggests that Smith didn't have enough discernment to know the source of his revelations. If this is true, then why couldn't this same thing have happened on other occasions such as when he received his infamous revelation on polygamy? All of Smith's revelations become suspect! Also, where in all of the scriptures do we read of a prophet receiving a revelation by putting a stone and his face into a hat? Did Noah, Moses or Abraham do this? Did Isaiah, Peter, or Paul do this?

Oliver Cowdery articulated his disappointment regarding the Toronto incident with the following words:

> But so great was my faith, that in going to Toronto, nothing but calmness pervaded my soul, every doubt was banished and I as much expected that Bro. Page and I would fulfill the revelation as that we should live. And you may believe, without asking me to relate the particulars, that it is no easy task to describe our desolation and grief. Bro. Page and I did not think that God would deceive us . . . exactly as came *The Book of Mormon.*[4]

Cowdery was puzzled and confused because he knew that the Toronto revelation came exactly the same way that Smith brought forth *The Book of Mormon* and Mormonism itself, out of his hat! It seems almost unbelievable that Cowdery was willing to accuse the Lord of deception before he would consider the possibility that Smith was a liar and a fraud. It is frightening to think how much hypnotic power Smith seemed to have over his followers!

"Translation" Without Any Gold Plates

Joseph Smith's father-in-law, Isaac Hale, described what happened when Joseph was boarding in his home:

> The manner in which he (Joseph Smith) pretended to read and interpret, was the same as when he looked

> for money diggers, with a stone in his hat, and his hat over his face, while the book of plates were at the same time hid in the woods.[5]

A Magic Stone

Willard Chase, a neighbor of the Smith family explained how the seer stone was found on his property:

> In the year 1822, I was engaged in digging a well. I employed Alvin and Joseph Smith to assist me. . . . After digging about twenty feet below the surface of the earth, we discovered a singularly appearing stone, which excited my curiosity. I brought it to the top of the well, and as we were examining it, Joseph put it into his hat, and then his face into the top of his hat. . . . The next morning he came to me, and wished to obtain the stone, alleging that he could see in it; but I told him I did not wish to part with it on account of its being a curiosity, but I would lend it.[6]

This stone, found on the property of Mr. Chase in 1822, when Smith was only seventeen years old, was never returned to its owner. After the death of Joseph Smith, it was taken to Utah. On May 17,1888, L.D.S. Church President, Wilford Woodruff, dedicated the new Mormon temple in Manti, Utah. After the dedication services he stayed in the temple by himself for a few hours. Woodruff later reported:

> I consecrated upon the altar the Seer Stone that Joseph Smith found by revelation some thirty feet under the earth, and carried by him through his life. This is the very Seer Stone that the Prophet Joseph Smith used part of the time when translating *The Book of Mormon*; the one he took from a well he was digging with his brother Hyrum, near Palmyra, for Mr. Chase, and which he was falsely accused of taking from the children of Mr. Chase . . .[7].

Although this magical stone is still in the possession of the L.D.S. Church, apparently none of the prophets, seers, and revelators succeeding Smith have been able to use it to translate strange languages nor to receive revelations for Church members, today. It seems that only Smith could make it work.

Chandlers Mummies And Scrolls

In 1835, while living in Kirtland, Ohio, Smith bought some Egyptian mummies and some scrolls of papyrus that were with these mummies from Michael Chandler. Smith then claimed to "translate" the hieroglyphics characters on these scrolls into English. He then published his "translation" as the Book of Abraham and also the Book of Moses which were both part of a larger book, Smith's *Pearl of Great Price*, another new scripture for the world.

But Smith's pretended translation of Chandler's scrolls demonstrates his complete ignorance of Egyptian. Facsimile #1:

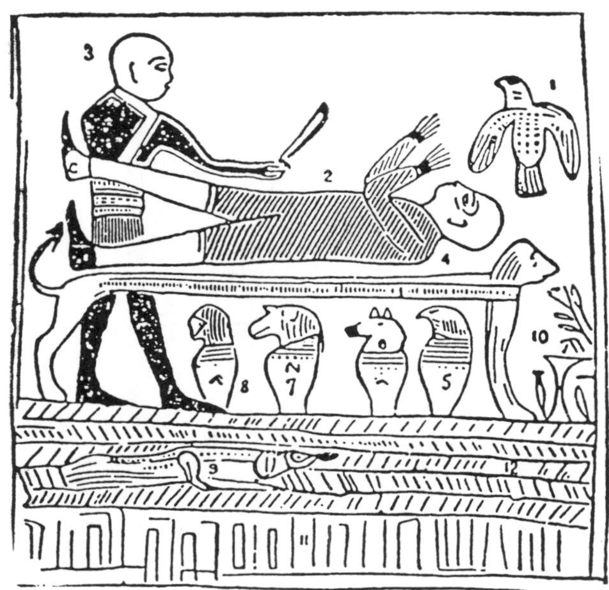

Joseph Smith's interpretation of facsimile No. 1 is as follows:

> Figure #1 is an angel of the Lord; Figure #2 is Abraham upon a sacrificial alter; Figure #3 is an idolatrous priest about to sacrifice Abraham; Figure #4 is a sacrificial alter; Figures #5, #6, #7 and #8 are the idolatrous gods of Pharaoh.[8]

Egyptologists unanimously agree that Facsimile No.1 is a common Egyptian woodcut dating from Roman times, many centuries **after** Abraham. It is an embalming scene showing the deceased on an embalming table. Over the dead person's head is a bird which represents his soul leaving his body. The jars below, closed with lids carved in the shape of animal heads, were used by the embalmer to contain the organs and entrails of the dead person.[9]

Not only does facsimile No. 1 have absolutely nothing to do with Abraham, as claimed by Smith, but his interpretation of Facsimile No. 3 is perhaps even more ludicrous:

> Figure #1 is Abraham sitting upon the throne of Pharaoh; Figure #2 is Pharaoh; Figure #4 is the prince of Pharaoh; Figure #5 is one of Pharaoh's servants; Figure #6 is a slave belonging to the prince.[10]

Egyptologists call all of this pure fabrication. They say that Facsimile No. 3 is a judgment scene in which the dead man (#5) is being led into his judgment by the Goddess Truth (#4) to be judged by Osiris (#1). A woman, the Goddess Isis, is standing behind Osiris. Figure #6 is the shadow of the dead person. **Even though figures #2 and #4 are obviously women, Smith claims that they represent Pharaoh and the prince of Pharaoh, both men!**

Joseph Smith contradicts prominent Egyptologists such as Dr. A. H. Sayce of Oxford, Dr. W.M. Flinders Petrie of London University, Dr. James H. Breasted of the University of Chicago, Dr. Arthur C. Mace, Curator, Metropolitan Museum of Art, New York, Dr. John Peters, University of Pennsylvania, and Dr. Edward Meyer, University of Berlin. I choose to believe these distinguished authorities on ancient Egyptian culture and language.

Smith's "Impudent Fraud"

These experts on Egypt are unanimous in stating that all three facsimiles published by Joseph Smith in his book, *The Pearl of Great Price*, relate to the mortuary religion of Egypt and have nothing to do with Abraham.[11] One of these authorities said, "It is difficult to deal seriously with Joseph Smith's impudent fraud."[12]

Kinderhook "Translation" Hoax

Another incident that proves that Smith's claimed ability to translate languages was just another imposition upon the trust of his followers is the Kinderhook hoax. Smith's journal for May 1, 1843 says:

> I insert facsimiles of the six brass plates found near Kinderhook, in Pike County, Illinois, on April 23, by Mr. Robert Wiley and others, while excavating a large mound. They found a skeleton about six feet from the surface of the earth, which must have stood nine feet high. The plates were found on the breast of the skeleton and were covered on both sides by ancient characters. I have translated a portion of them, and find they contain the history of the person with whom they were found. He was a descendant of Ham, through the loins of Pharaoh, King of Egypt, and that he received his kingdom from the Ruler of heaven and earth.[13]

After Smith declared the plates authentic and even translated a portion of them, Wilber Fugate, one of the men who "found" the plates admitted that he had helped make them out of copper. He also admitted making a mold out of wax and using acid to burn the engravings into the copper to make them look old.[14]

Even those who refuse to believe that Smith was taken in by this hoax have a difficult time explaining what a nine foot tall Egyptian pharaoh was doing in North America and why his life history was not written in Egyptian hieroglyphics instead of something that looks more like hen scratching.[15]

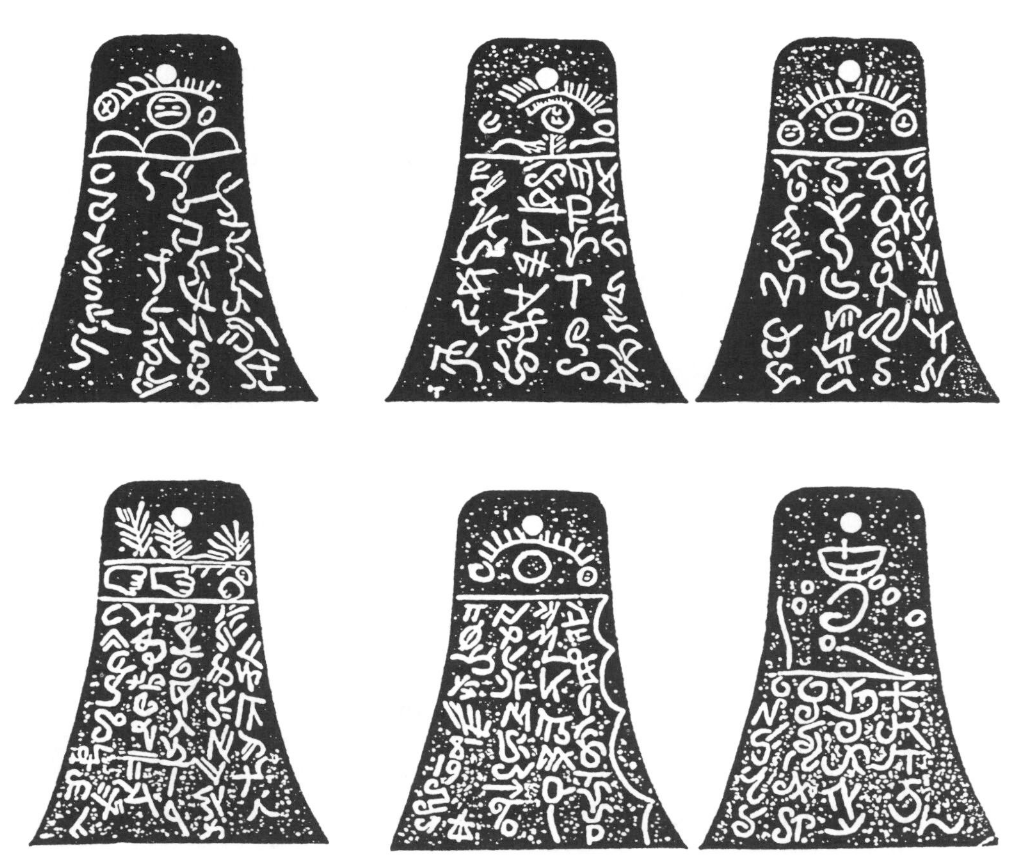

KINDERHOOK PLATES

Smith's Book of Abraham claims that the word "Egypt" was derived from a Chaldean word, "Egyptus." But ancient Egyptians never called their land "Egypt" nor is the word of Chaldean origin. It was derived from Aegyptus, a comparatively late Greek word for the land of the Nile.[16]

Smith's Book of Abraham claims that the Egyptians were cursed as pertaining to the priesthood.[17] If this is true, then why did Moses marry an Egyptian? And why has the L.D.S. Church never hesitated to offer the priesthood to Arabs, who are descendants of Abraham and his Egyptian wife, Haggar? And why have all racial restrictions pertaining to the priesthood now been entirely removed?

The Book of Abraham claims that the Egyptians learned mathematics and astronomy from Abraham after he learned these things from God. (see P. of G. P. facsimile no. 3) This is obviously just more of Smith's imaginary nonsense. The Egyptian civilization was highly advanced many centuries **before** Abraham. Their most magnificent structures were built long before Abraham was born.

Other Similar Books

Much of the information contained in *The Pearl of Great Price* can be found in the Bible. Other ideas pertaining to the eternal and unbegotten nature of "intelligences," the existence of greater and lesser intelligences, and ideas about a great planet (Kolob) that governs the universe apparently came from two books in circulation in Smith's time. One was Thomas Dicks's *Philosophy of a Future State*, published in 1830 and the other was Thomas Taylor's *The Six Books of Proclus, The Platonic Successor, on The Theology of Plato*, published in 1816.[18]

Overwhelmed by evidence against the authenticity of Smith's Book of Abraham and his Book of Moses, The Community of Christ (formerly The Reorganized Church of Jesus Christ of Latter-Day Saints) no longer considers *The Pearl of Great Price* to be part of its canon of scripture.[19] Isn't it about time the L.D.S. Church also admitted that this "scripture" is a fraud?

Unreadable Egyptian Hieroglyphics

Why did Smith tell everyone that his gold plates and other source material for his "translations" were written in Egyptian or "Reformed Egyptian"? Why didn't he translate anything from Hebrew, Greek, or Latin? Why was Egyptian the only language that Smith translated with his Urim and Thummim and his magical seer stone? The obvious reason is that Egyptian was considered a dead, untranslatable language, and therefore Smith thought that nobody would ever be able to expose his fraud.

But unfortunately for Smith, only a few years later, using the newly discovered Rosetta Stone and other resources, Jean Francois Champollian discovered the difference between ideograms and phonetic complements which established the connection between Coptic and Egyptian languages. And after only a few years, Egyptologists were able to read hieroglyphics and expose Smith's deception. His pretended translation of the facsimiles that came with the papyrus scrolls that he bought from Michael Chandler in 1835 have been called an "**impudent fraud**" by an expert in the Egyptian language.[20]

Chapter 6

ANACHRONISMS AND IMAGINARY GEOGRAPHY

> I believe that to recognize the truth is not primarily a matter of intelligence, but a matter of character.
> -Erich Fromm

Who would believe a book on Roman history that had Caesar's children talking on the telephone, watching television, and surfing the Internet? And yet, there are many anachronisms almost this serious in *The Book of Mormon.* Things happen before they could possibly have happened and in geographic locations that are impossible.

Nephi Quotes Old World Prophets Who Lived Centuries Later.

One example of this is when Nephi, living in the New World about 600 B.C., quoted Malachi, an Old Testament prophet, who would not say these words until about 200 years later!

> The day soon cometh that all the proud and they who do wickedly shall be as stubble, and the day cometh that they must be burned. (Compare I Nephi 22:15 with Malachi 4:1.)

On another occasion, Nephi quoted the Apostle Peter, who was paraphrasing some things that God had spoken to Moses. How did Nephi have access to words which Peter would not say in the

Old World until some 600 years later? (Compare I Nephi 22:20 with Acts 3:22-23 and Deuteronomy 18:15,18,19.)

Another *Book of Mormon* prophet apparently quoted the New Testament when he said, "For do we not read that God is the same yesterday, today, and forever, and in him there is no variableness neither shadow of changing?" (Compare Mormon 9:9 with Hebrews 13:8 and James 1:17). How did Mormon have access to the words of New Testament apostles Paul and James?

Michael Marquardt and other scholars have found over 300 quotations in *The Book of Mormon* that apparently came from prophets and apostles in the Old World who lived **after** 600 B. C. when Lehi and his family left on their migration to the New World![1] Most of these quotations appear in their King James wording, including the mistakes that were later corrected by scholars.

It is obvious that Smith's *Book of Mormon* prophets were quoting from a King James Bible. And yet this Bible, which was translated from Hebrew and Greek, was not published until 1611 A.D., about twelve centuries **after** Moroni supposedly inscribed his last words on the gold plates!

Joseph Smith said that he translated *The Book of Mormon* from ancient plates inscribed with "reformed Egyptian."[2] King James translators used Hebrew and Greek. And yet, much of the wording in The *Book of Mormon* is identical to that of the King James Bible. This includes entire chapters from Isaiah quoted in 2 Nephi and a large number of verses from Malachi and Matthew quoted in 3 Nephi. How can all of this be explained?

Another time and place problem involves some of the quotations from Isaiah that appear in *The Book of Mormon*. Isaiah was an Old Testament prophet who lived in the days of Uzziah, about 750 B. C. Isaiah, however, apparently did not write all of the chapters that appear under his name in the Bible. Starting with chapter 40 there is a sudden change of style, language, and background. Bible scholars believe that these later chapters were written by another person living after the exile, in the days of Cyrus, about 540 B. C.[3] These chapters refer to persons who lived and events that happened many years **after** the exile. And yet these last chapters of Isaiah are quoted frequently by *Book of Mormon* prophets who left Jerusalem **before** the exile. (compare 2 Nephi 7,8 with Isaiah 50 and 51. Compare Mosiah 12:21-24 with Isaiah 52:7-10. Compare Mosiah 14 with Isaiah 53. Compare 3 Nephi 22 with Isaiah 54).

Nephi Uses Words That will Not Be Known For Centuries.

Still another time and place problem is the frequent use of the terms "church", "synagogue", "gentile", "baptism", "Bible", and "Jesus Christ" by Nephite prophets about 600 B.C.[4] The word "church" is never mentioned in the Old Testament. It comes from a Greek word that refers specifically to followers of Jesus.[5] The "synagogue" was an institution created by the Jews **after** the exile in order to cope with the problem of being separated from their temple at Jerusalem. "Gentile" is a New Testament term. The word, "Bible" was not used until about 400 A. D. when Latin scholars borrowed this term from the plural Greek word "biblia" meaning rolls or scrolls. And yet Nephi talks about the "Bible" almost one thousand years earlier.

The words "baptism" and "Jesus Christ" cannot be found in the Old Testament and yet Nephi used them in his writing. How could Nephi have been familiar with all of these terms that were unknown to other prophets who were living about 600 B. C. when Lehi's family left Jerusalem for their promised land in America? How can all of these serious anachronisms be rationalized away?

Unknown Inventions

Anachronisms in *The Book of Mormon* also include references to window glass, spring steel (Nephi's bow was made of “fine steel”), submarines, scimitars and many other things centuries **before** they were invented. Joseph Smith's Nephites even had **machinery** about 2000 years before the industrial revolution![6] Archaeologists have never found any evidence of iron, steel, or machinery in ancient America.

Serious Geographical Errors

Smith's book not only reflects his ignorance about time but also about place. Lehi's family couldn't possibly have taken their provisions and traveled 170 miles from Jerusalem to the Red Sea in just three days.[7] Also, there is no River Laman flowing into the Red Sea. Smith's portrayal of desert travel and ocean voyages reflects his ignorance and lack of experience either on the desert or at sea.

His description of the promised land inhabited by the Nephites simply doesn't fit anywhere in the Americas despite great efforts by Church apologists to make it seem otherwise. I challenge any reader to take Smith's depiction of the land of the Nephites and Lamanites and make it fit somewhere into North, South, or Central America. (Smith's geography is found in Alma 22:27-32, Alma 50:7-15, and Helaman 3:8.)

Many L.D.S. scholars have tried to make sense out of Smith's geography and failed. For example, Smith's "narrow strip of wilderness" and his "small neck of land" which separates the major bodies of land "northward" (Desolation) from the land "southward" (Bountiful) does **not** fit Panama. His neck of land is far too narrow and the seas are in the wrong places. Panama is **not** "one and one half days journey for a Nephite." It is much larger. Also, the oceans bordering Panama are **not** east and west as in Smith's narrative, but north and south. Smith's landscape also includes "Sidon", a major river. But where is this river?

L.D.S. scholars have placed the hill Ramah (Cumorah) all over Central America, Mexico, and even in Western New York. But there is something wrong with every location.

If this were not such a serious matter, it would almost be comical to see B.Y.U. professors and other Church apologists falling all over each other trying to make Smith's geography fit somewhere into the real world. The most obvious solution for all of this is for everyone to simply admit that Smith did not know his Old World nor his New World geography and that his *Book of Mormon* is not real history but **fiction**. Authentic history does not contain any anachronisms nor does it include imaginary geography.

Chapter 7

CONFLICTS WITH SCIENTIFIC FACTS

> Whoever tells the truth, is chased out of nine villages.
>
> -Turkish proverb

Joseph Smith was **not** a scientist. He knew very little about mathematics, chemistry, physics, astronomy, biology, geology, anthropology, archaeology, or geography. His world was **not** the natural world of the scientist but rather the supernatural and mystical world of traditional religion.

Top Scientists Reject *The Book Of Mormon.*

Although pictures of great civilizations that once existed in Central America are often printed with *The Book of Mormon* and otherwise used by Church members in order to support its claim of authenticity, the scientific community does **not** accept that claim. Dr. Frank H.H. Roberts Jr., Director of the Bureau of American Ethnology at the Smithsonian Institution, wrote the following:

> The ancestors of the American Indians entered America probably 15,000 years ago and possibly much earlier. It is doubtful that any migrations occurred as late as 600 B.C. There is no evidence whatever of any migration from Israel to America, and no evidence that pre--Columbian Indians had any knowledge of Christianity or the Bible.[1]

Anthropologist Joseph Greenberg of Stanford University grouped the more than 1,500 American Indian tongues by looking for common sounds in simple words such as pronouns, the numbers one and two and the names for different parts of the human body. These are words that tend to change very little over time. Greenberg found that all Native American languages can be placed into one of three groups.[2] Not one of these languages even remotely resembled Hebrew or Egyptian, the languages in Smith's book.

Anthropologist Steve Zegura, an expert on blood types among the American Indians discovered these same three groups. Both researchers agree that the first of these groups migrated from Northeast Asia about 12,000 years ago. The other two groups came to the New World between 6,000 and 8,000 years later.[3] These findings clearly contradict the claims of Joseph Smith.

Dr. Michael D. Coe, Professor of Anthropology at Yale University and perhaps the world's leading authority on ancient American civilizations, wrote very pointedly concerning archaeology and *The Book of Mormon*:

> Mormon archaeologists over the years have almost unanimously accepted *The Book of Mormon* as an accurate, historical account of the New World peoples between about 2,000 B. C. and A. D. 421. . . . Let me now state . . . that as far as I know there is not one professionally trained archaeologist, who is not a Mormon, who sees any scientific justification for believing the forgoing to be true. . . . The picture of this hemisphere between 2,000 B.C. and A.D. 421 presented in the book has little to do with the early Indian cultures as we know them, in spite of much wishful thinking. . . . The bare facts of the matter are that nothing, absolutely nothing, has ever shown up in any New World excavation which would suggest to a dispassionate observer that *The Book of Mormon*, as claimed by Joseph Smith, is a historical document relating to the history of early migrants to our hemisphere.[4]

A Mormon Anthropologist Contradicts *The Book of Mormon.*

Even Mormon anthropologists and archaeologists are finding it more and more difficult to keep Joseph Smith's "keystone" from crumbling. John L. Sorenson, Professor of Anthropology at Brigham Young University, cites overwhelming evidence that there have been many cultures and languages in America dating back thousands of years. He makes it very clear that neither the Jaredites nor the Nephites could have come to an empty continent and lived in isolation as depicted in *The Book of Mormon*. Sorenson says:

> All this information boils down to the fact that *The Book of Mormon* is a partial record of events, emphasizing what happened to one group of people, put in their own ethnocentric terms, in the midst of other peoples each with its own version of events.[5]

This conclusion by a leading L.D.S. anthropologist clearly contradicts a statement made by the *Book of Mormon* prophet, Lehi, that his family was alone in their promised land:

> Wherefore, I, Lehi, have obtained a promise, that inasmuch as those whom the Lord God shall bring out of the land of Jerusalem shall keep his commandments, they shall prosper upon the face of this land; and they shall be kept from all other nations, that they may possess this land unto themselves. And if it so be that they shall keep his commandments, they shall be blessed upon the face of this land, and there shall be none to molest them, nor to take away the land of their inheritance; and they shall dwell safely forever.[6]

This promise made by the Lord unto Lehi about 570 B.C. does not make sense if major civilizations were already living in the New World as claimed by Sorenson and other leading scientists. Obviously, Smith did not know that there were many civilizations living in ancient America long before his Jaredites or Nephites supposedly came here.

When Smith published his *Book of Mormon,* he included an introduction entitled "Origin of *The Book of Mormon.*" This introduction quotes the Angel Moroni who supposedly came from Heaven for a visit with Smith: "He said there was a book deposited, written upon gold plates, giving an account of the former inhabitants of this continent and the source from whence they sprang."[7]

This quotation from Moroni does **not** indicate that Smith's Lamanites and Nephites were living among many other civilizations in ancient America as claimed by Sorenson and other scientists. Also, there is never any hint or suggestion in *The Book of Mormon,* itself, that any kind of political, economic, or social relationships took place with any other people. Apparently, the best minds in the L.D.S. Church cannot produce a reasonable answer to this dilemma.

The Mayas

Perhaps the most remarkable civilization in the New World was that of the Mayas of Central America. They built a large number of great cities, highways, and pyramids. Experts are now able to decipher their 800 hieroglyphic signs, including those of an amazingly accurate calendar. According to their own writings, Mayan history began about 3114 B. C. (our reckoning). It grew in power and complexity for thousands of years and did not crumble until late in the 9th Century A. D.[8] This 4000 year history clearly runs counter to *The Book of Mormon* narrative about the Jaredites (2000 B. C.) and the Nephites (600 B. C.) coming to an **empty** continent, growing in numbers until they filled the land and then being annihilated. It is very strange, indeed, that the Jaredites, Nephites, and Lamanites never met the Mayas!

Mayan hieroglyphics have no resemblance to Hebrew nor to "reformed Egyptian," the languages of the Nephites. The languages and cultures of the Incas, Aztecs, Toltecs, and other New World civilizations do not resemble that of the Nephites either. Again, an honest person is forced to choose between the claims of Smith and the overwhelming scientific evidence against him.

Books That Sell

Church bookstores have been making a lot of money selling books about archaeology and *The Book of Mormon.* B.Y.U Professor and Mormon anthropologist, John L. Sorenson says, "**Most L.D.S. literature on archaeology and *The Book of Mormon* ranges from factually and logically unreliable to truly kooky. In general, it appears that the worse the book, the more it sells**."[9] Apparently, Church members who desperately want to believe that Smith's *Book of Mormon* is authentic are buying thousands of these "unreliable" and "kooky" books.

Mayan Nephites

And yet, despite all of the evidence to the contrary, Joseph Smith claimed that the Mayas and the Nephites were one and the same culture! In September of 1842, after reading John Lloyd Stephens' book, *Incidents of travel in Central America, Chiapas, and Yucatan,* Smith made the following statement in his Nauvoo newspaper, *The Times and Seasons*:

> The foregoing extract has been made to assist Latter-Day Saints in establishing *The Book of Mormon* as a revelation from God. . . . Let us turn to our subject . . . to *The Book of Mormon,* where these wonderful ruins of Palenque are among the mighty works of the Nephites: and the mystery is solved.[10]

Thus, Smith commits himself that Palenque, an important Mayan city, was one of the mighty works of the Nephites. And yet Mayan history, language, and many other aspects of their culture refute this statement by Smith.

Other Problems With Smith's Book

Scientific information continues to contradict *Book of Mormon* claims over and over again. The Nephite missionary, Ammon, prepared horses and chariots for the Lamanite king, Lamoni.[11] And yet, archaeologists overwhelmingly agree that there were no horses or wheels, let alone chariots in ancient America.[12]

Joseph Smith claims that early Americans used gold coins called senines, seons, shums, and limnas and silver coins called senums, amnors, ezroms, and ontis in their business transactions. We are further informed that a senum of silver was equal to a senine of gold and that either of these was equal to a measure of barley or any other grain. And since all grains were tied to the monetary system, the Nephites also had a price support program for grain.[13]

All of this is very interesting except for the fact that no coins have ever been found despite over two centuries of digging. However, thousands of gold and silver coins much older than 400 A.D., when the Nephite Civilization ended, have been found in the Old World. Why did all of the Nephite money suddenly disappear?

Also, how could their money have been equal to a measure of barley when archaeologists claim that ancient Americans did not have barley until the coming of the Europeans?[14]

The Book of Mormon refers to silk and fine twined linen.[15] Again, scientists inform us that there was no silk and no flax to make linen in the New World.[16]

The Jaredites, the Nephites, and the Lamanites made thousands of steel swords and fought great battles of extermination. And yet, not one single iron or steel object has ever been found! Apparently, all of their steel swords and other objects made out of iron or steel mysteriously disappeared. Archaeologists now claim that ancient Americans did not have any iron or steel.[17]

The list of contradictions goes on and on and on. Perhaps the greatest irony is that not one of the ancient American civilizations knew the principle of the arch. **They didn't have a keystone!**[18]

Leaving the world of archaeology, anthropology, and world history to look for evidence of authenticity **inside** *The Book of Mormon* is not convincing either. Perhaps the most unique aspect of any civilization is its spoken and written language. Smith connected the Ancient Americans with two Old World languages, Hebrew and Egyptian. And yet, the strange names for people and places in *The Book of Mormon* refute these Old World connections.

Some of the most popular names among the Israelites were David, Abraham, Levi, Solomon, Judah, Manasseh, Saul, Joshua, Ruth, Miriam, and Naomi. Instead of these common Old World names, we find new names such as Lehi, Nephi, Mormon, Alma, Abinadi, Moroni, Helaman, Omni, Gadianton, Lamoni, Ammoron, Morianton, Corianton, and Shiblon.

New England colonizers coming to America named their children the same familiar names that had been in their families for generations. They also named many of their cities and towns after places left behind in the Old World such as Plymouth, York, Jersey, Manchester, Cambridge, Portsmouth, Lancaster, Dover, and Bedford. This seems like a natural and traditional thing for people emigrating to a new continent to do.

But instead of naming their cities after the ones they left behind in the Old World, the Nephites came up with names such as Zarahemla, Moronihah, Onihah, Gilgal, Moroni, Mocum, Gadiandi, Gadiomnah, Gimgimno, and Kishkumen.

Many Latter-Day Saints are partly convinced that *The Book of Mormon* is true because of the many strange sounding names it contains. Instead of proving authenticity, perhaps these unusual names for people and places actually serve to refute authenticity and prove only that Smith had a very creative imagination!

The Wrong DNA

And finally, DNA samples taken from a large number of Native American tribes closely match those taken from areas in the northeastern part of Asia. They do **not** match samples taken from Middle-Eastern cultures as claimed by Joseph Smith and his *Book of Mormon.* Native Americans are **not** Israelites.

One of the best DNA studies has been done by the University of Arizona Anthropology Department. If DNA evidence is reliable enough to convict criminals in a court of law, then it should also be good enough to convict Joseph Smith of fraud. (To access some of these scientific studies, go to the internet and type: DNA and Native Americans.)

Chapter 8

PLAGIARISM FROM OTHER BOOKS

> The exact contrary of what is generally believed is often the truth.
>
> - Jean De La Bruyere

Many of the names and events in *The Book of Mormon* came from Smith's own fertile imagination. But a considerable amount of material was obviously taken from other sources easily available to Smith before 1830 when he published his book. For example, whole chapters were copied from the King James Bible (mostly from Isaiah) word for word without giving credit to the source. These quotations were supposedly taken directly from Smith's gold plates, not the King James Bible.

Ethan Smith's *View Of The Hebrews*

Smith also had access to several very popular books about how Native Americans came to inhabit the New World. Most of these books connected the American "Indians" with the Ten Lost Tribes of Israel. Perhaps the most prominent of these books was Ethan Smith's *View of The Hebrews* which was published in 1823, seven years **before** Smith's *Book of Mormon.* (Ethan was not related to Joseph.)

Ethan Smith was a Congregational Minister living in Poultney, Vermont. Poultney also happened to be Oliver Cowdery's home town. Cowdery, a very close friend and associate of Smith, served as "scribe" while Smith dictated the manuscript for his *Book of*

Mormon. Ethan Smith's *View of The Hebrews* was widely read in all of the Eastern States including New York, the home of Joseph Smith. Ethan's book was so popular that a second edition was published in 1825, five years **before** Smith's book.

Many Similarities

As I read Ethan Smith's book, I was amazed by the many similarities between Joseph's and Ethan's books. Joseph's *Book of Mormon* and Ethan's *View of The Hebrews* are similar in that they both start out with the destruction of Jerusalem and the scattering of Israel.[1] Both are concerned with the Lost Ten Tribes and claim that these tribes have been preserved by the Lord as a distinct people.[2] Ethan quotes the eleventh chapter of Isaiah in his book. Joseph claimed that an angel, Moroni, quoted this very same scripture to him in his bedroom on September 12, 1828.[3] Isaiah is the favorite old testament prophet of both Smiths. Both authors use the allegory of the olive tree and the House of Israel.

Both men start out with a small group of people who cross the ocean to an uninhabited land, America.[4] In both books, those who migrate to the New World are all of one race and color.[5] In both accounts, a portion of the group become barbarians who occupy themselves primarily with hunting, stealing, and fighting. Eventually, these savages destroy their more civilized brethren in a great final battle on top of a hill! Both authors describe this desperate and frantic battle of extermination.[6]

Both books tell of sacred records which were handed down from generation to generation until they were finally buried in a hill where they were found many years later.[7] Both books identify Native Americans as the stick of Joseph or Ephraim which will some day be united with the stick of Judah or the Jews as prophesied by Ezekiel.[8]

Although the original language of both Ethan's and Joseph's migration was Hebrew, somehow both sacred records included Egyptian.[9] This was possibly an attempt on the part of both authors to combine their lost House of Israel theories with the Egyptian-like pyramids of Central America.

Both migrations had high priests who received revelations from God. These high priests had "breast plates" and the "Urim and Thummim."[10] Both books erroneously claimed that ancient Americans lived the law of Moses and that Christianity was later introduced to the inhabitants of the New World.[11] A golden age, a utopian society, was experienced by both groups after the introduction of Christianity.

Both Smiths use the terms "Zion" and "Mt. Zion" to designate the place of restoration and gathering of Israel.[12] Both books call upon the American people to preach the gospel to the Native Americans. Both refer to Native Americans by the term "remnants." Both remind the American people of the debt of gratitude that they owe to the House of Israel for giving them the Bible. Both predict the eventual conversion of the "remnants" and that they will become white before the burning of the world![13] Joseph used the terms, "white and delightsome."

Both books claim that in order to save their lives and retain their religious traditions, the industrious minority were forced to build high earthen walls, fortresses, and watchtowers around their cities.[14] Both accounts erroneously claim that ancient Americans had iron.[15]

Anticipating that readers would have doubts about his book, Ethan Smith said:

> Ye friends of God in the land addressed; can you read this prophetic direction of the ancient prophet Isaiah, without having your hearts burn within you?[16]

Joseph Smith makes a very similar statement:

> And when ye shall receive these things, I would exort you that ye would ask God, the Eternal Father, in the name of Christ if these things are not true; and if ye shall ask with a sincere heart, and with real intent, having faith in Christ, he will manifest the truth unto you, by the power of the Holy Ghost.[17]

Ethan Smith claimed that he translated his book from some old yellow parchments found buried in Indian Hill, a New England mound. These parchments were originally found by Mr. Joseph Merrick, Esquire, a highly respectable man in the Church of Pittsfield. Mr. Merrick later took these parchments to Reverend Sylvester Larned, an expert on foreign languages living in Boston. Mr. Merrick obtained an affidavit from Reverend Larned declaring that his parchments were authentic Hebrew scriptures.[18]

Again we see a striking similarity between the activities and claims of Ethan and Joseph. Ethan's **yellow** parchments were sent to Reverend **Larned** of Boston; Joseph sent a transcript from his **gold** plates to "one who is **learned**" to obtain an affidavit of authenticity. This was Charles Anthon of New York.[19]

Other similarities between these two books include the piety-prosperity theme, anti-Catholic ideas, monotheism, temples, copper breastplates, an Egyptian hieroglyphic language, and a great future in store for the "remnants."

It would be very difficult to find two books more alike in their basic ideas and content. There is far too much parallelism to be accidental. And since Ethan Smith published his book seven years **before** Joseph published his *Book of Mormon* and since there are so many similarities between these two books, it was obviously Joseph who plagiarized Ethan's ideas and not the other way around. If Joseph had published his book seven years earlier, a fair minded person would then be justified in accusing Ethan of transparent plagiarism.

Manuscript Found

Another source of information that may have been available to Joseph Smith in writing his *Book of Mormon* was a manuscript written by Reverend Solomon Spaulding, who died about fourteen years **before** the publication of Smith's book. Researcher Vernal Holley has found many similarities between Spaulding's *Manuscript Found* and *The Book of Mormon.*[20]

Both books claim to be an authentic history of the inhabitants of ancient America. Both manuscripts were obtained by using a lever to lift a heavy stone cover off from a depository in the ground. Both accounts tell of considerable difficulty in removing the record from the hill.

Both records claim to be an abridgment of a more detailed history. Both urge the reader to ponder their teachings with a pure heart and real intent. Both accounts include departure for the New World on a sea voyage. Both groups encounter a great storm and express fear of being buried in a "watery grave." Both groups sailed to the promised land under divine guidance.

Both authors include a change of skin pigmentation in their narratives. Spaulding has some of the descendants of his dark skinned people turning "fair and white" while Smith has a portion of his light skinned people turning "dark and loathsome."

Mr. Holley calls the similarities between the great speeches given by *Book of Mormon* prophets such as King Benjamin and the teachings of Spaulding's religious leaders (ohons) as "striking."

Both authors make the mistake of referring to wheat, horses, elephants, and steel, as being important aspects of the ancient American economy. Strangely, neither Smith nor Spalding ever mention pyramids, jade, jungles, corn, buffalo, jaguars, alligators, deer, elk, rabbits, llamas, and other things that actually were important in ancient America.

Both authors include an account of a divine reformer, a magical seer stone, fortified cities, and the seduction of stolen maidens. Both accounts dwell upon battles, wars and military strategy. Both authors conclude with a last great battle of extinction being fought upon a hill. Light skinned survivors are hunted down and killed in both accounts!

Nineteenth Century Concerns

Not only do the basic story line and many of the ideas presented in Smith's *Book of Mormon* resemble other popular books in circulation at the time, but the major concerns in his book reflect those of Joseph Smith's 19th century New England rather than those of the ancient Israelites.

Some of the major concerns in Smith's day include secret orders such as the Masons, the whereabouts of the Lost Ten Tribes, manifest destiny of the promised land of America, the piety-prosperity theories of the Calvinistic founding fathers of America, democratic government, the dislike for kings, the importance of freedom of speech and religion, and the origin of the "Indians." These were **not** concerns of the Israelites in 600 B. C. *The Book of Mormon* was obviously written by a person living in America in the 1800s A. D., not by Israelites who were living more than two thousand years earlier as depicted by Smith.

Alma And Paul

Smith's plagiarism from the King James Bible is also very transparent. For example, historian Michael Marquardt has pointed out the overwhelming similarities between the life and teachings of Smith's *Book of Mormon* prophet Alma and the life and teachings of the Apostle Paul.[21]

Both Alma and Paul were wicked men before their conversion. (Mosiah 27:8, I Timothy 1:12-13) Both were traveling about trying to destroy Christians. (Compare Alma 36:6, with I Corinthians 15:9) Both were on missions of persecution on the day of their conversion. (Mosiah 27:10-11, Acts 26:11-13) Both fell to the earth after a heavenly manifestation which, in both cases, was not understood by their traveling companions. (Mosiah 27:12, Acts 26:14 and 22:9) Both Alma and Paul were asked why they fought against the Lord. (Mosiah 27:13, Acts 9:4 and 22:7) Both became helpless and had to be helped by their friends. Paul was struck blind; Alma was struck dumb.

Both went without food for two or three days. (Mosiah 27:19-,23, Acts 9:8-9) Both were immediately converted and began to travel around preaching Christianity. (Mosiah 27,23, 24,32, Acts 9:18-20) Both healed a cripple. (Alma 15:11, Acts 14:10) Both were cast into prison. (Alma 14:22, Acts 16:23) Both Paul and Alma prayed unto the Lord who then loosened their bands and caused an earthquake which opened their prisons allowing miraculous escapes! (Compare Alma 14:26-28, with Acts 16:25-26).

Many of Alma's teachings are identical and others similar to the wording and phrases used by Paul. Compare Mosiah 27:26 with II Corinthians 5:17; Alma 5:42 with Romans 6:23; Alma 7:24 with I Corinthians 13:13; Alma 13:28 with I Corinthians 10:13; Alma 15:6 with Romans 1:16; Alma 40:3 with I Corinthians 15:51; Alma 41:4 with I Corinthians 15:53-54; and Alma 41:11 with Ephesians 2:12). It seems obvious that Smith used the life of Paul as a model for his *Book of Mormon* prophet, Alma.

Family Folklore

Another source of material for Smith's book was the visions, dreams, folklore, and myths of his own family. Some sections of his book had been part of the Smith family folklore many years before Joseph claimed that he received his gold plates. For example, In 1853, Joseph Smith's mother, Lucy Mack Smith, published a book entitled *Biographical Sketches of Joseph Smith the Prophet and His Progenitors For Many Generations.* This book contains information that is very damaging to the claims of her son, Joseph.

As a young woman living in Turnbridge, Vermont, Lucy married a young school teacher, Joseph Smith Sr. Lucy described her husband's problem in deciding which church to attend and support. In order to help her husband solve his dilemma, Lucy went out into a grove of trees to pray for her husband that he might be able to know which church was right.[22] All of this sounds very familiar to Latter-Day-Saints. But these things all took place when Lucy was just a young woman.

In answer to her prayer in the grove of trees, Lucy's husband (Joseph Smith Sr.) had the following miraculous experience:

> I thought, he said, I was traveling in an open desolate field, which appeared to be very barren. As I was thus traveling, the thought suddenly came into my mind that I had better stop and reflect upon what I was doing, before I went any farther. So I asked myself, what motive can I have for traveling here and what place can this be? My guide who was by my side, as before, said, "This is the desolate world; but travel on". The road was

so broad and barren, that I wondered why I should travel in it; for I said to myself, "Broad is the road and wide is the gate that leads to death, and many there be that walk therein; but narrow is the way and straight is the gate that leads to everlasting life, and few there be that go in thereat." Traveling a short distance further I came to a narrow path. This path I entered, and, when I had traveled a little way in it, I beheld a beautiful stream of water which ran from the East to the West. Of this stream I could see neither the source nor yet the termination; but as far as my eyes could extend I could see a rope running along the bank of it, about as high as a man could reach, and beyond me, was a low, but very pleasant, valley, in which stood a tree, such as I had never seen before. It was exceedingly handsome, insomuch that I looked upon it with wonder and admiration. Its beautiful branches spread themselves somewhat like an umbrella, and it bore a kind of fruit, in shape much like a chestnut bur, and as white as snow, or if possible, whiter. I gazed upon the same with considerable interest, and as I was doing so, the burs or shells commenced opening and shedding their particles or the fruit which they contained, which was of dazzling whiteness. I drew near, and began to eat of it, and I found it delicious beyond description. As I was eating, I said in my heart, "I cannot eat this alone. I must bring my wife and children, that they may partake with me. Accordingly I went and brought my family, which consisted of a wife and seven children and we all commenced eating, and praising God for this blessing. We were exceedingly happy insomuch that our joy could not easily be expressed. While thus engaged, I beheld a spacious building standing opposite the valley which we were in, and it appeared to reach the very heavens. It was full of doors and windows, and they were all filled with people, who were very finely dressed. When these people observed us in the low valley, under the tree, they pointed the finger of scorn at us, and treated us with all manner of disrespect and contempt. But their contumely we utterly disregarded. I presently turned to my guide, and inquired of him the

> meaning of the fruit that was so delicious. He told me it was the pure love of God, shed abroad in the hearts of all those who love him, and keep his commandments. . . . I asked my guide what was the meaning of the spacious building which I saw. He replied, "It is Babylon, it is Babylon, and it must fall. The people in the doors and windows are the inhabitants thereof, who scorn and despise the Saints of God, because of their humility." I soon awoke clapping my hands for joy.[23]

All of this happened to Joseph Smith Sr. when young Joseph Jr. was only six years old and some 19 years **before** publication of his book. And yet, this vision is almost identical to the vision of Lehi some 2400 years earlier as recorded in *The Book of Mormon*![24]

Is it reasonable to believe that God would give both Lehi and Joseph Smith Sr. the same vision over two thousand years apart? Or is it more likely that Joseph was fabricating a book from any source available to him including the Bible, *View of The Hebrews*, *Manuscript Found*, and other books, along with the folklore, dreams, visions, and other spiritual experiences that had been part of his family tradition for many years?

Perhaps the most important question a person can ask about all of this is whether Smith could have written *The Book of Mormon* using family folklore, scriptures from the Bible, information from other books, and his own remarkable imagination. I believe the answer to this question is yes, he could.

Other geniuses have been able to do amazing things. John Stuart Mill knew mathematics and languages when only a child. He could memorize almost as fast as he could read. Mozart created over 600 musical compositions. He could compose page after page of very complex material without ever changing a note.

The Book of Mormon is filled with serious mistakes. It is not nearly as remarkable as the works of Mozart, Mill, Jules Verne, or Shakespeare. Apparently, Joseph Smith had all of the intelligence, imagination, information, and motivation necessary to write his *Book of Mormon*, and he did so, plagiarizing freely as he went along.

Chapter 9

THE MOST CORRECT BOOK ON EARTH

> The truth knocks on the door and you say, "Go away, I'm looking for the truth," and it goes away, puzzling.
>
> - Robert M. Pirsig

Joseph Smith described his *Book of Mormon* as ". . . the most correct of any book on earth . . ."[1]. Many Latter-Day Saints consider it sacred scripture, something from God that couldn't possibly have been written by Smith or any other human being. The fact that it was presented to the world by a relatively uneducated twenty five year old man, only adds to their faith and testimony. But many of those who feel this way have never even read *The Book of Mormon*!

Serious Errors

But upon closer observation, this reverent assessment begins to unravel and serious flaws become apparent. In previous chapters we have already observed a large number of errors in Smith's book. This chapter presents a brief summary of those findings and then presents additional reasons why Smith's claims are ludicrous and arrogant.

No Law of Moses In Ancient America

The Book of Mormon starts out with many inconsistencies and contradictions. The narrative begins by telling readers that Lehi and his family are Israelites who left Jerusalem for a promised land

(America) about 600 B.C. We are then informed that they were strictly living according to the law of Moses until they were all converted to Christianity, about 600 years later. But there is no evidence within Smith's book that his people were living the law of Moses. Also, there is no scientific evidence in our world today that ancient Americans knew anything about the law of Moses nor Christianity.

Tall Tales, A Fantasy World

This "most correct of all the books on earth" then asks readers to leave their rational world and accompany Smith into his fantasy world of tall tales where almost anything can happen. Smith's fantasy world included steel bows, magic balls, submarines, stone lights, young supermen, gold plates, trances, mass conversions, and all kinds of other mystical and magical things.

False Prophesies

Next we are given a long list of false prophesies. The Ten Lost Tribes do not live as a group in the "north country" or anywhere else on this earth; it has all been explored. These same Ten Tribes have not made a triumphant return to Zion bringing their sacred scriptures with them as prophesied by Smith. And very few Native Americans have been converted to Mormonism. And those who have been converted have not become "white and delightsome," nor have they become an instrument in the hand of God in tearing American gentiles into pieces like a young lion as prophesied five times in *The Book of Mormon.*

The great and abominable Church (whatever that is) has not gathered all of the nations of the world together to fight against the Mormons. The cities of the gentile nations that have refused to accept Mormonism have not been thrown down and their chariots destroyed. Smith's false prophesies go on and on and on. They do not belong in the most correct of any book on earth.

Bad Theology And Racism

Smith's book then presents us with some false doctrine and bad theology. We are told about a whimsical God who changes skin pigmentation to dark, to white, and then back to dark again depending on the righteousness of the people. Smith's God changed the skin color of **all** Lamanites, even innocent little children, to "dark and loathsome," but He never changed the skin color of the Nephites even when they became extremely cruel and sinful. Why didn't God change the skin color of the people who accepted or rejected the gospel back in the days of Abraham, Moses, or Jesus? And why didn't He change the skin color of Hitler and his white skinned Nazi exterminators? Smith's *Book of Mormon* God is a whimsical, unjust racist!

Geographical Errors

The most correct book on earth then presents the reader with some serious geographical errors. The geography of the earth changes very slowly. Continents, seas, major rivers, and mountains have stayed about the same for thousands, even millions of years. *The Book of Mormon* contradicts this scientific fact. Rivers, mountains, and seas are said to be where they do not exist.

Despite Smith's account of Old World geography, there is no river "Laban" on the east coast of the Red Sea. The great Rub al Khali Desert is not a game preserve where Nephi could have killed enough wild animals with his steel bow to feed his father's family for eight years. In 600 B. C. there was no such place as "Bountiful," an uninhabited and fertile area on the west coast of the Persian Gulf where Nephi could have found all of the materials he needed to make tools and build a ship that could sail half way around the world.

Smith's New World geography isn't any better. Everything is in the wrong place. And where is the illusive and infamous Hill Cumorah anyway? Most Church members believe that Cumorah is a hill located near Palmyra in Western New York where Smith found the gold plates and where the L.D.S. Church presents a pageant every year.

But if the Nephites were Mayans, as claimed by Smith, and their homeland was in Central America and Mexico, then why did the Lamanites allow the conquered Nephites to take their old people, their children, and great quantities of supplies and march thousands of miles over deserts, mountains, and great rivers (like the Mississippi) to a small hill in the northeastern part of North America? Why would the Lamanites have agreed to such a costly and ridiculous scheme? And why did the Nephites want to fight their last battle on this small hill in a strange land? What is there about this ordinary hill that was supposed to give the Nephites some hope for a military victory? None of this is logical nor reasonable. Why would the most correct of any book on earth contain such nonsense?

Historical Errors

Smith was not only lacking in his understanding of geography, but also of history. His *Book of Mormon* contains major historical errors and anachronisms. The Jaredites, and later the family of Lehi couldn't possibly have come across the ocean to an **empty** America as claimed by Smith. The Mayans and other civilizations had been here for thousands of years.

Smith's inaccurate and simplistic prophecy about the discovery of America by "white and delightsome" gentiles further demonstrates his ignorance of American history. The earliest explorers and conquistadors coming to America were not white. Smith's account of elephants, horses, steel, chariots, silk, gold and silver money, barley, and machinery being present in ancient America is strongly rejected by some of our best scientific minds.

Anachronisms

Smith's sense of time and place was very poor. His prophets quoted Old World prophets long before these prophets were even born. His *Book of Mormon* prophets also used words such as "Bible," "baptism," "church," and "Jesus" long before these words came into existence. Smith's account of everyday life among his people also includes many objects long before they were invented. Real history does not contain anachronisms. Since Smith's book does contain anachronisms, it must be fiction.

Poorly Written

The “most correct of any book on earth” is also very confusing and poorly written. It does not have a good chronological flow. Smith’s narrative starts about 600 B. C. when Lehi is commanded by the Lord to call the people of Jerusalem to repentance. Instead of taking him seriously, they tried to kill him. But why wasn’t such an important prophet as Lehi ever mentioned in the Bible?

Lehi is then commanded to take his family and depart for a “promised land.” After spending about eight years in the Arabian wilderness, Lehi's family (mostly boys) and Ishmael's family (mostly girls) supposedly came to America on their ship. God then made Lehi a promise that they could have their promised land all to themselves. But that, of course, would have been impossible.

Almost 500 pages later, and right in the middle of Smith's narrative about Nephites and Lamanites, he begins a new story about some "Jaredites" who supposedly came to the New World in the days of The Great Tower, about fourteen centuries **before** Lehi. Smith then interrupts his story about the Jaredites , Nephites, and Lamanites to give a brief account of a still another group, the “Mulekites,” who were also brought to the promised land by the Lord. All of this is very confusing.

Repetition

Another serious problem with “the most correct of any book on earth” is repetition. The words "and it came to pass" are used hundreds of times. In some places almost every sentence begins with "And it came to pass . . ."

There are other kinds of repetition as well. There are several anti-Christs in the narrative, but they are all alike. The Jaredite civilization came to an end in a great battle of extermination upon the very same hill (Ramah-Cumorah) as the Nephites! The piety-prosperity theme and the anti-Masonic themes are repeated over and over again. Also, the wars and war heroes are all similar. Apparently, Smith thought that if he said something over and over and over again, people would begin to believe it. And this actually seems to have happened! There are now millions of believers.

Chloroform In Print

Mark Twain called *The Book of Mormon* "chloroform in print," "imaginary history," and "tedious plagiarism." He then went on to say that if Smith had left out the words "And it came to pass," his book ". . . would have been only a pamphlet."[2]

Twain apparently read the first (1830) edition. As a brilliant writer and a good judge of literature, Mark Twain was offended by Smith's repetition, confusion, tall tales, historical inaccuracies, bad grammar, poor sentence construction, and copious plagiarism.

Poor Grammar

Jerald and Sandra Tanner's book, *3913 Changes in the Book of Mormon*, includes many examples of Smith's poor writing style and bad grammar. A few of these along with the corresponding page numbers from the **first edition** of *The Book of Mormon* are as follows:

> And he beheld that they did contain the five books of Moses, which gave an account of the creation of the world, and also of Adam and Eve which was our first parents . . . (p.15).
>
> And he saith unto me, Behold, there is save it be, two churches; one is the church of the lamb of God and the other is the church of the Devil. . . (p.33).
>
> And the words which he shall write, shall be the words which is expedient in my wisdom, should go forth unto the fruit of thy loins. (p.67)
>
> And it came to pass that the servant of the Lord of the vineyard, done according to the word of the Lord of the vineyard, and grafted in the branches of the wild olive tree. (P.132)
>
> And he preached many things which were flattering unto the people; and this he done, that he might overthrow the doctrine of Christ. (p.140)

And they were surrounded by the kings guard, and was taken, and was bound and was committed to prison. (p.169)

. . . and all this he done, for the sole purpose of bringing this people into subjection or into bondage. (p.170)

And a Prophet of the Lord have they slain; yea, a chosen man of God, who told them of their wickedness and abominations, and prophesied of many things which is to come . . . (p.171).

And after Alma had said these words, both Alma and Helam was buried in the water. (p.192)

And it came to pass that Gideon sent men into the wilderness secretly, to search for the king and those that was with him. (p.195)

Now there was a place in Shemlon, where the daughters of the Lamanites did gather themselves together for to sing, and to dance, and to make themselves merry. (p.196)

And it came to pass that king Limhi and many of his people was desirous to be baptized; but there was none in the land that had authority from God. (p.200)

And behold, they had found those priests of king Noah, in a place which they called Amulon; and they had began to possess the land of Amulon, and had began to till the ground. (p.204)

And it came to pass that they did appoint judges to rule over them, or to judge them according to the law; and this they done throughout all the land. (p.220)

And now behold, I say unto you, that the foundation of the destruction of this people is a beginning to be laid by the unrighteousness of your lawyers and your judges. (p.251)

. . . he met with the sons of Mosiah a journeying toward the land of Zarahemla. (p.269)

. . . nevertheless they departed out of the land of Zarahemla, and took their bows, and their arrows, and their slings; and this they done that they might provide food for themselves while in the wilderness . . . (p. 269).

And it came to pass that when the multitude beheld that the man had fell dead, who lifted the sword to slay Ammon, fear came upon them all, and they durst not put their hands to touch him or any of those which had fallen . . . (p.278).

. . . they did lay down the weapons of their rebellion, that they did not fight against God no more . . . (p.290).

And it came to pass that the curse was not taken off of Korihor; but he was cast out, and went about from house to house, a begging for food. (p.309).

Now this he done that he might preserve their hatred towards the Nephites . . . (p. 340).

And thus ended the record of Alma, which was wrote upon the plates of Nephi. (p.347).

Yea, verily, verily, I say unto you, if all men had been, and were, and ever would be like unto Moroni, behold, the very powers of hell would have been shaken forever; yea, the Devil would never have no power over the hearts of the children of men. (pp. 358-9).

> Now Moroni was compelled to cause the Lamanites to labor because it were easy to guard them while at their labor . . . (p.375).
>
> Behold we have escaped from the Nephites, and they sleepeth; and behold we have took of their wine, and brought with us. (p.379).
>
> And it came to pass that when the Lamanites saw that Moroni was a coming against them, they were again frightened and fled before the army of Moroni. (p.403).
>
> . . . therefore I have wrote this epistle, sealing it with mine own hand, feeling for your welfare . . . (p.457).
>
> . . . and I have wrote them to the intent that they that they might be brought again unto this people, from the Gentiles . . . Behold I were about to write them all which were engraven upon the plates of Nephi, but the Lord forbid it . . . (p.506).
>
> And I did endeavor to preach unto this people, but my mouth was shut, and I were forbidden that I should preach unto them . . . (p.519).

These quotations from Smith's original *Book of Mormon*, published in 1830, are but a small sample of hundreds of grammatical errors contained in his first edition. And yet, Smith claimed that he dictated **every word** of his book as directed by the Lord. He wouldn't allow John H. Gilbert, the man who set the type for the original *Book of Mormon*, to change anything, even to correct punctuation or grammatical errors.

If we take Joseph Smith at his word, that he translated **every word** of his *Book of Mormon* from gold plates by the gift and power of God, then we also have to believe that God is an inconsistent, unjust, racist, who is ignorant about geography, history, science, and even English grammar!

Embarrassed Church scholars have made almost 4,000 corrections to *The Book of Mormon* since 1830.[3] If every word of the first edition was given and approved of God, then it would seem that there are **now** about 4000 errors put into this book by uninspired men! Most of the changes that have been made have been grammatical but some have been changes of substance. For example, a prophesy in the 1830 edition concerning the remnants (American Indians) reads as follows:

> And then shall they rejoice: for they shall know that it is a blessing unto them from the hand of God; and their scales of darkness shall begin to fall from their eyes; and many generations shall not pass away among them, save they shall become a white and delightsome people. (p.117)

This wording stayed in Smith's book until it became too much of an embarrassment for the Church. It now reads:

> And then shall they rejoice; for they shall know that it is a blessing unto them from the hand of God; and their scales of darkness shall begin to fall from their eyes; and many generations shall not pass away among them, save they shall be a pure and a delightsome people. (2 Nephi 30:6)

Another significant change is the title page which read:

BY JOSEPH SMITH, JR,

AUTHOR AND PROPRIETOR

PALMYRA:

PRINTED BY E. B. GRANDIN, FOR THE AUTHOR
1830

This same part of the title page now reads:

TRANSLATED BY JOSEPH SMITH, JUN.

PUBLISHED BY

**THE CHURCH OF JESUS CHRIST
OF LATTER-DAY SAINTS**

SALT LAKE CITY UTAH, U.S.A.

The title page of the first edition named Joseph Smith, Junior as the **author** of *The Book of Mormon*, which undoubtedly was true. Now, the title page claims that Smith was only the **translator**.

Most Corrected Book On Earth

But why should Church leaders need to make major changes or even minor changes in the wording and grammar of God? Obviously, *The Book of Mormon* is **not** the most correct of any book on earth. The thousands of changes that have been made since 1830 certainly places it in contention for recognition as the most corrected book on earth!

Dark Depravity

And finally, Smith's "most correct" book includes many revolting accounts of violence, war, carnage, bloodshed, and the most unthinkable atrocities. Smith dwells on these things throughout his book. Here is but one example:

> . . . the Lamanites have many prisoners, which they took from the tower of sherrizah; and there were men, women, and children. And the husbands and fathers of those women and children they have slain; and they feed the women upon the flesh of their husbands, and the children upon the flesh of their fathers; and no water, save a little do they give unto them. And not withstanding the great abomination of the Lamanites, it does not exceed that of our people in Moriantum. For behold, many of the daughters of the Lamanites have

> they taken prisoners; and after depriving them of that which was most dear and precious above all things, which is chastity and virtue - And after they had done this thing, they did murder them in a most cruel manner, torturing their bodies even unto death; and after they have done this, they devour their flesh like unto wild beasts because of the hardness of their hearts; and they do it for a token of bravery.[4]

It is not easy to come up with a more revolting story than first starving women and little children almost to death and then feeding them upon the flesh of their own husbands and fathers! But then Smith's Lamanite atrocities seem to be outdone by the Nephites who first raped the Lamanite girls and then tortured them to death "in a most cruel manner" and then ate them as a token of bravery! Perhaps Smith actually succeeded in coming up with something even more sickening than his first story about Lamanite atrocities.

And since there never were any Nephites or Lamanites in ancient America, **all of this fictitious rape, torture, murder, and cannibalism came out of the darkness of Smith's own imagination**. And yet this man is almost worshipped by millions of Church members all over the world, many of whom have never even read his book.

Chapter 10

CREDIBILITY OF WITNESSES

> As a rule people are afraid of truth. Each truth we discover in nature or social life destroys the crutches on which we used to lean.
>
> - Ernst Toller

Many Church members are impressed by the eleven men who signed their names as witnesses to the existence of Smith's elusive gold plates and also to his inspired translation. The written testimonies of these witnesses have always been published in the introduction to Smith's book. But how much credibility do these men have? Were they objective witnesses or part of a conspiracy?

Biased Witnesses

Smith's witnesses included his father, two of his brothers, and eight of his closest friends. All of these men were very anxious to see Smith succeed. Two of his witnesses, Martin Harris and Oliver Cowdery, had invested a great deal of time and money toward publication of Smith's book. Cowdery spent hundreds of hours as Smith's scribe writing page after page of *The Book of Mormon* in longhand. Harris sold part of his farm in order to finance the publication of Smith's book. The three Smiths, the five Whitmers, Oliver Cowdery, and Martin Harris all had a great deal to gain if Smith's book succeeded and a lot to lose if Smith was exposed as a fraud. Would these men be considered objective in a court of law?

Joseph Smith Discredits His Own Witnesses!

Strange as it may seem, the person who casts the most doubt upon the honesty of his witnesses is Joseph Smith, himself! A few years after publication of his book, Smith told a congregation of Church members that Martin Harris, John Whitmer, David Whitmer, and Oliver Cowdery, (four of his witnesses) were full of "wickedness and hypocrisy" and "too mean to mention."[1] He also referred to David Whitmer as a "dumb ass."[2] Statements like these do not strengthen a person's faith in the credibility of these men.

Martin Harris Lies.

Apparently, Smith was right about the dishonesty of his witnesses. For example, in 1827, Martin Harris took some of Smith's "reformed Egyptian" hieroglyphics to Charles Anthon, a language expert at Columbia College in New York. Harris said that Anthon declared the hieroglyphics authentic and then certified that Smith's translation " . . . was correct, more so than any he had before seen translated from Egyptian."[3]

There are some serious problems with this story. Anthon was an expert only in Greek and Latin. Egyptian was considered a dead, unreadable language until the French scholar Jean Francois Champollian, using the Rosetta Stone and other resources, discovered the difference between ideograms and phonetic complements which established the connection between Coptic and ancient Egyptian.

Most of Champollian's work, including a book on grammar and a dictionary on Egyptian hieroglyphics (picture language), were published several years **after** Harris made his visit to Anthon.[4] It is very doubtful that Anthon could have read **any** Egyptian, let alone Smith's "reformed Egyptian." And how could Anthon have certified that Smith's translation was the most correct that he had ever seen translated from Egyptian? It would have been impossible. Harris was obviously lying in order to promote the sales of Smith's book.

Later, when word got back to Anthon that Harris was using his name to prove the authenticity of Smith's book he became very angry and told his version of their meeting:

> He requested an opinion from me in writing, which of course I declined. . . . This paper was in fact a singular scrawl. It consisted of all kinds of crooked characters disposed in columns, and had evidently been prepared by some person who had before him . . . a book containing various alphabets. Greek and Hebrew letters, crosses and flourishes, Roman letters inverted or placed sideways, were arranged in perpendicular columns, and the whole ended in a rude delineation of a circle divided into various compartments, decked with various strange marks and evidently copied after the Mexican calendar, given by Humboldt, but copied in such a way as not to betray the source whence it was derived.[5]

Not only this statement but the fact that Anthon could not have read Smith's "reformed Egyptian" anyway is strong evidence that Anthon was telling the truth. After all, Harris had a financial interest in *The Book of Mormon*, but Anthon had no reason to lie.

A Conspiricy

Apparently, Smith and Harris were both in on this deception. It seems that they were pretending to fulfill a prophesy recorded in the twenty-ninth chapter of Isaiah:

> And the vision of all is become unto you as the words of a book that is sealed, which men deliver to one that is learned, saying, Read this I pray thee: and he saith, I cannot; for it is sealed: and the book is delivered unto him that is not learned, saying, Read this, I pray thee: and he saith, I am not learned. . . . Therefore, behold, I will proceed to do a marvelous work among this people, even a marvelous work and a wonder: for the wisdom of their wise men shall perish, and the understanding of their prudent men shall be hid.[6]

But the story told by Harris and Smith does **not** fulfill Isaiah's prophesy. Isaiah said that some "men" would first deliver "a book that is sealed" to a learned man who would say that he could not read a sealed book. Later, these men would deliver this same book to a man who was not learned who would at first say, "I am not learned", but then would read it by the power of God. Anthon never saw these men nor any sealed book. All he ever saw was Harris and his piece of paper.

Also, Isaiah said that **after** the learned man had his chance to read the sealed book, it would be "delivered unto him that is not learned." But Smith obtained the book **first**, not after Anthon had his chance as Isaiah prophesied.

Despite all of these problems, conflicts, and contradictions, the Martin Harris and Joseph Smith version of this event is still canonized in *The Pearl of Great Price* as sacred L.D.S. scripture.[7]

Oliver Cowdery Accuses Smith Of Adultery.

Oliver Cowdery, another witness to the gold plates, fell out of favor with Smith in 1838 when he accused Joseph of adultery.[8] If Cowdery was lying, this creates a serious question about his personal honesty. If he was telling the truth, it calls into question the honesty and morality of Smith. Whether Cowdery was lying or telling the truth, the position of *The Book of Mormon* is weakened. **Smith loses either way**.

Most of Joseph Smith's eleven witnesses eventually turned against him and left the Church. David Whitmer even claimed that God commanded him to leave. Some of Smith's witnesses later claimed that they had seen the gold plates with their spiritual eyes, which may simply have meant their imaginations. But would these men have left Mormonism if they really believed that Smith had exclusive priesthood authority from God necessary for their eternal salvation and exaltation?

Chapter 11

REASON VS. TESTIMONY

> A thing is not necessarily true because a man dies for it.
>
> \- Oscar Wilde

Joseph Smith told his followers that they could know the truth about his revelations and his *Book of Mormon* by sincere prayer.[1] Sometimes both fasting and prayer were necessary. If a person prayed with real intent in the name of Christ, God would cause a certain feeling to come over him or her. Smith always stressed the importance of feelings and emotions as a way to discern truth.

A Testimony

And even now, after all these years, many Church members still say, "I don't care how much scientific evidence there is against the authenticity of *The Book of Mormon*, what really matters to me is the feeling that I have in my heart when I read that book and attend testimony meetings."

Even at the highest levels of the Church, testimony, not scientific evidence or logical reasoning, predominates. A good example of this was in 1922, when B.H. Roberts, perhaps Mormonism's greatest historian and most celebrated intellectual, presented five questions about *The Book of Mormon* to The First Presidency, The Quorum of Twelve Apostles, and his own Council of Seventy:

1. How could there be such great diversity of Indian languages in the Western Hemisphere when Lehi and his followers were only here a short period of time.

2. Why were there no horses in America upon arrival of the Spaniards when the followers of Lehi had such animals.

3. Nephi had a bow of steel when history records that the Jews had no knowledge of steel in 600 B.C.

4. The words, "swords" and "scimitars" appear in *The Book of Mormon* and yet the word "scimitar" does not appear in literature until well after the Christian era.

5. The Nephites possessed an abundance of silk when apparently silk was not known in America.

Roberts expected the collective wisdom of these men and perhaps a revelation from the Lord to answer his questions. After three days of meetings, Roberts reported, "In answer, they merely one by one stood up and bore testimony to the truthfulness of *The Book of Mormon*."[2] This is the same reaction that most Church members give today when confronted with scientific evidence against *The Book of Mormon*. Testimony takes priority over science.

Some Questions About Testimony

But what is a testimony anyway? Is it divine communication or just a powerful psychological experience? How can a testimony be trusted when sincere testimonies often contradict each other? And why is testimony considered more reliable than scientific evidence and logical reasoning by many Church members?

Despite overwhelming evidence against the authenticity of *The Book of Mormon*, many Church members claim to have a spiritual witness or "testimony" that transcends science. Many of those who feel this way are not aware that throughout world history many people have believed strongly enough about various ideologies to die for their convictions. Many religious groups have fought and killed each other while fervently praying to God for help. Thousands of men and women have had a strong enough "testimony" to offer their own sons and daughters as human sacrifices to pagan idols. **A personal testimony in action can be a very frightening thing**. Human reason may not be perfect, but irrational and emotional behavior has filled the pages of history with a sad legacy of violence, intolerance, hatred, and war.

Creation Of A Strong Emotional Response

Despite its laborious and repetitive literary style, *The Book of Mormon* has an amazing ability to create powerful spiritual and emotional responses. These feelings may be what many people call "testimony." To them, it rings true; it has a familiar spirit; it brings tears to their eyes. They seem to reason that if some of its doctrines are edifying, then the book itself must be authentic.

Perhaps *The Book of Mormon* touches the hearts of many people because it reassures them that some of their deepest convictions are true. If a person desperately wants to believe something, it usually creates a strong emotional response when he hears or reads anything which satisfies this longing.

For example, **wealthy people** sometimes feel guilty when they observe the relative poverty and deprivation which surrounds them on all sides. They often live in exclusive neighborhoods and gated communities. They move in social circles where they are spared the pain of observing the poverty and human degradation of others. Rich people may find comfort in reading one of the most often repeated themes in *The Book of Mormon*, the Calvinist doctrine that riches are a blessing from God. Righteous people have a divine promise that they will "prosper in the land" while those who do not keep the commandments of God will be "cut off." [3]

According to *The Book of Mormon*, material prosperity is an indication of grace and favor with God not only in this world but in the next. God and mammon are not incompatible after all. They are not the enemies that apostate "Christian" asceticism (and the New Testament) would have us believe. Many country club Mormons experience a strong emotional response to this piety-prosperity theme that is repeated over and over again in *The Book of Mormon*.

On the other hand, **the poor** may respond to the powerful share-the-wealth sermons of Benjamin, Alma, and Moroni.[4] The small book, 4 Nephi, describes a utopian society where there are no rich and no poor. Everyone shares like real brothers and sisters. The brotherhood of man is a reality, not just something talked about on Sunday. This doctrine is enough to touch the hearts and bring tears to the eyes of those who have lived in degrading poverty all of their lives. Many early converts came from the ghettos of the Old World hoping to share the wealth with the saints in Zion.

Mystics, spiritualists, and visionaries are immediately attracted by Lehi, Nephi, and other New World prophets' dreams, visions, and conversations with God and angels. Lehi was so overcome by the spirit that he went into a trance.[5] He apparently saw no difference between his own dreams and a vision from God. On one occasion Lehi said:

> Behold I have dreamed a dream; or in other words I have seen a vision.[6]

Although Lehi claimed to be a true prophet, his wife and two of his sons turned against him calling him a visionary man. His two sons even tried to kill him.[7] Any person who has had supernatural experiences and then suffered ridicule, rejection, and persecution would probably relate to Lehi.

Smith's narrative includes a magic ball, glowing stones, trances, visions, mass conversions, slippery treasures, and all kinds of miracles.[8] One of the major messages of *The Book of Mormon* is that visions, trances, speaking in unknown tongues, and other spiritual experiences are to be taken seriously. Those who ridicule or persecute mystics and visionaries may be fighting against God. All of this is very comforting to visionary men and women.

Many **Christians** are pleased to have another witness that Jesus is the Christ. Nephi and other *Book of Mormon* prophets predicted the virgin birth of Jesus and the divine nature of His mission.[9] The book of 3 Nephi includes a touching and powerful account of the visit of the resurrected Christ to the New World.[10]

Some of the teachings in the New Testament are repeated. All of this provides a strong emotional response, comfort, and reassurance to Christians. Smith's references to a great and abominable church brings additional comfort to many protestants who see this as support for their belief in the corruption and apostasy of medieval Catholics.[11]

Nationalistic Americans may be gratified to learn that America is "a land choice above all other lands," that it has a special mission to perform in the world, and that no one will be permitted to come here without permission from God.[12] Manifest destiny was not just a political slogan of early American patriots but the mind and will of God.

Strangely, American "gentiles" were also reassured by *The Book of Mormon* that killing the remnants (Native Americans) and taking their land was justified as part of God's punishment for the sins of their progenitors![13]

Mormons, of course, think that America's mission is to create a safe political climate that will permit them to grow strong enough to convert everyone in the world to pure Christianity (Mormonism). Church members also have an obligation to teach Native Americans (Lamanites) about the gospel and also about their past and their glorious future.[14]

Racists can find comfort in the doctrine that God punishes sinful people with a dark skin.[15] The terms "white and delightsome," and "dark and loathsome" are music to the ears of a racist. They have known all along that a light skin color is an indication of favor with God.

The Anti-Masons were a very important social and political group in 1830 when *The Book of Mormon* was published. The condemnation of secret societies along with their secret signs, tokens, handclasps, and passwords is one of the major themes of Smith's book. It claims that Satan, himself, first introduced these things to Cain, thus tempting him to become a murderer.[16] Thus, Smith's book strongly appealed to anti-Masonic sentiments.

At the top of our list of those who are most likely to experience a strong emotional response (testimony) when reading *The Book of Mormon* are Latter-Day Saints, themselves. **Mormons have an overpowering need to believe in the authenticity of this book. The alternative is unthinkable!**

Even those who have never read Smith's book sometimes stand up in meetings and bear a sincere testimony that they **know** it is true. How can a Latter-Day Saint, a teenager, for example, who is reading *The Book of Mormon* for the first time, approach it honestly and objectively when so much depends upon its truthfulness? Rejecting *The Book of Mormon* could mean turning against ones parents, friends, and neighbors and having all of them turn against you. It would mean the great sacrifices made for Mormonism by pioneers and other ancestors were in vain. It would mean that Joseph Smith and other Church leaders were, and are, guilty of fraud and deception on a level almost beyond human comprehension.

Objectivity Almost Impossible

Before most young Latter-Day Saints ever start reading *The Book of Mormon*, they have seen hundreds of people, including their own parents, stand up in Church meetings and with conviction in their voices and even tears in their eyes say that they "know" that this book is true and that Joseph Smith was a prophet of God. This makes it very difficult for a young, first time L.D.S reader, to consider *The Book of Mormon* honestly, objectively, and with real intent as suggested by Moroni.[17] It is almost impossible.

Objectivity and honesty become even more difficult for young L.D.S. men and women who go on full time missions. These young people soon become very uncomfortable unless they have a testimony. When everyone else in a testimony meeting is saying, "I know beyond a shadow of a doubt that Joseph Smith was a true prophet and that *The Book of Mormon* is the word of God," it would be very embarrassing to get up and say, "I am not even sure that there were any gold plates." It would also be embarrassing to say, "I

believe that Joseph Smith was a true prophet and that this Church is true." Belief isn't good enough. A missionary is expected to **know**.

Many missionaries experience great pressure from their families to go on a mission. Once out on their missions, they are placed into a position where they simply have to obtain a testimony in order to escape the pain of uncertainty and also to avoid feeling like a hypocrite for telling other people about Joseph Smith and his *Book of Mormon* when they don't even know if these things are true. Under these stressful circumstances, almost every missionary somehow comes up with a testimony.

A Missionary Experience

A returned missionary privately told me of an experience he had while serving on a mission. This young man was working closely with his mission president in the mission home when suddenly two General Authorities from Salt Lake City arrived. After interviewing the mission president and some of the lady missionaries, one of these General Authorities left on a plane for Salt Lake City taking the mission president with him. The other stayed as acting mission president until someone else could be called.

It seems that the mission president, a very spiritual man, had secretly called seven lady missionaries into his office, one at a time. After swearing them to secrecy, he told each of them that the president of the Church was going to change Church policy and restore plural marriage (polygamy). The mission president also told each of these young ladies that he had personally received a revelation from the Lord that she was to marry him.

Following the example of Joseph Smith, he told these young ladies that they were entitled to know the truth for themselves. He counseled each of them to fast and pray with a sincere heart and a desire to know the will of the Lord.

Then an amazing thing happened. Six out of the seven lady missionaries returned to the mission president's office within a few days and told him with tears in their eyes, that their prayers had been answered. They had received a testimony that he had spoken the truth. Each of these young ladies expressed their love and agreed to marry him, a man three times their age!

The mission president was excommunicated. All of the lady missionaries were sent home except the one who could not make up her mind, broke her oath of secrecy and called her parents to ask for their advice. When her parents called the General Authorities to find out what was happening to their daughter, two General Authorities were immediately sent to solve the problem.

But how can all of this be explained? Where did the six lady missionaries get their testimonies? Their mission president was **lying** and yet these young ladies somehow received a testimony that he was telling them the **truth**. How did all of this happen? Part of the answer could be that it is dangerous for any person to trust an authority figure more than they trust their own thinking.

Mind Games

Perhaps something snaps when a person fasts, goes without sleep, prays by the hour, and experiences great physical, mental, emotional, and spiritual stress. Many people who have had this experience describe a feeling of great peace that comes over them after they finally make their decision. They usually interpret this psychological peace as a sign of divine approval, an answer to their prayers. But is putting great mental and emotional pressure upon a person the Lord's way of breaking the human will and forcing people into obedience and conformity? Would Jesus do this? Or is this just another mind game played consciously or even unconsciously by manipulators?

I believe that early in his life, while attending religious revivals, Joseph Smith observed the powerful psychological, emotional, and spiritual experience called "testimony." Later on, he put this strange phenomenon to good use in his new Church. It was really quite simple. All Smith had to do was put people into a stressful position where they had to make a very important decision affecting their lives and then tell them to fast and pray about it. In most cases they somehow came up with a testimony that pleased Smith. This could be about gold plates, *The Book of Mormon*, a mission call, polygamy, or just about anything else. Joseph Smith made "testimony" the cornerstone of his new religion.

Cults And Testimony

But testimony and spiritualism are also the power behind cults and fundamentalism. Thousands of cult members and Mormon fundamentalists are dedicated and sincere in their faith. Where do they get their testimonies? And what is the explanation for conflicting testimonies? I have heard men and women from many different religions explain why they **knew** that their particular religion was the only one approved of God. The answer to all of this has to be that testimonies are not reliable.

My Personal Testimony

I have personally experienced the strange phenomenon of a testimony. I gained most of my testimony while in the Northern States Mission. Somehow I came to "**know**" that Joseph Smith was a prophet and that his *Book of Mormon* was true. I was so sure of these things that I would have given my life for my Church. It felt wonderful to be certain about religion. Now, I realize that first I was indoctrinated, and then I was placed into a situation where I was forced to come up with a testimony for my own mental health.

Overwhelmed by new information that I did not have before, I have now become convinced that I was wrong about Smith, his gold plates, and his *Book of Mormon.* My testimony was based upon ignorance, feelings, emotions, deception, and self-deception.

The Truth Or Just A True Principle?

Some Latter-Day Saints say that they gained their testimony while reading a particular part of *The Book of Mormon.* But these readers do not seem to make any distinction between the truths contained **in** this book and the truth or authenticity **of** the book itself. They do not seem to understand that *The Book of Mormon* and many other books may contain touching and beautiful truths that can bring tears to a person's eyes without being authentic. It may be that the reader is having a strong emotional reaction or even receiving a divine witness that the principle being taught in those particular pages is true. But this does not mean that *The Book of Mormon* or any other book that can produce this response is factual and based upon real events.

For example, who can read Charles Dickens' account of Ebenezer Scrooge, a mean spirited old miser, and his miraculous transformation into a loving and generous person at Christmas time without having an emotional response? But does this mean that Scrooge and Tiny Tim were real people that existed at some time and place in history?

Reason Vs. Emotion

And finally, to emphasize the importance of reason and the danger of reliance upon emotions and feelings, I would like to use a quotation from a master of manipulation and opportunism, Adolf Hitler:

> Reason can treacherously deceive a man, but emotion is always sure and never leaves him.[18]

Hitler's first deputy, Rudolf Hess, echoed the words of his Fuhrer when he told a large audience of Nazis:

> Do not seek Adolf Hitler with your brains, you will find him with your hearts.[19]

This irrational, anti-intellectual, and emotional climate resulted in a moral vacuum and a holocaust where as many as twelve million people were killed in concentration camps while over forty five million others were killed on the battlefields of World War II. This is what can happen when large numbers of people rely on emotions and allow an authoritarian leader to do their thinking! **And finally, let's never forget those evil words of Adolf Hitler, "Reason can treacherously deceive a man, but emotion is always sure and never leaves him."**

Chapter 12

SOCIAL PATHOLOGY

> All that the human race has achieved, spiritually, and materially, it owes to the destroyers of illusions and the seekers of reality.
> -Erich Fromm

When a person makes a significant departure from reality as defined by the society in which she lives, she is said to be insane. But sometimes it is society that departs from reality and the individual who refuses to go along with this madness is more sane than her social environment. Who can watch a film of Hitler projecting his psychopathic illusions upon thousands of people and then see how skillfully he was able to turn decent men and women into mobs of screaming barbarians without understanding that **insanity can be contagious**. Individual pathology can easily become social pathology when communicated effectively by a charismatic leader.

Joseph Smith was a dreamer, a visionary man who didn't always distinguish between reality and fantasy. His world view included a number of illusions shared by other religious ideologies and some unique to Mormonism.

Ethnocentrism

One of Smith's illusions shared by many other religions is ethnocentrism. This is a strong conviction that a person's religion, political ideas, traditions, race, language, and homeland are special in the eyes of God, and that all other cultures are not just different but **wrong and in need of conversion**. This is one of the most seductive of all illusions.

One example of ethnocentrism is the Jews who consider themselves a "chosen people," the children of Abraham. Another is the Protestants who claim that they are the "elect" of God predestined for salvation. Moslems claim to be "messengers of Allah." And Latter-Day Saints claim special lineage through Ephraim and the "House of Israel." They also claim to have the only true religion and exclusive priesthood authority to perform ordinances and give blessings in the name of God.

One of the most ethnocentric statements that it is possible to imagine is the claim made by Joseph Smith that the Lord told him in 1820 that the churches of the world were "all wrong," their creeds were "an abomination in His sight," and that the ministers of these religions were "all corrupt."[1]

This statement helped create a climate of confrontation, intolerance, bigotry, hatred, and persecution. This claim made by Smith was obviously untrue. He was lying. God never told him those things because they were untrue. There were many dedicated, loving, and sincere ministers of religion in 1820, just as there are today. Many were helping the sick, the poor, and the discouraged. They were also conducting funerals, performing marriages, and teaching high moral principles. Some were diligently seeking to discover new aspects of the gospel in the Bible, and even translating ancient scriptures.

Some of these "corrupt" religious leaders were even risking their lives to create a new government of freedom and liberty in America. How can anyone believe that God would tell Smith that these ministers were all corrupt? And how can any person or church that makes such insulting claims expect a warm reception from others?

In her autobiography, *Quicksand and Cactus*, Juanita Brooks gives a powerful and moving example of how Mormon ethnocentrism influenced her world view as a child. Juanita grew up in

Bunkerville, Nevada, a small agricultural community about four miles downstream and across the Virgin River from Mesquite, Nevada. Every person in town was a Mormon. Almost all visitors to Bunkerville were L.D.S. Church authorities from Salt Lake City.

As a small child, Juanita often heard her parents praying for the L.D.S. missionaries who were out in the world trying to share the light of Mormonism with those who were "sitting in darkness." Only the Mormons had the true Church and the priesthood. It was their obligation to share the gospel with those not fortunate enough to be born into the true Church.

One day Juanita's father came into the house, announced that there was an "outsider" in town, and said that this man would be coming to their home for dinner. Juanita was both excited and frightened. She had never seen an outsider before. She expected him to be ignorant, underprivileged, and inferior. How else could he be after all those years sitting in darkness? Mormon girls were strictly forbidden to have anything to do with outsiders. And every Mormon girl knew that she would be better off dead than to marry one!

To Juanita's great astonishment, the man who came into the house with her father was tall, handsome, well dressed, highly educated, and a world traveler. He immediately memorized the names, ages, and interests of all the children. He seemed especially impressed with Juanita. He started talking to her about books, literature, and poetry. He quoted long passages from prominent authors. Juanita was spellbound. She had never met such an interesting person in her entire life. And this outsider could even play the piano!

Later that evening, the outsider danced very gracefully with Juanita while everyone else stomped around the community dance floor. Suddenly, the full impact of Mormon ethnocentrism came to Juanita. **She realized that she had been deceived**. She wrote in her autobiography, "Sitting in darkness indeed! . . . Surely he was not the one who had been sitting in darkness, and whatever light he had I wanted some of."[2] It was this outsider who lit Juanita's intellectual fire. She later went to Columbia University and became one of the greatest and most courageous historians in Western America. Her life was changed by spending a few hours with an outsider who had spent his entire life "sitting in darkness," from the Mormon ethnocentric perspective.

Each ethnocentric group stresses its uniqueness and its differences in order to maintain its vitality and identity. Each builds walls against outsiders and foreigners. Ethnocentrism creates iron curtains, Zion curtains, and all kinds of barriers to keep out those who are different.

People who are caught up in the social illusion of being better and special usually try to become closer to God by becoming more Catholic, more Baptist, more Moslem, more Jewish, or more Mormon. But does all of this division please God? Is this world made a better place as each ethnic community becomes more narrow, more radical, more divided, and more militant, or has this been the major cause of persecution, hatred, and conflict for thousands of years?

The Pharisees were very religious. They were also self-righteous, unloving, unkind, and intolerant. The Good Samaritan forgot about ethnic hatred and saw the dying Jew simply as another human being. Jesus praised the humanistic Samaritan and condemned the pious Jews. One of the greatest struggles in our world has been between ethnocentrism and humanistic empathy. Unfortunately, ethnocentrism has almost always won.

But is this social illusion logical? Is it reasonable that God would judge a person by whether he believes this or that, eats this or that, worships on Friday, Saturday, or Sunday, or prays with his hat on or off, when a person's belief system, like the language he speaks, is largely determined by his cultural heritage? For example, why are nearly all Arabs Moslem and almost all Italians, Roman Catholic? And most people who are born into a religion (including Mormons) live their entire lives and then die as members of that same religion. Does this mean that they will be exalted or condemned by a just God in an afterlife because their cultural heritage was different on this earth?

The parables of Jesus clearly teach that a person will be judged by his love for others and his generosity of spirit, not by his belief system. Was the Good Samaritan sent to hell because he believed false doctrine while the Priest and the Levite were saved in the kingdom of God because they had the true religion? This is not logical, reasonable, merciful, nor just.

It is not easy for a Moslem to escape the confines of the mosque, the Koran, Ramadan, and the veil. It isn't easy for a Catholic, Jew, or Mormon to escape his or her walls of ethnocentrism. **Perhaps the most difficult challenge a person can ever have in this life is to transcend the limitations, narrowness, and ethnocentrism of his own cultural heritage in pursuit of truth.**

Social Paranoia

Another of Smith's illusions that is shared by other religious groups is social paranoia. This illusion cements the religious, political, or ethnic community together by convincing them that there is safety and security only within their group. It is a dangerous world out there! Outsiders cannot be trusted. Everyone hates people like us. We must stick together and unite behind our leaders in order to survive. Anyone who questions or criticizes our leaders is an enemy and a threat to our very survival.

The person who accepts this illusion soon begins to believe that the worst thing that could possibly happen to him is ostracism, disfellowship or excommunication. It would be like being thrown overboard into a raging sea full of sharks. Erich Fromm said:

> Man as man is afraid of insanity, just as man as animal is afraid of death. Man has to be related, he has to find union with others, in order to be sane. This need to be one with others is the strongest passion, stronger than sex and often even stronger than his wish to live. . . . For this reason the individual must blind himself from seeing that which his group claims does not exist, or accept as truth that which the majority say is true, even if his own eyes could convince him that it is false. The

> herd is so vitally important for the individual that their views, beliefs, feelings, constitute reality for him, more so than what his senses and his reason tell him. . . . There is almost nothing a man will not believe or repress when he is threatened with the explicit or implicit threat of ostracism.[3]

More than a century earlier, Joseph Smith said something very similar:

> Nothing will have such influence over people as fear of being disfellowshipped by so goodly a society as this.[4]

Smith used fear of ostracism very effectively. And even today, many Latter-Day Saints would rather see a loved one die than be excommunicated from the Church! And yet, the very idea of excommunication seems foreign to Christianity. When did Jesus ever cast anyone out or send them away? When asked by the Pharisees why He ate with publicans and sinners, Jesus said, "They that be whole need not a physician, but they that are sick."[5] If Jesus is the Great Physician and His church is a hospital, it makes about as much sense to cast sinners out of a church as it does to throw heart attack victims out of an intensive care unit.

Even the possibility of ostracism creates a perversion of Christian love by making love conditional. The church or the family will love and include a person **if** he or she thinks, feels, and behaves in a certain way. This twisted "love" becomes a powerful instrument of control. It suffocates and enslaves the human spirit.

The Amish have a social control mechanism called "**shunning**." Amish leaders have the power to officially declare any man or woman a non-person. They cease to exist. If this non-person is a man, his wife and children refuse to talk or eat with him. His wife refuses to sleep with him. Nobody will hire him, work for him, or do any kind of business with him. He is completely rejected until he conforms to the rigid requirements of the Amish community.

Erich Fromm explains how Smith's "disfellowship" or Amish "shunning" effects the individual:

> To put it briefly, the individual ceases to be himself; he adopts entirely the kind of personality offered to him by cultural patterns; and he therefore becomes exactly as all others are and as they expect him to be. The discrepancy between "I" and the world disappears and with it the conscious fear of aloneness and powerlessness. This mechanism can be compared with the protective coloring some animals assume. They look so similar to their surroundings that they are hardly distinguishable from them. The person who gives up his individual self and becomes an automation, identical with millions of other automations around him, need not feel alone and anxious any more. But the price he pays, however, is high; it is the loss of his self.[6]

The belief that a person's happiness, worthiness, survival, and even his eternal salvation depends solely upon being a Catholic, Jew, Moslem, or Mormon is an illusion, a departure from reality, a social pathology. It is a social control mechanism giving wealth and power to certain religious leaders. It creates chains and walls for people. It divides one group against another.

Certainty

The illusion of certainty is another popular social pathology. Certainty brings a sense of peace and security. It helps a person make sense out of this world and avoid the painfulness of ambivalence. A strong leader is one who **knows** where he is going and what he is talking about. The person who can only make tentative assertions, state opinions, and speculate does not inspire deep loyalty nor great enthusiasm.

Human nature seems to crave certainty. This tendency has created serious problems for the world. The more certain a person is that his ideas are "true," the more radical and less tolerant he usually becomes.

The spirit of freedom and liberty is a genuine respect for the values and opinions of others. But how can a person have this kind of respect for others unless he honestly believes that other people may be right or at least partly right and that his own ideas and values may be wrong or at least partly wrong?

Oliver Cromwell wrote a letter to the General Assembly of The Church of Scotland before the great Battle of Dunbar in which he pleaded:

> My brethren, I beseech you, in the bowels of Christ, think it possible that you may be mistaken.[7]

The famous American jurist, Learned Hand, said:

> The spirit of liberty is the spirit which is not too sure that it is right; the spirit of liberty is the spirit which seems to understand the minds of other men and women.[8]

Jacob Bronowski condemned the illusion of certainty and warned the world of its tragic consequences when he said:

> The Principle of Uncertainty or, in my phrase, the Principle of Tolerance fixed once for all the realization that all knowledge is limited. It is an irony of history that at the very time when this was being worked out there should rise, under Hitler in Germany and other tyrants elsewhere, a counter conception: a principle of Monstrous Certainty. When the future looks back on the 1930's it will think of them as a crucial confrontation of culture as I have been expounding it, the ascent of man, against the throwback to the despots' belief that they have absolute certainty. It is said that science will dehumanize people and turn them into numbers. This is false, tragically false. Look for yourself. This is the concentration camp and crematorium at Auschwitz. This is where people were

> turned into numbers. Into this pond were flushed the ashes of some four million people. And this was not done by gas. It was done by arrogance. It was done by dogma. It was done by ignorance. When people believe they have absolute knowledge, with no test in reality, this is how they behave. This is what men do when they aspire to the knowledge of gods.[9]

Oliver Wendell Holmes said:

> The longing for certainty and repose is in every human mind. But certainty is generally an illusion and repose is not the destiny of man.[10]

True believers rather than doubters have caused most of the trouble in the world. The more certain a person is, the more susceptible he becomes to self-deception and radical behavior. The organization must survive and grow at all costs. The cause becomes worth dying for and killing for. The New York World Trade Center bombings are but one example. **Those airliners were piloted by certainty**. Those young Islamic terrorists truly believed in what they were doing. They were quite certain as they died in flames.

The spirit of radicalism created by certainty frightened non-Mormons in New York, Ohio, Missouri, Illinois, and The Utah Territory. These "gentiles" came to believe that there was no limit to what Mormon men and women would do for Joseph Smith and Brigham Young.

Even though true believers have caused most of the trouble in the world, ironically, doubters have suffered most of the guilt. Consider the guilt feelings of medieval Catholics who didn't believe in killing heretics or going on the Crusades against Moslems. The young Japanese who didn't believe in fascism and refused to become a Kamikaze pilot during W.W.II probably felt ashamed. Many Germans who did not believe Hitler's Nazi propaganda were afraid and perhaps even ashamed to express their feelings. Those responsible for torturing and killing millions of people have apparently suffered very little guilt or remorse. After all, why should any person feel guilty when he "knows" he is right and contributing to so great a cause?

Jesus commanded his followers to live by faith. Faith is **not** certainty; it includes an element of doubt. But the Pharisees did not need faith; they had certainty. They were quite sure they were doing God a favor by killing Jesus. Would the Jews have dared risk the eternal consequences of killing the Son of God if they had any doubts? **Jesus was killed by certainty** and its natural consequences, self-righteousness, bigotry, self-deception, intolerance, and radicalism.

And yet, despite all of the evil caused by the illusion of certainty, many Latter-Day Saints claim to **know** that Joseph Smith was a true prophet and **know** that *The Book of Mormon* is true beyond a shadow of a doubt. Missionaries are encouraged to appear certain whether they are or not. People are more easily seduced by a person who appears certain.

Freedom

Still another illusion that is part of Mormonism and also other religions is that of freedom. Erich Fromm refers to a psychological experiment in which a man was hypnotized and then told that upon awaking from his hypnotic sleep he would have a strong desire to read a manuscript that he brought with him. He would not be able to find this manuscript because a close friend had stolen it and he would become angry with his friend. When the man was brought out of hypnosis, he started to look for his manuscript. When he couldn't find it, he angrily accused his friend of stealing the manuscript. The man who had been hypnotized honestly thought that it was his own idea to read the manuscript and that it had also been his own idea to accuse his friend of taking his papers.[11] Fromm then goes on to say:

> Man, so proud of his freedom to think and to choose is, in fact, a marionette moved by strings behind and above him which in turn are directed by forces unknown to his consciousness. In order to give himself the illusion that he acts according to his own free will, man invents

> rationalizations which make it appear as if he does what he has to do because he has chosen to do so for rational or moral reasons.[12]

Fromm claims that society can indoctrinate a person to a point where he loses his own identity. He may express "his" opinion and not even realize that he is simply repeating a slogan or a party line. He is listening to the inner voices of his mother, father, church leader, or political propagandist. He has been conditioned to respond in a certain way to these voices. He has lost the power of independent thought. He has become an automation, an organization man. He thinks and feels the way he is supposed to think and feel. And yet, he sincerely believes that he is free!

If a child can be so thoroughly indoctrinated that he or she becomes incapable of spontaneous, independent thinking, this extinguishment of individuality may be considered a serious form of child abuse. And yet it is practiced freely by parents and teachers who were also abused in this way as children.

If we really believe in freedom, does it make sense to lock our children behind walls of ideology and ethnocentrism which cannot help but bring them into conflict with other children who have been taught opposing values and illusions? Perhaps the hope of the world is for parents in every nation and culture to teach their children **how** to think but not **what** to think. But what are the chances of this ever happening?

America's founding fathers fought and died to provide future generations with freedom and human dignity. Their new constitution included freedom of religion for all American citizens. But among many churches, including the Latter-Day Saints, this freedom is quite limited. L.D.S. Church history includes many examples of authorities taking away a man's Church membership, his wife and children, his farm, his business, and even threatening his life if he tried to exercise his constitutional right to freedom of religion."[13]

And even today, when a close friend of mine who no longer believes in Mormonism asked his wife if she believed in freedom of religion, she said, "Not for you, I don't. You owe it to me and to our children to go along with things and at least pretend to believe in the Church. You have no right to cause trouble and embarrassment for our family." This man is faced with a divorce and serious financial trouble if he insists upon his constitutional right to freedom of religion. It appears that his wife is free to practice her religious ideas, but he is not free to practice his.

The doctrine that religion is a family matter rather than one of individual preference and private conscience is an important aspect of Mormonism. One reason the L.D.S. Church places so much importance upon the family is Church **power**. A brave man, who is willing to face an enemy's guns, may be overwhelmed by his mother's tears when she pleads, "Son, stay close to the Church, attend your meetings, pay your tithing, and go to the temple. I want our whole family to be together in the next world. It would break my heart if you were not there in the celestial kingdom with the rest of us." This awesome power, a mother's love and tears, is at the disposal of the Church.

Jesus understood that a person's family could be a powerful obstacle in the path of finding truth. He announced:

> For I am come to set a man at variance against his own father, and the daughter against her mother, and the daughter in law against her mother in law. and a man's foes shall be they of his own household. He that loveth father or mother more than me is not worthy of me: and he that loveth son or daughter more than me is not worthy of me.[14]

Perhaps Jesus meant that any person who loves his or her own family members more than they love the truth is not worthy of Him. What else could He have meant by these words?

Millenialism

Still another common illusion and social pathology is millenialism. Smith and many other religious leaders believed that the Second Coming of Christ was very near. Early Mormon missionaries were instructed to warn people to flee to Zion for protection from the wrath of God that was about to be poured out upon Babylon (the world) without measure. This was about 170 years ago. Many religious leaders have been predicting the quickly approaching Second Coming for almost 2000 years.

Families Are Forever.

An illusion that is somewhat unique to Mormonism is the notion that "families are forever" and that certain Church ordinances can help save and exalt one's ancestors. However, the Bible does **not** teach eternal marriage nor that a person can do anything to help save his dead relatives. And yet, genealogy, baptisms, ordinations, endowments, and sealings for the dead in an L.D.S. temple are considered some of the most sacred obligations of Church members today.

Other Mormon Illusions

Other uniquely Latter-Day Saint illusions include the reality of Joseph Smith's gold plates, Nephites, Lamanites, Jaredites, and Gadianton Robbers. According to some of the best scientific minds in the world, these are illusions, part of Smith's dream world. If these scientists are right, anyone who sincerely believes in these things, has, to some extent, departed from reality. And when thousands of Church members gather in meetings and refer to Native Americans as Lamanites and solemnly bear testimony to each other that Smith's other dreams and illusions constitute reality, social pathology becomes an important part of these meetings.

Chapter 13

A LEGACY OF DECEPTION

Take heed that no
man deceive you.
- Jesus Christ

Early in his life, young Joseph Smith learned that most people are trusting and gullible. He soon became known for his skill with seer stones, witch-hazel sticks, mineral rods, and incantations.[1] In his well researched book, *Early Mormonism and the Magic World View*, D. Michael Quinn has documented Smith's lifelong association with the occult.

In 1826, Joseph Smith was tried and convicted in a New York courtroom of being a "glass looker," a money digger, and a disorderly person. This trial and Smith's conviction is a matter of public record.[2]

Joseph was often hired to discover the location of hidden treasures and lost articles. He sometimes told his greedy and gullible employers about vast underground treasures that were once hidden by ancient Americans. These treasures were still guarded by old spirits who could move their treasures around unless tricked or persuaded into relinquishing their wealth.[3]

Slippery Treasures

Smith's ideas about slippery underground treasures guarded by old spirits or demons are also found in his *Book of Mormon*. The thirteenth chapter of Helaman contains the following lamentation:

> O that we had remembered the Lord our God in the day that he gave us our riches, and then they would not have become slippery that we should lose them; for behold our riches are gone from us. . . . Yea, we have hid up our treasures and they have slipped away from us because of the curse of the land. . . . Behold we are surrounded by demons . . .[4].

Smith claimed that demons were still guarding those slippery Nephite treasures in his day. And only a person with great skill, such as Smith, could locate these underground treasures and then trick the old demons into giving up their valuables. But why were these spirits so determined to hang onto their treasures? And what use could an old spirit possibly have for gold, silver, or anything else of great earthly value?

The Master Manipulator

Smith was never able to find any of the vast underground treasures he talked about, but he became very skillful in explaining his failures. He also learned how to place men and women into a position where they desperately wanted to believe his explanations no matter how ludicrous.

For example, after a man had paid Smith for his skill in locating hidden treasures and had also paid other men for actually digging deep holes in the ground, he was not anxious to admit to his wife and neighbors that he was a fool who had been taken in by a confidence scheme. Smith could usually count on this man to either keep quiet or else to defend him. Otherwise this man would open himself up to serious family trouble and ridicule from friends.

Later on, after Smith had organized his Church, he continued to use his remarkable manipulative skills. After a man had gone on several missions, donated money and property to the Church, worked hard, and suffered great persecution for Mormonism, he would be very reluctant to admit that he had been duped. He would probably defend Smith or else keep quiet.

Also, a woman who became a polygamous wife was almost forced to remain a loyal defender of Smith. Otherwise, she would have to admit that her marriage was not valid, that she was living an adulterous life, that her children were not legitimate, and that she may even suffer the wrath of God in an afterlife. How could any woman face up to that much shame, guilt, and condemnation? She was securely caught in Smith's trap.

You Can't Prove He's Wrong.

Another method of deception and manipulation soon developed almost to perfection by young Joseph was to make claims or allegations that other people had no way of disproving. For example, how could anyone prove that Smith did not see the Father and the Son in a grove of trees near his father's farm? How could anyone prove that Smith did not have gold plates, visitations from angels, or revelations from God?

This also explains why Smith claimed to translate his *Book of Mormon* from "reformed Egyptian," and why he felt confident that his explanation of Chandler's Egyptian writings and facsimiles would never be exposed as a fraud. Smith, and most other people, believed that Egyptian was a dead, untranslatable language. And even if scholars were eventually able to decipher Egyptian, Smith would already be famous and have power and authority over a large following of committed believers. How could Joseph possibly lose a game where other players desperately wanted him to win and where others were never permitted to see his cards or test his claims?

Smith Betrays The Hales.

In 1828, Smith fell in love with Emma Hale, daughter of Isaac and Elizabeth Hale. The Hales were bitterly opposed to this marriage because of Smith's occupation as a glass - looker.[5] But this didn't stop Joseph. One day while the Hales were away, Smith eloped with Emma. The Hales were heartbroken and angry.

A few months later, in an effort to patch up his in-law problems, Joseph admitted that he had never been able to see anything in his seer stone and promised Emma's angry parents that his career in deception was over.[6] If they would only accept him into their family, he would go out and make an honest living. Smith candidly admitted to the Hales that he was a liar and a con-man, and that he had been making money by deception and promised to repent.[7]

Isaac Hale took Joseph at his word and even gave the young couple a house and some land. But Joseph's heart was not in farming. He was a storyteller, a glass-looker, magician, author, politician, military leader, land speculator, banker, womanizer, city planner, and church leader but certainly **not** a farmer.

Smith did not keep his promise to his in-laws; his career in deception was not over but just beginning. He soon left his farm and went back to glass-looking. A few months later Smith announced that he had discovered some gold plates. Some of Smith's associates in the buried treasure business were angry at him, not because of his religious claims, but because they wanted their share of the gold. Smith refused to share his gold plates with his old treasure hunting partners. This created feelings of anger and betrayal and resulted in the "persecution" of Smith.

The Fear Of God And Of Smith

In 1830 Smith organized his new church calling it "The Church of Christ."[8] By now he had discovered another method of deception that added to his manipulative powers. Smith pretended to have revelations from God instructing certain individuals to do this or that. Smith observed that almost everyone desperately wants to believe in God. He also learned that almost everyone wants to believe that he or she is favored of God and important enough to be noticed as an individual. This made people vulnerable to Smith's revelations which directed specific individuals to do certain things. Church members tended to be simple and honest people who were so humbled and honored by God's personal attention that they would do whatever Smith's revelations instructed them to do.

Joseph learned as a young boy attending religious revivals that most people had a great fear of offending God and jeopardizing their eternal souls. It became quite a simple matter to transform this fear of God into fear of Smith. All he had to do was say his magic words, "Thus saith the Lord" and strong men broke down and cried, went on missions, gave him their property and money, voted in elections as instructed, and even brought Smith their wives or daughters.[9]

"Revelations" From Secret Informers

About this time Smith discovered still another powerful method of deception and manipulation. An illustration of this is when an early convert to Mormonism, Parley P. Pratt, went to New York and told Smith some intimate details about the lives of his close friends living in Kirtland, Ohio. Later, when Smith went to Kirtland, he pretended that God had revealed these secret things to him.

Sidney Rigdon (a Campbellite minister), Orson F. Whitney (a prominent businessman), and other residents of Kirtland were so astounded by Smith's intimate knowledge of their personal lives that they were easily converted to Mormonism. Rigdon brought most of his congregation with him. Whitney also brought a considerable number of friends and relatives into the Church when he bore strong testimony to the truthfulness of Smith's "revelations." Joseph continued to have these "revelations" gleaned from secret informers throughout the remainder of his life.

Smith's Kingdom Was Of This World.

Unlike Jesus, Smith's kingdom was very much of this world. He was mayor of a city, a land developer, a military general, and a candidate for President of The United States. His revelations were not limited to theology, the kingdom of Heaven, or the next world. Property, money, political voting, a private army, and even which men and women were to be married to each other were all important enough for the Lord's direct and explicit instructions. Smith's "Thus saith the Lord," covered almost every aspect of a Church member's life.

Revelation On Polygamy, A Floodgate Of Deception

In 1843, Smith recorded a revelation that had apparently been dreamed up much earlier. This would soon cause serious trouble for Smith and his followers. Now canonized as section 132 of

The Doctrine and Covenants, this revelation establishing polygamy is still considered sacred scripture by Latter-Day Saints, today. **Thus, polygamy is still an official aspect of Mormonism.**

Smith's revelation on polygamy opened floodgates of lies and hypocrisy. Hundreds of honest women and honorable men were forced to become liars by circumstances created by Smith, Young, and other Church leaders.

In the first place, polygamy was a violation of section 121 of the Illinois State law of 1833. This law provided for a $500 fine and one year in prison for each violation.[10] Smith had to swear his new wives and also his friends and their plural wives to oaths of secrecy in order to stay out of prison.

Noted Church historian, B. H. Roberts, admitted that secret marriages were performed by early Church leaders and that this practice resulted in duplicity and hypocrisy:

> This enforced secrecy which a reasonable prudence demanded gave rise to apparent contradictions between public utterances of leading brethren in the Church and their having a plurality of wives.[11]

The official Church policy of lying about polygamy, called "reasonable prudence" by B.H. Roberts, nevertheless proves that Apostle John A. Widstoe was lying when he said, "The Church ever operates in the full light. There is no secrecy about its doctrine or work."[12]

Let's consider a typical secret Mormon marriage in Nauvoo. A young woman, probably a convert from England who has been taught to almost worship the Prophet Joseph and other Church authorities, is taught "the principle" and then sworn to secrecy. What does she tell her parents when she comes home from this meeting with Smith? She can't tell them the truth without violating her oath of secrecy. She is forced to deceive them. She must lie to her own parents.

When she leaves the house to spend time with her secret husband, where does she tell her parents that she is going? Again she is forced to lie. And what does she tell a young man who happens to take a romantic interest in her? Can she tell him that she is secretly married to a man old enough to be her father or grandfather? Again, she is forced to make up excuses and lies.

How long can this young lady and her husband continue to meet secretly as husband and wife in a small community without being seen by someone who likes to gossip? Is this what the Apostle Paul meant when he said that a Christian should avoid even the "very appearance of evil"?[13] Is it any wonder that Joseph Smith was accused of adultery by his own counselors and closest associates including Oliver Cowdery and William Law?[14]

What would this secret wife tell her parents and her friends if she became pregnant? She couldn't tell them the truth about the child's father without violating her oath of secrecy. She would again be forced to lie and to also bear the shame of being an unwed mother.

What would she name her child? She couldn't give her baby the last name of Smith, Kimball, or Young without violating her oath. And when the child grew up and asked who her father was, could this polygamist wife be honest and trust the child to keep the secret? Could she expect her child to never acknowledge her father in public and want to be with him or would this young mother be forced to lie to her own child?

A man who became involved in a secret Mormon marriage also found himself in a situation where he had to make excuses and pretenses. He couldn't be open and honest. He had to worry about the feelings of his first wife and about the fact that polygamy was against the law. He was forced to deceive his new wife's parents who continued to support their daughter in their own home and who could also be forced to share the shame of her unwed pregnancy. This man had to be willing to deny everything and make public statements against polygamy. He was trapped in Smith's world of lies and hypocrisy. There was no easy way out.

This man had to ignore his plural wives and children in public. Acknowledging them would be a violation of his oath. A

Mormon man also had to be willing to leave his wives and families without any financial support in order to go on a Church mission should he receive a "call."

How can anyone believe this web of secrecy, deception, hypocrisy, rumors, accusations, denials, anger, jealousy, and even criminal behavior came from the Lord? L.D.S. scriptures clearly state the God cannot lie and that Satan is the father of **all** lies.[15] There was plenty of lying taking place in Nauvoo.

In 1838, Smith compiled some information for publication in the *Elders Journal.* Question number seven was, "Do you Mormons believe in having more wives than one?" His answer was: "No, not at the same time. But they believe that if their companion dies, they have a right to marry again."[16] Missionaries used this question about polygamy and Joseph Smith's answer in the *Elders Journal* for many years after polygamy had been adopted to prove that the Church was being misrepresented.

On February 1, 1844, seven months after Smith finally recorded his earlier revelation on polygamy, the following notice was published in the *TIMES AND SEASONS*, the official Church newspaper, in Nauvoo:

> As we have lately been credibly informed, that an Elder of the Church of Jesus Christ of Latter-Day Saints, by the name of Hiram Brown, has been preaching polygamy, and other false and corrupt doctrines, in the county of Lapeer, state of Michigan. This is to notify him and the Church in general that he has been cut off from the Church, for his iniquity; and he is further notified to appear at the Special Conference, on the 6th of April next to make answer to these charges.
>
> JOSEPH SMITH
> HYRUM SMITH
> Presidents of said Church

Official Church records indicate that at the time this notice appeared, Smith and nearly all of his close associates had several wives. Thus, while calling polygamy a false and corrupt doctrine in public, both Joseph and Hyrum were teaching and living it in their private lives.

The August, 1842 edition of the *MILLENNIAL STAR*, a newspaper edited and published by Apostle Parley P. Pratt for the saints in England also contains a denial that Church leaders were living polygamy.[17] Apostle Pratt was simply lying. Smith taught the Apostles, including Pratt, "the principle" in 1841, a year before this deceptive editorial was published.[18] My ancestors were among those living in England who were deceived by all of this. This makes me feel angry and betrayed. My trusting ancestors and all of their descendants have been victimized by Apostle Pratt's lies.

Another denial of polygamy was published by Hyrum Smith in the *TIMES* AND SEASONS, on March 15, 1844, only three months before he and Joseph were killed:

> To the brethren of the Church of Jesus Christ of Latter Day Saints, living on China Creek, in Handcock County, Greeting: Whereas Brother Richard Hewett has called on me to-day, to know my views concerning some doctrines that are preached in your place, and stated to me that some of your elders say, that a man having certain priesthood, may have as many wives as he pleases, and that doctrine is taught here: I say unto you that that man teaches false doctrine, for there is no such doctrine taught here; neither is there any such thing practiced here. And any man who is found teaching privately or publicly any such doctrine, is culpable, and will stand a chance to be brought before the High Council, and lose his license and his membership also: therefore he had better beware what he is about.
>
> I am
> Your obedient servant,
> HYRUM SMITH

In May of 1844, only a month before he was killed, Joseph Smith answered a leading citizen of Nauvoo, who charged him with adultery and polygamy by saying:

> **What a thing it is for a man to be accused of committing adultery, and having seven wives, when I can only find one.**[19]

Church records and sworn affidavits prove that at this time, Joseph Smith had many wives. Again, he was lying. How much evidence does it take before a person begins to gain insight into the true character of Joseph Smith?

A few of the prominent Church leaders in Nauvoo who finally had enough of Smith's duplicity, decided to expose him. They published a newspaper called the *NAUVOO EXPOSITOR*. The first (and only) edition of this newspaper was published on June 7,1844.

Joseph said that the *NAUVOO EXPOSITOR* was full of lies and slander. He ordered all of the newspapers confiscated and the printing press destroyed.[20] I have read this newspaper from beginning to end and have been unable to discover one single lie. (The most important parts of this publication appear as appendix A in this book.) History has vindicated the publishers of the *NAUVOO EXPOSITOR* and exposed the duplicity and hypocrisy of Smith and his friends who destroyed this press.

Even after the death of Joseph Smith, John Taylor, editor and publisher of *The Times and Seasons,* a man who would become the third president of the L.D.S. Church, continued Smith's legacy of deception. On May 1, 1845 about a year after the death of Smith, the following editorial was published:

> The Latter-Day Saints are charged by their enemies with the blackest crimes. Treason, murder, theft, polygamy, and adultery are among the many crimes laid to their charge. . . . Most of the stories against the Mormons have been propagated by apostates and traitors. Sidney Rigdon, I see by the papers, has made

> an exposition of Mormonism, charging Joseph Smith and the Mormons with Polygamy. . . . Mr. Rigdon's spiritual wife system was never known until it was hatched by John C. Bennett who was cut off from the Church for seduction. As to the charge of polygamy, I will quote from the book of *Doctrine and Covenants*, which is the subscribed faith of the Church and strictly enforced. . . . "Inasmuch as this Church of Christ has been reproached with the crime of fornication and polygamy, we declare that we believe that one man should have but one wife and one woman but one husband except in case of death when either is at liberty to marry again."[21]

This quotation by Apostle Taylor was from section 101 of the original *Doctrine and Covenants* published in 1835. This along with quotations from *The Book of Mormon* against polygamy and Joseph Smith's statements in the *Elders Journal* were used by Church leaders and missionaries for many years to prove to the world that they were not living polygamy when they actually were.

By the time Taylor published this editorial, Brigham Young had at least ten wives and other Church leaders were not far behind.[22] The spiritual wife system "hatched" by apostate John C. Bennett is now called eternal marriage and is probably the most sacred principle of the L.D.S. Church.

Polygamy Officially Announced

Finally, in a general conference in Salt Lake City in 1852, after more than ten years of denial, an official announcement of polygamy was made by Apostle Orson Pratt under the direction of Church President Brigham Young. Brigham said that it was time to "let the cat out of the bag."

Soon after this happened, two of Joseph Smith's sons and a few others who refused to follow Brigham Young and the Mormon Pioneers in their migration West, came to Salt Lake City to claim their right to lead the Church. Part of their program was an effort to convince the Saints that it was not Joseph Smith but rather Brigham Young who instigated the practice of polygamy.

In order to protect his position, Brigham countered by producing the sworn affidavits of twenty women who said that they had been married to Joseph Smith and lived with him as husband and wife.[23] This oath of Lucy Walker was typical:

OATH OF LUCY WALKER SMITH,
WIFE OF JOSEPH SMITH, JR.

UNITED STATES OF AMERICA
STATE OF UTAH
COUNTY OF SALT LAKE

LUCY WALKER SMITH, being first duly sworn says:

I was a plural wife of the Prophet Joseph Smith, and was married to him in the State of Illinois, on the first day of May, 1843, by Elder William Clayton. The Prophet was then living with his first wife, Emma Smith, and I know that she gave her consent to the marriage of at least four women to her husband as plural wives, and that she was well aware that he associated and cohabited with them as wives. The names of the women were, Eliza and Emily Partridge, and Maria and Sarah Lawrence, all of whom knew that I too was his wife.

When the Prophet Joseph Smith first mentioned the principle of plural marriage to me, I felt indignant and so expressed myself to him, because of my feelings and education were averse to anything of that nature. But he assured me that this doctrine had been revealed to him of the Lord, and that I was entitled to receive a testimony of its divine origin for myself. He counseled me to pray to the Lord, which I did, and thereupon received from Him a powerful and irresistible testimony of the truthfulness and divinity of plural marriage, which testimony has abided with me ever since.

LUCY WALKER SMITH

Subscribed and sworn to before me this
24th day of October, 1902.

JAMES JACK

Notary Public

My Commission Expires August 6th, 1905

Things that Smith had declared "apostate lies and slander" only a few years earlier, now became the sworn testimony of twenty women! How can Church members today rationalize all of this deception and duplicity? After all, Jesus saved his strongest condemnation for the hypocrites.

Apostle Orson Hyde justified official Church lying on the grounds that it was necessary. After the Church had moved west, Hyde told a congregation of Mormons in Salt Lake City:

> What would it have done for us if they had known that many of us had more than one wife when we lived in Illinois? They would have broken us up, doubtless, worse than they did. They may break us up and rout us from one place to another, but by and by, we shall come to a point where we shall have all the women and they shall have none.[24]

Most of the Mormon Pioneers believed the public statements made by their leaders and sustained them against the "lies" of apostates and traitors. It is interesting to speculate what percentage of the pioneers would have followed the brethren west with "faith in every footstep," if they had known the truth about polygamy and other secret practices of their leaders. **Sadly, most of the Mormon Pioneers were following a trail of lies**.

In the 1880s when federal marshals came to the Utah Territory to enforce federal laws against polygamy, the tradition of lying continued. Men lied about who was and who was not their wife. Women lied about their marital status. Many of these women, even under oath, said, "I do not know who the father of my child is." What a degrading experience this must have been for women. Children were also taught to lie. They were given fictitious names to say if a stranger ever approached and asked who they were. My own mother was taught to do this because her father and mother were polygamists.

Finally, in 1890, under extreme pressure from the United States Government, President Wilford Woodruff, the fourth president of the L.D.S. Church, issued the "Manifesto" which seemed to discontinue the practice of polygamy. But this document only perpetuated the legacy of lies.

Woodruff's 1890 Manifesto is as follows. I have underlined the portions that couldn't possibly have been true:

OFFICIAL DECLARATION

To Whom it may Concern:

Press dispatches having been sent for political purposes, from Salt Lake City, which have been widely published, to the effect that the Utah Commission, in their recent report to the Secretary of the Interior, allege that plural marriages are still being solemnized and that forty or more such marriages have been contracted in Utah since last June or during the past year, also that in public discourses the leaders of the Church have taught, encouraged and urged the continuance of the practice of polygamy.

I, therefore, as president of the Church of Jesus Christ of Latter Day Saints, do hereby, in the most solemn manner, declare that these charges are false. We are not teaching polygamy or plural marriage, nor permitting any person to enter into its practice, and I deny that either forty or any other number of plural marriages have during that period been solemnized in our temples or in any other place in the Territory. One case has been reported, in which the parties allege that the marriage was performed in the Endowment House, in the Spring of 1889, but I have not been able to learn who performed the ceremony; whatever was done in

> this manner was without my knowledge. In consequence of this alleged occurrence the Endowment House was, by my instructions, taken down without delay. Inasmuch as laws have been enacted by Congress forbidding plural marriages, which laws have been pronounced constitutional by the court of last resort, I hereby declare my intention to submit to those laws and use my influence with the members of the Church over which I preside to have them do likewise. There is nothing in my teachings to the Church or in those of my associates, during the time specified, which can reasonably be construed to inculcate or encourage polygamy; and when any Elder of the Church has used language which appeared to convey any such teaching, he has been promptly reproved. And I now publicly declare that my advice to the Latter-Day Saints is to refrain from contracting any marriage forbidden by the law of the land. (D. & C, pp. 256-257)
>
> WILFORD WOODRUFF
> President of the Church of Jesus Christ
> of Latter-Day Saints
> October 6, 1890

Church records prove that the underlined portions of this statement were lies. Polygamy **was** being taught and plural marriages **were** being performed in the Utah Territory during the period of time specified. Elders were **not** reprimanded for teaching this doctrine. The Endowment House was **not** torn down because an unauthorized plural marriage was performed there. It was torn down because the Salt Lake Temple was almost complete thus making the Endowment House obsolete.

Accurate records are kept by the Church of **all** ordinances. It would **not** have been difficult for President Woodruff to find out who was married in the Endowment House during the previous spring and also who performed the weddings. Woodruff also had the power not only to reprimand but to release or even excommunicate anyone who performed unauthorized ordinances since he alone held the keys and sealing power. He was simply lying.

Plural marriages continued to be performed long after Woodruff's Manifesto. President Joseph F. Smith found it necessary to issue a second Manifesto in 1904. This applied not only to Church members within the United States but also to the saints in Canada, Mexico and other countries as well. The next year two apostles, John W. Taylor and M. F. Cowley resigned their apostleships rather than stop performing plural marriages.[25] My own grandfather (John Reese Evans) was married to his second wife by Church authority in the Manti, Utah L.D.S. Temple on October, 9, 1907, three years after the second manifesto.

The Mormon Battalion Deception

Another example of official deception by Church leaders has to do with the Mormon Battalion. I was taught in Sunday school, seminary, and priesthood meetings that on the 26th of June in 1846, the U.S. Government demanded the services of five hundred able bodied Mormon men to help fight the war with Mexico. This cruel act, while the saints were camped in Iowa on their way west, caused great hardships and many deaths among the poor saints crossing the plains. The women and older men who were left had no choice but to continue their struggle without help from these five hundred younger and stronger men.

I was about forty years old before I learned that this distortion of Mormon history was all part of a legacy of deception. Prominent Church leader and historian, B.H. Roberts, finally told the truth about the Mormon Battalion in his six volume *Comprehensive History of the Church*. But since this truth is not faith promoting, it has been ignored by those who write lesson manuals intended to indoctrinate young people. **The ultimate test of all official Church publications is not whether something is true but whether it is faith promoting.**

The truth is that Brigham Young secretly sent Jesse C. Little to Washington D.C. to see President James K. Polk and other federal officials with the proposal that the U.S. Government send a company of one thousand Mormons with the U.S. Army going to fight the war with Mexico. These men were to be paid for a one year enlistment, in advance, and be able to keep all of their weapons and equipment at the end of their service.

President Polk didn't want any Mormons in his army. The quota of 50,000 men had already been oversubscribed by three times, and besides, Polk didn't trust the loyalty, patriotism, or military training of the Mormons. But after much persuasion, he **reluctantly** agreed to send five hundred Mormons.[26]

When Captain James Allen, representing General Stephen W. Kearny of Ft. Leavenworth, entered the encampment of Mormons at Council Bluffs (Winter Quarters) Iowa in June of 1846, Young pretended to be surprised and angry but promised to raise the recruits as a demonstration of Mormon patriotism. Five hundred men were enlisted and paid one year in advance. The money was turned over to Brigham Young .

The great hardships, suffering, and even death that sending these five hundred men caused would have been much greater if President Polk had granted Young's original request to send one thousand men! In order to divert the anger and resentment of Church members away from himself, Young lied to his people and blamed the U.S. Government for the entire episode. On September 13, 1857, Brigham Young told a congregation of Mormons in Salt Lake City:

> There cannot be a more damnable, dastardly order issued than was issued by the Administration to this people while they were in an Indian country in 1846. . . . While we were doing our best to leave their borders, the poor, low, degraded curses sent a requisition for five hundred of our men to go and fight their battles! That was President Polk; and he is now weltering in hell with old Zackary Taylor, where the present administrators will be if they do not repent.[27]

On February 17,1861, Brigham Young, the Man who was President of the L.D.S. Church for thirty years, and a man who is still revered by Mormons as a prophet of God again lied when he told a congregation of Church members assembled in the Tabernacle at Salt Lake City:

> Did Thomas H. Benton aid in gathering the Saints? Yes, he was the mainspring and action of governments in driving us to these mountains. He obtained orders from President Polk to summon the militia of Missouri, and destroy every man, woman, and child, unless they turned out five hundred men to fight the battles of the United States in Mexico. He said that we were aliens to the Government, and to prove it he said, "Mr. President, make a requisition for five hundred men, and I will prove to you that they are traitors to our Government. . . . We turned out the men and Mr. Benton was disappointed.[28]

Neither Thomas Benton nor the Missouri militia had anything to do with enlistment of the Mormon Battalion. Nor was the U.S. Government threatening to exterminate all of the Mormons. This entire sermon is but another example of the many, many lies told by Brigham Young and other Church leaders in order to deceive and manipulate their people.

As it turned out, despite high U.S. Military casualties in this war, the Mormon Battalion was not used by field commanders. The Mormon Battalion didn't have to kill anyone nor did they suffer any casualties. But Brigham Young didn't know in advance that many of these young men wouldn't get killed when he volunteered their services. He was willing to jeopardize not only their lives but also the lives of their families who were left short handed crossing the plains for his own selfish purposes. Then he lied about it. What kind of a person does it take to do something like this?

The Mountain Meadow Massacre

Young and other Church leaders also lied about many other things, including who really instigated and took part in the

Mountain Meadows Massacre, the real reason that the U.S. Army was coming to the Utah Territory in 1857, and the separation of Church funds from Young's own personal property. The list goes on and on and on. As I read the twenty six volume *Journal of Discourses*, I was saddened and shocked by the level of deception practiced by men claiming to be prophets of God.

In more recent times, L.D.S. Presidents haven't added any "thus saith the Lord" revelations to Smith's *Doctrine and Covenants*. But modern prophets, seers, and revelators have pretended to have revelations establishing correlation programs, giving blacks the priesthood, making major changes in the temple endowment and sacred garments, opening missions here and there, and all sorts of other things. Many of these modern revelations contradict those of previous prophets, but that doesn't seem to matter. Perhaps Joseph Smith said it best when he said, "We believe all things, . . ."[29].

Mark Hofmann

Also in more recent times, court records indicate that Church leaders did not tell the truth about their relationships with forger and murderer Mark Hofmann. First Counselor Gordon B. Hinckley and other Church leaders had frequent contacts and made a number of secret financial deals with Hofmann. Yet, when I watched the news conferences on television, these Church leaders pretended that they hardly even knew who Hofmann was. This dishonest behavior is but a continuation of the time-honored policy that a Church member has a sacred duty to lie, if necessary, to protect the Church and Church leaders.

Truth Over All?

Contrary to claims made by many Latter-Day Saints, truth is **not** the most important thing in their lives. Other things are more important. For example, a close friend of mine who no longer believes in Mormonism, asked his mother if she would rather have him be honest with himself and with others about his questions and doubts about Mormonism or whether she would be more proud and much happier with him if he just pretended to believe and continued to live a life of hypocrisy and deception. Without hesitation, she said,

"I want you to be active and loyal to the Church regardless of what you may think about it." Family relationships, loyalty to the Church, and a number of other things are more important than personal integrity to this faithful Mormon mother and thousands of others just like her. Mormonism is responsible for creating this climate of hypocrisy by putting Church and family loyalty above honesty and integrity. I have personally experienced this unhappy situation on many, many occasions.

Sadly, the legacy of deception is not over. It will persist for many generations to come. It will continue as long as helpless little children and trusting adults are taught that *The Book of Mormon* is authentic, that Joseph Smith was a true prophet and his revelations were from God, that only Mormons have any authority to perform ordinances valid in the sight of God, that the L.D.S. temple ritual is a revelation from God, that only L.D.S. Church leaders receive revelations from God, that the creeds of all other churches are an "abomination" in the sight of God, and that their ministers are "all corrupt."

As long as these and other falsehoods are taught and believed, this sad legacy of lies will continue. And yet, Smith had the audacity to say that Satan is "the father of all lies," and "Wo unto the liar, for he shall be thrust down to hell."[30]

Pointing out even these few examples of deception by Joseph Smith, Brigham Young, and other Church leaders has caused many people including some members of my own family to become angry with me. Sadly, I have come to understand the words of the Apostle Paul to the Galatians, "Am I therefore become your enemy, because I tell you the truth?" (Gal.4:16)

Chapter 14

THE OUTLAWS

Tell the truth and run.
-Yugoslav proverb

In 1842 Joseph Smith wrote a letter to John Wentworth, Editor of the *Chicago Democrat.* This letter included a summary of Mormon beliefs. Number twelve of Smith's thirteen articles of faith reads as follows:

> We believe in being subject to kings, presidents, rulers, and magistrates, in obeying, honoring, and sustaining the law.[1]

And yet, Smith and other Church leaders were continually in violation of both state and federal laws.

Glass-looker Conviction

One of Smith's earliest encounters with the law has been mentioned earlier. This was his arrest, trial, and conviction as a "disorderly person" and a "glass-looker" in the courtroom of Judge Albert Neely.[2] This trial took place on March 20, 1826 in Bainbridge, New York and is a matter of public record.

Smith's Private Army

In 1834, Smith organized his own private army and called it Zion's Camp. He even had a revelation that stated, "Behold I say unto you, the redemption of Zion must needs come by power."[3] This army and an even larger private army that he organized later in Nauvoo were clearly illegal. They were not subject to federal or state authority but only to the commands of Smith. But what would happen in America if Mormons, Moslems, Catholics, Lutherans, Methodists, and Baptists each had their own private armies not subject to civil authorities?

An Illegal Bank

In November of 1836, Smith decided to start his own bank and print his own currency. This new bank was to be called the Kirtland Safety Society. When the Ohio legislature denied Smith's petition for an act of incorporation, he didn't let this stop him from organizing his bank and printing money. He simply ignored the laws of Ohio and went ahead with his bank.

Smith even had a convenient revelation from God advising Church members to buy stock in his illegal enterprise:

> It is wisdom and according to the mind of the Holy Spirit, that you should . . . call on us and take stock in our Safety Society.[4]

About one year later Smith's bank went broke costing some of his gullible followers their life's savings. Smith blamed this failure on the state of Ohio, his enemies, and almost everyone else. He took no responsibility and made no apologies. Apparently, he couldn't even seem to understand why many of those who lost all of their money were angry with him. Ironically, Smith's Safety Society proved to be anything but safe.

When Ohio authorities finally realized what Smith had done, they sent a sheriff and a deputy to arrest Joseph Smith, Sidney Rigdon, and other Church leaders who had violated Ohio State Laws. Smith and Rigdon escaped arrest by secretly leaving for Missouri in the middle of the night of January 12, 1838.[5] Other officials in the bank were not so lucky. Josiah Butterfield, Jonathan Dunham, and Jonathan Hale were arrested and thrown into jail for circulating illegal currency and for other unlawful banking activities.[6]

The Danites

After arriving in Missouri, Smith continued his outlaw ways. He organized a group of Mormon secret police called Danites to fight against outside enemies and also to rid the Church of dissenters (apostates). Each Danite took a blood oath to support the First Presidency, whether right or wrong, even to the shedding of blood. Each member was given secret signs, handclasps, and passwords to identify other members. The Danites were told by Smith and Rigdon, "You have been chosen to be our captains to rule over this last kingdom of Jesus Christ."[7]

On June 17, 1838, Rigdon told a large audience:

> "When men embrace the gospel and afterward lose their faith, it is the duty of the saints to trample them under their feet."[8]

Apostle Heber C. Kimball told the saints that the Bible was wrong about how Judas died. He said that the other eleven apostles actually kicked Judas until his bowels came out. Kimball went on:

> I know the day is right at hand when men will forfeit their priesthood and turn against us and against the covenants they have made and will be destroyed as Judas was.[9]

Where did first counselor Rigdon and Apostle Kimball learn such shocking things? If they didn't learn them from their file leader, Smith, then why didn't he correct them? Apparently, Mormonism, under Smith and later under Brigham Young, was a one way street where a person was welcome to come in but not free to get out. All of this sounds more like the ground rules for a street gang or the Mafia than the gospel of Jesus Christ.

In Smith's kingdom of God, apostates were guilty of treason and thus deserved to be killed. Never mind that no religious organization in America has any legal authority to kill someone. Again, Smith's behavior was that of an outlaw.

Dissenters including prominent men such as Oliver Cowdery, Lyman Johnson, David Whitmer, John Whitmer, and a number of others were given three days to get out of Western Missouri or face the wrath of the Danites.[10]

Danites were told by Smith and Rigdon that the kingdom spoken of by the prophet Daniel (thus the name Danites) that was to crush all other kingdoms had been set up by the Lord in these latter days in preparation for the imminent return of Jesus Christ. Since the kingdom of God takes precedence over the governments of men, the Lord's prophet and his followers were above the laws of Missouri, any other state, or even the government of The United States.[11]

This "above the law" attitude soon caused Smith and his partners in crime serious trouble. While in Missouri, Smith, Rigdon, Pratt and other Church leaders were arrested for a large number of crimes including treason against the state of Missouri, murder, burglary, arson, robbery, and larceny.[12] While being transferred from Liberty Jail to another location, they escaped and fled to Commerce (Nauvoo), Illinois. But these old Missouri charges would haunt these fugitives from the law for many years to come.

Despite testimony and sworn affidavits by several men including two of Smith's own apostles (Marsh and Hyde), Smith maintained that he had no first hand knowledge nor any responsibility for the Danites. John Taylor, a close friend of Smith's and a man who would later become third president of the L.D.S. Church also denied any knowledge of Mormon Danites:

> I have heard a good deal about Danites, but never have I heard of them among the Latter-Day Saints. If there was such an organization, I was never made acquainted with it.[13]

But Smith, Rigdon, Taylor, and other Church leaders **were** in control of the Danites. They organized this secret military organization and gave them their orders. By denying involvement, they were simply lying.

Smith's personal history claims that in order to get out of his legal trouble in Missouri, he paid legal fees and bribes of over $50,000![14] But how did Smith come up with that much money in 1839?

"Above The Law"

At first, Church leaders blamed their troubles in Missouri upon religious persecution, but later on, Smith's first counselor, Sidney Rigdon, admitted that the main reason that Mormons had so much trouble in Missouri was that they would not obey the laws of the land. He said, "We did not break them, we were above them."[15]

Rigdon also spoke candidly about the attitude that he, Smith and other Church leaders began to assume:

> . . . we began to talk about the kingdom of God as if we had the world at our command. We talked with great confidence, and talked big things. . . . We began to talk like men in authority and power. We looked upon the men of the earth as grasshoppers.[16]

Smith agreed with Rigdon's outlaw mentality when he said:

> I am above the kingdoms of the world, for I have no laws.[17]

Eventually the lawless Smith became so intoxicated with power that he began to exhibit some very bizarre behavior. For example, he started ordering other Church leaders to bring him their wives and daughters. This became Smith's ultimate test of obedience and loyalty. Many of these men, including Apostle Heber C. Kimball, did as they were told![18]

Astonishing Arrogance

Smith's lawless arrogance was apparently unbounded. In May of 1844, one month before he died, he said:

> **I have more to boast of than ever any man had. I am the only man that has ever been able to keep a whole church together since the days of Adam. A large majority of the whole have stood by me. Neither Paul, John, Peter, nor Jesus ever did it. I boast that no man ever did such a work as I. The followers of Jesus ran away from Him; but the Latter-Day Saints never ran away from me yet.**[19]

Smith made this astonishing statement to a congregation of saints in Nauvoo and later recorded it in his journal. **He claimed to have more to boast about than any man who ever lived including Jesus Christ**! It is not easy to think of a more arrogant and offensive statement than to proclaim oneself greater than Abraham, Moses, Peter, and even Jesus! Smith's arrogance and pride are a shocking contrast to the Savior's sermons on humility.

Joseph Smith's hunger for power and his preoccupation with military imagery are well documented. On January 25, 1842, Lieutenant General Joseph Smith, as commanding officer of about two thousand members of his private army, the Nauvoo Legion, held one of his many military reviews. As usual, he was dressed in splendid military clothing and riding a magnificent white stallion. In his address to his troops he said, ". . . that his soul was never better satisfied than on this occasion."[20] This is a strange comment from a man who claimed that he had seen and talked with God The Father, Jesus Christ, Peter, James, John, Moses, Elijah, Moroni, and other heavenly beings!

Smith's illegal army apparently helped satisfy his insatiable hunger for power. By promoting himself to the office of Lieutenant General, Smith offended many patriotic Americans since that high office had also been held by George Washington.

Treason Against The United States

By 1841, U. S. President John Tyler had finally had enough of Smith's private army, arrogance, and outlaw behavior. On March 31st, he issued a proclamation charging Joseph Smith with treason:

Joseph Smith, Esq.
Washington D.C., March 31,1841.

Sir: You stand accused of high treason. You will deliver yourself up to the governor at Springfield, Illinois, in order to be tried before the Supreme Court of The United States next term.

The governor of Illinois will be directed to take you in custody, if you will not deliver yourself up.

The President will deliver a proclamation against you, if you obey not this order by May 1,1843.

Respectfully yours,

Hugh L. Legare, Attorney-General
By Order of J. Tyler, President
of the United States[21]

This federal arrest warrant for treason was still outstanding when Smith was killed at Carthage, Illinois in June of 1844.

Bid For Vast Military Powers

On March 26,1844, even after being charged with treason by the President of the United States, Smith had the arrogance and audacity to send a memorial to the U.S. Congress requesting them to pass a law giving him authority to raise a military force of 100,000 men to take over the western part of America. The proposed law would punish anyone who tried to "hinder or molest" Smith in his military campaign. It called for a fine of $1000 or two years in prison for anyone who tried to oppose him. Smith's Army was not to be part of the regular United States Army.[22] Congress, of course, refused to have any part of Smith's unconstitutional bid for military power.

Candidate For President

Incredibly, during this same period of time, Smith became a serious candidate for President of The United States. In a flagrant violation of an important American legal tradition, Smith tore down Thomas Jefferson's wall of separation of church and state and called hundreds of priesthood holders to go into every state of the Union to campaign for his election.[23]

And what would Smith have done if elected, resign as Mormon prophet or hold both positions at once? Why not hold both positions? After all, Smith didn't seem to see any problem with being Church president and Mayor of Nauvoo at the same time. And later, Brigham Young didn't seem to see any problem with being both Church President and Governor of the Utah territory. Obviously, neither Smith nor Young believed in Jefferson's separation of church and state.

Illegal Polygamy Secretly Introduced

In 1841 Joseph Smith secretly introduced polygamy to some of the leading men and women in Nauvoo. Two years later he recorded his infamous revelation on polygamy which later became canonized as section 132 of his *Doctrine and Covenants*. Finally, in 1852, after many years of secrecy and denial, Church leaders admitted that they had been living "the principle" for over ten years.

But polygamy was against the law in most states. Section 121 of the Illinois State Law of 1833, provided a fine of $500 and one year in prison for each violation of its law against bigamy and polygamy. Since Joseph Smith had as many as fifty wives, he could have been fined $25,000 and been sent to prison for 50 years! Many of the other Church leaders were also guilty of breaking the Illinois law against polygamy. This "partners in crime" atmosphere, created by Smith, served to unite Church leaders and members for many years to come.

Smith's Nauvoo, A Law Unto Itself

In December of 1843, the Mayor of Nauvoo (Joseph Smith) and the City Council passed an ordinance making it illegal for any person to serve any county, state, or federal writ upon any person in Nauvoo or to search or seize any property in the city without permission of the mayor (Smith).[24] This action was intended to take Nauvoo out of the jurisdiction of any other governmental authority in the entire United States. Eventually, many serious students of Mormon history begin to realize how much time Smith actually spent in his dream world.

Nauvoo Expositor And Press Destroyed, A Rampage

On June 7th, 1844, the first and only edition of the *Nauvoo Expositor* was published. This paper exposed polygamy and some of the other illegal activities of Church leaders. Smith ordered this printing press destroyed. He also ordered all copies of this newspaper to be confiscated and burned. The next day a mill and some other buildings belonging to the Laws, Higbees, Fosters, and others who printed the *Nauvoo Expositor* were also destroyed. These men and their families who dared to question Smith's unlimited power were forced to flee Nauvoo for their lives! Smith and his outlaws were on a rampage.

Soon after the *Nauvoo Expositor* incident, several warrants were issued by state and county authorities for the arrest of Joseph, Hyrum, and a number of other Church leaders. Charges included treason against the State of Illinois, polygamy, adultery, resisting arrest, destruction of property, and perjury. These new charges, in addition to the old Ohio and Missouri charges along with the still outstanding warrant for high treason by the President of the United States certainly justify calling Smith an "outlaw." Unfortunately, Smith was turned into a martyr before he could stand trial for his crimes.

After the Smith brothers were killed during the afternoon hours of June 27, 1844, Arza Adams, one of Smith's many bodyguards, delivered a letter with the sad news to Church members in Nauvoo. This shocking letter came from Apostle John Taylor who was in jail with Smith and who was wounded at Carthage.

Above The Law Attitude Continues

But outside of a brief power struggle between Brigham Young, Emma Smith, William Smith, Sidney Rigdon, and a few others for leadership power, things didn't change very much. Church leaders and members had been converted to the idea that they alone had the true religion and authority to perform ordinances acceptable to God. They strongly believed that as members of the kingdom of God, they were answerable only to God and not to secular authorities. This "above the law" attitude would continue to cause them serious trouble in years to come.

Mormons Leave Illinois

The citizens of Illinois who, only a few years earlier had welcomed Mormon refugees from Missouri and had given them considerable help and encouragement soon came to resent Mormon arrogance, lawlessness, and militarism. They no longer considered the Mormons to be good neighbors.

Finally, the Mormons were forced to leave Illinois just as they had been forced to leave Ohio and Missouri where they had also refused to obey the law. They migrated west into an area occupied only by Native Americans near The Great Salt Lake. This territory, which belonged to Mexico, became part of the United States only one year later, in 1848, thus making the Mormons once again subject to the laws of the United States Government.

The Utah Territory

In 1850, Congress passed a law creating the Utah Territory. Federal appointees to govern this new territory were selected and sent west. This angered Church leaders who had already chosen the name, Deseret, for their territory and elected their own leaders including Brigham Young for Governor.

Church leaders refused to accept the new federal appointees and eventually drove them out of the territory. Brigham Young even threatened to kill these officers.[25] When the "runaway appointees" went back to Washington D.C. and reported their experiences to President Buchanan, the angry Commander-in-Chief sent part of the United States Army west to establish law and order and depose Brigham Young as king of his Great Basin Kingdom. A New Governor for the Utah Territory, Alfred Cumming, was appointed and sent west with the Army.

No Separation Between Church And State

While all of this was going on, the sermons by Church leaders in the Salt Lake tabernacle continued their "above the law" themes. Early saints were told that the Mormon priesthood was the only legitimate power in heaven or upon the earth.

Typical comments by Church leaders include:

> The government of God is upon the earth. I allude to the Church which it dictates; and then the whole earth which it will dictate.[26]

> The Priesthood upon the earth is the legitimate government of God, whether in the heavens or on the earth . . . and it is the only legitimate power that has a right to rule upon the earth.[27]

> We used to have a difference between church and state, but it is all one now. Thank God we have no more temporal and spiritual. We have got church and state together.[28]

Brigham Young told Mormon women assembled in the Salt Lake Tabernacle not to worry whether their husbands had other wives or whether their husbands loved them or not because their children would soon rule the nations of the world.[29] Apparently, Young was so intoxicated with the love of power that he thought political power was more important than close family relationships.

Church leaders and members took all of this very seriously. They even sent a proclamation to the kings, queens, and presidents of governments all over the world asking them to give up their positions before the Lord took vengeance upon them![30]

Outlaw Utah

Also, during this period of time, some of the most cruel and lawless acts imaginable took place in The Utah Territory. One of these acts was The Mountain Meadows Massacre near Cedar City in Southern Utah where about 100 disarmed men, women and children were killed in cold blood. This atrocity was committed by local Mormons along with some Native Americans in September of 1857.[31]

Seventeen children were spared because Mormons considered them to be innocent and still members of the kingdom of God. Sixteen of these orphans were later sent back to relatives in Arkansas.[32] Of course, saving these small children caused credibility problems later on when Church leaders tried to blame the entire incident upon Native Americans who cared nothing about sparing small children.

This wagon train, led by Captain Charles Fancher, was relatively wealthy. Most of the livestock stolen from them was given to Native Americans who helped with the massacre, but the wagons, firearms, jewelry, clothing, and other property were confiscated by local Church authorities. The $4,000 in gold that the Fanchers were taking to California to buy property was taken by William Stevens and given to the traveling bishop, Amos Milton Musser, who in turn, took it to Salt Lake City and gave it to Brigham Young.[33]

There may be some question about whether this massacre was committed under orders from Brigham Young, but the local leaders were strictly under his control. Also, there is no question that Young was an accessory after-the-fact since he protected the participants from prosecution and even rewarded them in many ways including additional wives.

Another outlaw incident that took place about this time was the massacre of Captain John W. Gunnison and seven other men in his survey party on the Sevier River in Millard County in 1853. Gunnison had written a book, *The Mormons,* that offended Young.[34]

Others who were killed during this outlaw era include the Aikens (1857) and the Parrish family (1857). The Aikens had property worth an estimated $25,000 which was never found. The Parrish family was killed on the eve of their departure out of the Church and out of the Utah Territory bound for California.[35]

These incidents are but a small sample of the murders and robberies that took place during the outlaw era in Brigham Young's Great Basin Kingdom. Orrin Porter Rockwell and William A (Bill) Hickman both admitted killing a number of people under orders from Brigham Young.[36]

The U.S. Army Comes To The Utah Territory.

When Young found out that President Buchanan was sending an army and a new Governor to replace him, he ordered General Daniel Wells, a commanding officer of Young's private army, still called the Nauvoo Legion, to attack these U.S. troops in the mountains before they were able to reach Salt Lake City.

Young counseled Wells to spare as much human life as possible and concentrate on destruction of supplies and confiscation of livestock. Wells, ever obedient to his master, did as he was told. His Nauvoo Legion conducted guerilla warfare in the mountains and plains east of Salt Lake City. They burned a large number of supply wagons and took thousands of unprotected government cattle and horses to Salt Lake City and gave them to Brigham Young.[37]

Brigham Young Is Charged With Treason.

Federal officials charged Brigham Young and other Church leaders with treason, theft, and a number of other crimes. One hundred and forty years later, in 1997, Church President Gordon B. Hinckley dedicated a monument honoring Wells and the other outlaws who burned and stole U.S. Government property east of Salt Lake City in 1857!

When the U.S. Army, after almost freezing and starving to death in the mountains, finally got started toward Salt Lake City, Brigham Young did one of the most evil and cowardly things that can be imagined. He told U.S. Army officers that if they came into his Great Basin Kingdom, that he would burn all of the homes and barns and leave nothing but ashes. Young told Captain Van Vliet:

> . . . for when the time comes to burn and lay waste our improvements, if any man undertakes to shield his, he will be sheared down . . .[38].

This was no idle threat. Young ordered everyone to put straw and other flammables into their houses and barns and prepare to burn everything upon a moment's notice. A frightened, angry, and sad column of Mormons started south in their wagons with no destination and very few supplies. But they were angry at the U.S.

Government, not at Young and other Church leaders who had created their plight. This was because Church leaders had, once again, lied by telling them that the U.S. Army had come to destroy their religion, kill their men, and rape their wives and daughters.[39]

President Buchanan and the new governor finally began to see the dark side of Young and began to realize that they were not dealing with an ordinary person but with a power-hungry fanatic who was willing to lie, hide behind women and children, kill any man who didn't follow orders, and send Church members off into the desert and almost certain death rather than give up his power!

Amnesty Offered

After charging Brigham Young and other Church leaders with treason, destruction and theft of government property, violence, threatening to kill federal appointees, and a number of other crimes, U.S. President James Buchanan offered these Mormon outlaws a general pardon, provided Young step down as Governor and the citizens of the Utah Territory begin to obey federal laws.[40] Buchanan made this offer because he didn't want to see so many innocent men, women, and children suffer the desolation of war.

Young Steps Down But Retains His Power.

Young bitterly accepted this amnesty and gave up his position as governor but **not** his power. He continued to control the government of the Utah Territory through his "ghost legislature." Since almost all elected members of the legislature were faithful Mormons, Young simply held a meeting prior to each legislative term and told his obedient followers which laws to pass and which ones to defeat. Some claim that L.D.S. Church leaders still control State Government in Utah since almost all legislators are Mormons who are well aware of the Church position on major legislation.

Young also continued to control the court system through his power over Mormon jurors. He could convict or acquit any person as he pleased. For example, John D. Lee was given additional wives by "Brother Brigham" as a reward for his loyalty even after his admitted participation in the Mountain Meadows Massacre.

It was not until about twenty years later (1877) when Young needed a scapegoat that a mostly Mormon jury convicted Lee of murder. Lee was executed even though he was obviously not acting alone and wasn't even in command of those who participated in this terrible crime.[41] This was an example of flagrant jury tampering.

Federal Law Against Polygamy

On July 8,1862, Abraham Lincoln fulfilled one of his Republican campaign promises to "abolish the twin vestiges of barbarism in America, slavery and polygamy."[42] When Lincoln signed this new federal law against polygamy, Young and other Church leaders were outraged. They still hated Lincoln for his negative attitude toward the Mormons and their Nauvoo City Charter, when Lincoln was a member of the Illinois Legislature.

Church leaders and members who claimed, " We believe in . . . obeying, honoring, and sustaining the law," simply ignored this new law. Church members who were charged with the crime of polygamy simply demanded a jury trial and were then acquitted by their Mormon "peers." This law against polygamy was considered an unenforceable joke.

In 1875, George Reynolds, private secretary to Brigham Young, was charged and convicted of polygamy in the Third District Court. He was sentenced to two years imprisonment at hard labor.[43] Young encouraged the Mormon jury to convict Reynolds because he wanted to appeal the conviction through the federal court system in order to have the U.S. Supreme Court declare the 1862 law a violation of the Bill of Rights provision for freedom of religion.

Four years later (1879), and two years after Brigham Young died (1877), The United States Supreme Court upheld the 1862 law against polygamy stating that there are limits to freedom of religion, assembly, speech, the press, and all of the other constitutional rights. The court held that none of our constitutional rights are absolute. For example, if a person's religious beliefs included human sacrifice or the Hindu custom of burning a man's wife when he dies, freedom of religion does not extend this far nor does it extend to polygamy, the court declared. (C.H.C. Vol. V, pp. 468-473).

Thus, the law against polygamy was upheld by the court of last resort in America and became the law of the land. But still the Mormon outlaws refused to honor or obey it. Church authority was considered superior to federal or state laws. Smith's "above the law" mentality still prevailed.

Tough New Federal Laws

In 1882, the United States Congress, by a vote of 199 to 42, passed the Edmunds law, an amendment to the 1862 law against polygamy. This new law defined polygamous living or "unlawful cohabitation" as a federal crime punishable by a $300 fine and imprisonment not to exceed six months. It also made it unlawful for any polygamist to hold any public office, vote, or serve on a jury in any territory of the United States.[44]

Now Church leaders and members started to pay attention. They could no longer serve on juries and prevent convictions. Some of those who still refused to obey the law were convicted and imprisoned. This included one of my own grandfathers. (Both of my grandfathers were polygamists.) But even the hiding, lying, suffering, fines, and imprisonment were not enough to force Church members to obey the law. **There was a higher law, God's law**.

It was not until 1887, when the Edmunds-Tucker law was passed, which designated the L.D.S. Church as a subversive organization, abolished the Nauvoo Legion, dissolved the Church as a corporation, and confiscated Church property, did Church leaders realize that their "above the law" attitude meant serious trouble.[45]

Individual Church members and even Church leaders were expendable, but the organization itself had to be protected at all costs. But even then, it took three years for Church President Wilford Woodruff to issue his "Manifesto" officially advising all Church members to "obey the laws of the land."[46] But why was this even necessary if Church members really believed Smith's twelfth article of faith which says, "We believe in being subject to kings, presidents, rulers, and magistrates, in obeying, honoring and sustaining the law"?

But major changes in attitudes and value systems do not take place quickly. It took a long time before Church leaders began to give up Smith's "above the law", and "kingdom of God," ideas in order to become part of the larger American culture.

Despite claims to the contrary, the L.D.S. Church does not have a proud tradition of law abiding, patriotic behavior. After all, how many leaders of other churches have been charged with high treason, murder, theft, destruction of government property, threatening to kill government officials, arson, and polygamy? And how many other churches have officially been declared subversive organizations or had their property confiscated by the U.S. government?

Chapter 15

A LUST FOR POWER

> Power will intoxicate the best hearts, as wine the strongest heads. No man is wise enough, nor good enough to be trusted with unlimited power.
>
> - Charles Caleb Colton

I believe that one of the fundamental evils in our world has always been the lust for power. It has contributed to war, political strife, authoritarianism, chauvinism, divorce, racism, murder, rape, spouse and child abuse, assault, street gangs, organized crime, and a long list of other sources of human misery. Unfortunately, world history includes a sad legacy of men and women lusting for power and willing to do almost anything to gain and keep it.

Sadly, the long list of men intoxicated with power includes Joseph Smith, Brigham Young, and a number of other Church leaders. Smith had a compelling need to dominate everyone around him. This included his parents, his wife, his brothers, his friends, and Church members in general. He became a master of manipulation and control. Brigham Young learned the secrets of power from his mentor and ruled his Great Basin Kingdom like a dictator for about thirty years.

Even from his grave, Smith still dominates the lives of millions of men and women who sing his praises every Sunday, go on missions to win converts to his myths and illusions, pay millions of dollars to build chapels and temples to perform his sacraments and rituals, and even wear the regulation underwear. I know men and women who no longer believe in Mormonism who have taken second jobs in order to send a son or daughter on a two year mission for Smith and his Church. That is a lot of power. Directly or indirectly, Smith still controls the lives of most Mormon men and women. A person who doubts this should consider what would happen to him or her if he or she were to turn against Smith, stop going to Church, stop paying tithing, and stop going to the temple. The probability is very high that this person's husband or wife would divorce them. Mormons who turn against Smith stand a good chance of losing their marriage and family, their home, and perhaps even their job or business.

Power Defined

A good definition of power is the ability to control and manipulate other people. A person with power can coerce others into doing things they don't want to do, even things that are clearly against their own self interest. Extreme power can force people to give up their own life for a cause, kill other people when told to do so, suffer extreme persecution, and give away all of their money and property. It can force a man to give another man his wife or daughter, and leave his home and family to go away on a mission and stay there until "released." It can force a woman to share a husband with other women, and give themselves to a man who they may fear or hate when told to do so. Smith and Young were able to do these things. No one should be trusted with that much power.

Lust For Power Is Condemned As Satanic.

And yet, ironically, Mormon scripture says that the reason Satan's plan of salvation was rejected and the thing that made Satan so evil was his great desire for power:

> Wherefore, because that Satan rebelled against me, and sought to destroy the agency of man, which I the Lord God, had given him, and also that I should give unto him mine own power, . . . I caused that he should be cast down.[1]

Another Mormon scripture says:

> The rights of the priesthood are inseparably connected with the powers of heaven, and the powers of heaven cannot be controlled nor handled only upon the principles of righteousness. . . . but when we undertake to cover our sins, or to gratify our pride, our vain ambition, or to exercise control or dominion or compulsion upon the souls of the children of men, in any degree of unrighteousness, behold, the heavens withdraw themselves, the Spirit of the Lord is grieved; and when it is withdrawn, Amen to the priesthood and authority of that man. . . . We have learned by sad experience that it is the nature of almost all men, as soon as they get a little authority, as they suppose, they will immediately begin to exercise unrighteous dominion.[2]

Both Smith And Young Exercised Almost Unlimited Power.

And yet, Smith, Young, and other Church leaders exercised control, dominion, and compulsion with a passion. They controlled almost every aspect of a Church member's life including property, marriage and family relationships, political activities, meetings, the media, who was to be fellowshipped or ostracized, who would be called to go on a mission and when they would be "released," and who was to be exalted in the celestial kingdom of God and who was to be damned in hell. **It is not easy to find men in world history who have exercised more raw power than Joseph Smith and Brigham Young.**

But how were these men able to manipulate strong and intelligent men and women and get them to do almost anything they were asked to do, including many things that were clearly against their own self interest? And how do these men continue in our day to control Mormon men and women even from their graves? What is the secret of their great power?

Internal Controls

Smith and Young used a large number of internal and external power techniques to control Church members. Internal controls included (1) the strong need that most people have to believe in God and an afterlife, (2) the attractiveness of Smith's illusions and myths, (3) the seductiveness of authoritarian certainty and freedom from painful ambivalence, (4) the need for community, to belong to a church, group, club, or gang, (5), The need to be part of a cause and have a meaningful life, (6) the authoritarian need to be important and share power, (7) the need for identity, to be special in the eyes of God, to be a chosen people, the House of Israel, a master race, and (8) the sacrifice trap.

Conversion

Internal controls are usually more effective than external control mechanisms. If a person is truly converted to something, then very little external pressure will be necessary because the person wants to do what his manipulator wants him or her to do.

First a person was converted to Mormonism. Then they were cut off from their old social support system by coming to Utah and perhaps living polygamy. Then they were fellowshipped with open arms into their new Mormon community and usually given a position of responsibility and authority in the Church.

Conversion was the first and most effective internal control mechanism used by Smith and Young. Once a person accepted the assumption that Joseph Smith was a prophet who spoke for God, then whatever he said became the will of God. This mental process convinced many converts that doing things that were illegal, immoral, or clearly against their own self interest really **were** in their self interest because by doing these things, they pleased Smith and God and earned eternal glory and happiness in the celestial kingdom.

Thus, Smith's great deception gave him remarkably persuasive powers. Men lived for him and died for him. Heber C. Kimball, John Taylor, and others proved their absolute loyalty and obedience by giving Smith their wives and daughters.[3] Married women gave themselves to Smith or allowed their husbands to take other wives in order to please God and earn so great a reward.

Mormon women were told that neither they nor their husbands could be exalted in the celestial kingdom of God unless their husbands lived the law of celestial marriage and took other wives. One Mormon woman, who went looking for another wife for her husband, was asked, "Doesn't it almost break your heart to have your husband take another wife?" She answered, "If my heart stands between me and the kingdom of God, it ought to break."[4]

This kind of reasoning, encouraged by Smith and Young, caused Mormon men and women to stop doing their own thinking and just turn their lives over to their authoritarian masters. This spiritual slavery is a clear contradiction to any notions of individualism and free agency. But isn't this the same method of redeeming humanity with power and force that Mormon theology claims that Satan advocated and God rejected in the first place?

Church members were told that they belonged to the only true Church, were members of the House of Israel, were special in the eyes of God, and that they had a very important work to do in building up the kingdom of God on the earth and the establishment of Zion. They had identity, community, authority, importance, a purpose in life, the approval of God, and wonderful, comforting certainty. All of this was, and still is, very seductive. What more could a person ask in this life?

The Sacrifice Trap

Another internal control mechanism used very effectively by Smith and Young was the sacrifice trap. A person tends to value that for which he or she has paid a very dear price. For example, let's consider Sarah, a twenty five year old woman who, in 1856, joined the L.D.S. Church in Liverpool, England. Sarah joined the Mormons despite the tears and pleading of her parents, her husband, and her friends.

Sarah left her husband, her parents, her friends, and her homeland to migrate to America with her three small children. She sacrificed almost everything she had for the Church. Sarah pushed a handcart over 1,000 miles across the plains, buried two of her children in shallow graves, and shared her new husband with four other women. All of this broke her heart. She didn't know life could hurt so bad.

Sarah worked hard to support herself and her children during the years that her husband was away on a Church mission. She spent most of her time alone and lonely. She had no one to share her hopes and dreams and fears. And even when Sarah's husband came home, it was almost a week before he got through visiting his other wives and finally got around to her.

After a new federal law was passed against polygamy, Sarah had to teach her children to lie when anyone asked who their father was in order to keep her husband out of trouble. After all, any stranger could be a federal marshal. When this didn't succeed, she lied in court under oath to protect her husband. But despite all of this lying, her husband was convicted and sent to prison. Again, Sarah was left alone to fend for herself.

After her husband got out of prison, Sarah and her "sister wives" took their families and moved to Mexico in order to avoid more trouble. Colonization in a strange land was very painful. Poverty, sickness, and death again were part of Sarah's life. A few years later, Sarah's husband was called to an important Church position in Utah. Since he could only take one of his wives with him to the states, he took Amanda, his youngest and prettiest wife. Sarah was left alone in Mexico.

What kind of evidence would it take to get Sarah to see that her sacrifices, work, pain, and tears had been in vain? What would it take to convince her that she had dedicated her life and the lives of her children to a fraud. She would probably die first!

Smith and Young understood how their sacrifice trap could lock converts into Mormonism. Brigham Young said:

> **Well, do you think that persecution has done us good? Yes. I sit and laugh, and rejoice exceedingly when I see persecution.**[5]

This is not an isolated quotation. There are over one hundred similar statements in the *Journal of Discourses*. And why did Young welcome persecution and why did it even make him laugh? This and many other of his statements indicate that Young had very little human compassion even for his own people. But the more important reason that both Smith and Young gloried in persecution was that they both knew that it created a powerful sacrifice trap.

Mormonism has always demanded great sacrifices. Many faithful members make a covenant to sacrifice all that they have, even their own lives, if necessary, to the building up of the kingdom of God upon the earth and the establishment of Zion.

Some people are born into the sacrifice trap. From childhood they hear stories about the great price their parents and ancestors have paid for their membership in the Church. Many who are born into this trap spend their entire lives paying tithing, going on missions, serving in bishoprics, serving in other Church callings, sending their own children on missions, doing genealogy and temple work, and in other ways paying a higher and higher price for their Church membership.

How can a person be objective about Mormonism when she and her ancestors have paid so dearly for their "pearl of great price"? How can a person even consider the possibility that her treasure is not a real pearl but only a cheap imitation? But this person is more likely to become angry at the person who tells her the truth than at the con-man (Smith) who sold her a fake pearl.

Responsibilities In The Church

Another important internal control is that Mormonism is **not** a spectator religion where a priest, minister, or rabbi gives the prayers and sermons and does nearly all of the work while Church members mostly sit and listen. Almost every member is called to at least one position in the Church. These positions are in the Sunday school, priesthood quorums, Relief Society, youth programs, scouting, home teaching, visiting teaching, missionary programs, temple work, genealogy, and ward choir. There are also many leadership positions in bishoprics, stake presidencies, and General Authorities. The fact that individual Church members feel responsible for doing a good job (magnifying their callings) creates a great source of talent, energy, and money for Mormonism.

External Controls

But what happens when a Church member no longer believes in *The Book of Mormon*, Joseph Smith, and the myths of Mormonism? Even when conversion, the sacrifice trap, and other internal controls have broken down, the Church has some very powerful external controls that can keep a person who no longer believes in line for many years.

The Family

Perhaps the strongest external pressure comes from a person's own family. It is not easy to resist the pressure from a husband, wife, parent, grandparent, or child to remain active and at least pretend to believe. For example, when a man's daughter wants to get married in the temple, how does he explain to her that he can not be there to see her get married because he no longer believes in Joseph Smith. And it seems that almost everyone blames the man for this situation and not the cruel Church policy that will not allow him to see his own daughter get married unless he pays his tithing and convinces his bishop that he still believes in Smith's illusions.

And what does a man say to his wife when she cries at night because he will not take her to the temple for an eternal marriage and she is afraid that she will be left single and separate for all eternity? What does a person say when a son or daughter comes home from Church asking why their parents don't love them enough to be married in the temple and create an eternal family? And how embarrassing is it to a man who is not allowed to bless or baptize his own child when the entire family has gathered together for such an important occasion. I have experienced this humiliation.

When a person has been taught all of his life to honor his father and his mother, what does he say when, with tears in their eyes, his parents plead with him to become active in the Church, pay his tithing, go to the temple, and put his garments back on in order to stay a part of their eternal family. This kind of pressure is almost more than a person who dearly loves his parents can take.

The Church is very much aware of this external control and the great power it has over those who no longer believe in Mormonism. But the abuse of this power has caused many tears and a great deal of pain for so many, many people. What other church does not allow loving family members to witness a wedding and participate in other ordinances?

The L.D.S. Church claims to be a kind, loving, and family oriented organization. In spite of that, it hurts many people and tears many families apart in order to maintain its power. But those who have been deeply hurt are not supposed to become angry, upset or bitter. If they do, loyal Church members think that there is something wrong with them, but not with heartless Church policies.

Economic Power

Another weapon in the external control arsenal of the L.D.S. Church is power over a person's job, property, and ability to support one's family. There are many men and women in the L.D.S. Church today who would lose their jobs or important business relationships if they were to admit that they no longer believe in Joseph Smith and his *Book of Mormon*. This certainly includes all of those men and women who work in Church offices, the Church "education" system, or at Brigham Young University.

In the early days of the Church, Smith's program of consecration and stewardship (also called the united order) gave him this kind of economic power over almost everybody. Church members were required to deed all of their property over to Smith in exchange for his goodwill.[6]

Smith's communistic, authoritarian theocracy gave him control over everyone's property. If followers did what they were told, they would be given the best land, employment, and marriage partners. If they didn't follow counsel or turned against Smith, they were excommunicated and forced to leave town with almost nothing.

The freedom of religion, speech, assembly, and association provided in the Bill of Rights are almost meaningless without economic freedom (private property and freedom of enterprise). If someone else controls a person's economic life and decides whether his family will eat and have a place to live, then whoever has this power over him becomes his master, and he must do as he is told. Smith had this power. And yet, he claimed to believe in free agency and said that Satan was the one who sought the power to destroy the agency of man. It seems that Smith and Young did a pretty good job of destroying the freedom of Church members all by themselves.

Women And Marriage

Another external control used very effectively by Smith and Young was their control over women and marriage. They each claimed to be the only man on earth with the sealing power of God. No one was married for all eternity without their permission. Their sealing power was superior to any other civil or religious marriage. They claimed absolute power over marriage and divorce.

If a man turned against Church authorities, he was excommunicated and lost not only his property but also his wives and children. They were given to someone else. If the infraction was not too serious, a man sometimes lost his position in the Church and one or two of his wives and some of his children.

One example of this was when John D. Lee hesitated to accept Brigham Young's mission call to the Iron Mission in Southern Utah. Lee's favorite wife, Louisa, and also their only son was taken away from Lee and given to General Daniel Wells, a commanding officer in Young's private army, the Nauvoo Legion of the Church.[7]

Wells was also rewarded for his absolute obedience and loyalty to Young with another woman, Hannah Hotchkiss. Hannah was taken away from her husband, Sterne Hotchkiss, when he refused to accept Young's mission call to Siam.[8] Wells was the officer commanding the Nauvoo Legion in the Utah Territory when they burned U.S. Government supply wagons and stole several thousand head of government livestock east of Salt Lake City in 1857. Wells was well rewarded by his master, Brigham Young.

In 1855, Brigham Young Said:

> No Man has a right to a wife or wives, unless he honors his Priesthood and magnifies his calling before God.[9]

George A. Smith, one of Young's counselors, told a conference of Church members:

> . . . There is not a "Mormon" sister who would live with a man a day who would refuse to go on a mission. There is no other way for a man to save his family; and in order to save himself, he must fulfill his calling and magnify his priesthood in proclaiming the fullness of the gospel to the nations of the earth . . .[10].

If Smith, Young, or some other Church leader wanted to get rid of a man, all they had to do was call him on a mission to a country on the other side of the Earth and leave him there as long as they felt necessary. If the man refused to go, he was branded an apostate, thus losing his wife and family. Poor Sterne Hotchkiss refused Young's call to Siam and lost his wife, family, and his Church membership. His wife was given to Wells, one of Young's friends. She had no choice but to give herself to Wells. If she refused to become the wife of anyone she was given to, she also become an evil apostate and lost her Church membership in this life and could expect to go to hell after she died. Not many Mormon women could stand up to that much pressure.

Another example of Young's abuse of power was when he decided that he wanted Zina Jacobs, the beautiful wife of Henry B. Jacobs. Young, exercising his power to take the wife of any man lower than him in the priesthood pecking order (see Smith's preemptive wives doctrine in chapter 16), not only took Zina for his wife but ordered Henry to stand as a witness to the wedding ceremony. Then Young sent the poor brokenhearted Jacobs on a Church mission to England. Jacobs was so sick that he had to be carried in a blanket to start on his way to England. Both Zina and the Jacobs children now belonged to Brigham! In April of 1850, Zina gave birth to Brigham Young's daughter.

Six years later, Jacobs, who still loved Zina, wrote her a heartrending letter:

> Oh how happy I would be if I only could see you and the little children, bone of my bone, flesh of my flesh. I am unhappy, there is no peace for poor me, my pleasure is you, my comfort has vanished. . . . Oh Zina, can I ever, will I ever get you again, answer the question please. Zina my mind never will change from worlds without ends, no never, the same affection is there and never can be moved. I do not murmur nor complain of the handlings of God no verily, no but I feel alone and no one to speak to, to call my own. . . . I do not blame any person or persons, no - May the Lord our Father bless Brother Brigham and all pertains unto him forever. Tell him for me I have no feelings against him nor never had, all is right according to the law of the celestial kingdom of our God Joseph.[11]

Apparently, poor Jacobs had been so brainwashed that he not only gave up his wife and children to Brigham Young, but then honored and blessed the man who had emasculated him and considered Joseph Smith to be his God! Jacobs was not alone in referring to Smith as "our God." A number of sermons by Church leaders in the tabernacle at Salt Lake City refer to Smith this way and say that no person in this last dispensation can enter the kingdom of God without the permission of Joseph Smith.[12]

When a person considers the realities of this situation where Smith and Young could take any woman they wanted, and do it by the power of their pretended priesthood and in the name of God, it is horrifying! These men were walking roughshod over the lives of real people with sensitive feelings and real emotions, not just fictitious characters in some paperback novel.

Perhaps Brigham Young experienced great satisfaction in having sex with Zina and the other women that he pre-empted since this was a culmination of his lust for women and his lust for power. But what about the feelings and emotions of Zina and the other women who were caught up in this system of interchangeable partners and spiritual beds? How did they feel about being taken away from their husbands and becoming the newest member in the harem of Smith, Young, Kimball, Wells, or Pratt? And what about their heartbroken husbands?

When a woman feels powerless and is forced to give herself to a man because of his power, whether the source of that power is a gun or God, this is usually called rape. And if this is true, then Smith, Young and other Church leaders were guilty of adultery and rape on a massive scale. These men didn't have to be romantic, loving, or even kind. They simply used the promise of exaltation and threats of ostracism and damnation to create fear and submission thereby getting whatever and whoever they wanted.

Smith and Young not only controlled their female converts but also the men. Men were required to attend priesthood meetings and conferences, but these men never knew if they would be called from the pulpit to go on a proselytizing or a colonizing mission. They never knew if someone higher in authority wanted to take their wife and children. And if they refused counsel or a mission call, they faced excommunication and the loss of everything they had, even their souls.[13] Mission calls to remote, dangerous, or undesirable places were often used as a form of punishment or even banishment for men who were not submissive enough. This was the Mormon Siberia.

Men who were pronounced apostates and traitors in the kingdom of God, were often ordered out of town or even threatened with execution. Smith and Young both threatened to kill apostates and were apparently willing to back up these threats with action.[14] Fear of death has always proven to be a very effective external control mechanism for authoritarians including Smith and Young. Very few men or women were willing to openly speak out against them no mater how cruelly they were treated. And even today, most Church members are afraid to say anything against Joseph Smith. He is considered sacred, beyond criticism.

Condemnation In An Afterlife

Church leaders not only claimed the right to control all of the property and to own men and women but also the souls of Church members. In other words, Church members really "belonged" to the Church, body and soul, both in this life and in the next! A Church member who was excommunicated lost all of his or her blessings and ordinances including their eternal marriage, their temple endowments, baptism, and their priesthood. Since all of these were necessary for exaltation in the celestial kingdom of God, an excommunicated person was in big trouble in the next world. And even today, most Church members will do almost anything to avoid excommunication.

Fortunately, today, most Church members own their own homes, farms, businesses and other property and some of the most flagrant abuses of power of early Mormonism have been discontinued. But the Church still has a great deal of power and control over the lives of faithful Church members and also the lives of many of those who no longer believe in Mormonism. And it still claims the power to determine the punishment or reward Church members can expect to receive from God in the next world.

Joseph Smith's God Makes Death Threats!

It is interesting to note that although Joseph Smith claimed that the Lord gave man his free agency, Smith also claimed that God forced him into polygamy against his will. When approaching Mary Elizabeth Rollins Lightner about becoming one of his wives, Smith told her:

> An angel of God came to me three times between the years 1834 and 1842 and said that I was to obey that principle or he would slay me.[15]

Benjamin Johnson explained why he gave his sister, Almira, to become a polygamous wife to Smith:

> I know that Joseph was commanded to take more wives and he waited until an angel with a drawn sword stood before him and declared that if he longer delayed fulfilling that command, he would kill him. . . . the prophet again came to my house and occupied the same room and bed with my sister Almira that the month previous he had occupied with the daughter of the late Bishop Partridge as his wife.[16]

In Smith's infamous revelation on polygamy, canonized by the L.D.S. Church in section 132 of its *Doctrine and Covenants*, God threatens to destroy any woman who does not accept polygamy and refuses to give her husband other wives:

> And again verily, verily, I say unto you, if any man have a wife . . . and he teaches unto her the law of my priesthood as pertaining to these things, then she shall administer unto him, or she shall be destroyed, saith the Lord your God . . .[17].

Apparently, Smith's God sends angels who threaten to kill people with drawn swords if they don't follow orders. His God also threatens to destroy any woman who will not accept polygamy. Who is this God Smith is worshipping? Certainly it is **not** Jesus, the Christian God, who gave man his free agency and who is kind and loving to all of His sons and daughters.

Secrecy And Deception

Another powerful external control mechanism used very effectively by Smith and Young was deception. If Smith had not lied about his gold plates, his ability to translate, his visions and revelations, his restoration of "true Masonry", polygamy, his secret wives, his secret police (Danites), and his secret world government (The Council of Fifty), it is unlikely that many people would have followed him or made great sacrifices for him.

If Brigham Young had told Church members the truth about polygamy, the Mormon Battalion, the Mountain Meadows Massacre, his illegal and immoral activities, and his great personal wealth, it is doubtful that many of them would have followed him and become part of his Great Basin Kingdom. Deception was a very important source of power for Smith, Young, Taylor, and a number of other Church leaders. As I read the twenty six volume *Journal of Discourses*, I was saddened and shocked by the level of deception practiced by men claiming to be prophets of God.

Control Of The Media And The Pulpit

In order to maintain power through deception it becomes necessary to control the media. Smith controlled the pulpit, the newspapers, and other media in Nauvoo until the *Nauvoo Expositor* came to town. Smith clearly understood that this publication could expose his secrecy and deception. Apparently, this is why he found it necessary to not only destroy this newspaper but also its building and presses. He also destroyed considerable other property of the publishers and drove them out of town.

Following the example of his mentor, Brigham Young controlled the pulpit and the media in his Great Basin Kingdom for many years. And even today, L.D.S. leaders understand the importance of controlling the media. Effective indoctrination is of critical importance in maintaining the growth and power of the Church. It is still not easy to get anything published or distributed in Utah if it goes against Mormonism.

Eternal Oaths And Covenants

Another effective and powerful external control mechanism very skillfully used by Smith was requiring Church members to make sacred oaths and eternal covenants of loyalty to him and to Mormonism. Melchizedek priesthood holders and all of those receiving their temple endowments and ordinances were required to pledge eternal loyalty to Mormonism and to Church leaders. This requirement is still part of Mormonism today.

Smith's eternal oaths and covenants were intended to bind a person to Mormonism and its leaders even after internal controls such as conversion were no longer effective. According to Smith there is no forgiveness in this life nor the next for covenantbreakers. Just as the old Catholic marriage system was intended to force men and women to remain married even after they no longer loved each other or wanted to be together, Mormon covenants were intended to force Church members to stay loyal to the Church even after they no longer believed in Mormonism.

But making an eternal covenant of loyalty to any ideology is fundamentally anti-intellectual and essentially dishonest. It is promising to never learn anything in the future that may change a person's mind. But how can an honest person promise to never learn anything in the future that may change his or her mind? The very essence of science and the search for truth is for a person to remain open minded and willing to change even one's most basic ideas and values when presented with enough good evidence. This is what open-mindedness is all about. Again, we see an example of Smith's fundamental dishonesty.

Unpredictable Behavior

Being unpredictable gives a person power since it puts other people into a position where they do not know what to expect. An unpredictable person can twist and turn another person back and forth like a wire until they break. This is part of the power that an abusive or alcoholic husband has over his wife. Sometimes he is kind and loving and other times he is angry and abusive. Eventually she breaks, becoming compliant and docile. Smith used his different personalities to break the will of Emma, his brothers, his apostles, and many others.

Smith's Violent Temper

A very important aspect of Smith's unpredictability was his violent temper. His own written history includes several accounts of physical fights that he got into even after becoming president of his Church. One incident was a fight that he got into with his brother William in a meeting right in front of other Church members.[18]

Joseph and William were both about six foot two inches tall and very husky, powerful men. Unlike Hyrum who Joseph loved because he was "meek," "humble," and "possessing the mildness of a lamb," William was not so submissive and easily dominated.[19]

William said to his brother, Joseph:

> I have not done anything wrong. You are always determined to carry your points whether right or wrong, and therefore, I cannot stand an equal chance with you.[20]

William not only accused Joseph of dominating everyone and every situation but also accused him of being an "imposter" and false prophet.[21] Joseph's reply was revealing:

> I brought salvation to my father's house, as an instrument in the hands of God when they were in a miserable situation. . . . and if at any time you should consider me to be an impostor, for heaven's sake leave me in the hands of God, not to take vengeance upon me yourself.[22]

Another example of Smith's temper, recorded in his own history, was when he kicked Josiah Butterfield "out of the house, across the yard, and into the street.[23] He also recorded an incident when Mr. Bagby, a tax collector in Nauvoo, offended Smith:

> . . . I followed him a few steps, and struck him two or three times. Esquire Daniel H. Wells stepped between us and succeeded in separating us. I told the Esquire to assess the fine for assault, and I was willing to pay it.[24]

Later in his journal history, Smith admits that during the Bagby altercation he had, "Seized him by the throat to choke him off."[25] Smith's journal also includes his threat to whip Sylvester Smith, a member of Zion's Camp, and also his threat to kill Hiram Kimball.[26] Smith's threat to kill Hiram Kimball was because Kimball refused to obey Smith's order to blow up any riverboat that refused to pay the Nauvoo City wharfage fee!

Later on, in his Great Basin Kingdom, when Brigham Young was accused of being an authoritarian with a bad temper, Young responded by comparing himself to Joseph Smith:

> Some may think that I am rather too severe, but if you had the Prophet Joseph to deal with, you would think that I am quite mild. There are many here that are acquainted with brother Joseph's manner. He would not bear the usage I have born, and would appear as though he would tear down all the houses in the city, and tear up trees by the roots, if men conducted to him in the way they have to me.[27]

Apparently, even the powerful Brigham Young had experienced the anger and rage of Joseph Smith and wanted everyone to know how fortunate they were to have Brigham to deal with instead of Joseph.

Smith's Preoccupation With Power

Additional evidence of Smith's preoccupation with power is found in some of the comments he made in Church meetings. In June of 1843 he told a congregation of saints:

> I feel as strong as a giant. I pulled sticks with the men coming along, and I pulled up with one hand the strongest man that could be found. Then two men tried, but they could not pull me up. . . . I wish you to know and publish that we have all power; and if any man from this time forth says anything to the contrary, cast it into his teeth.[28]

A final example of Smith's obsession with power is the story line in his *Book of Mormon*. It starts out with a power struggle between Nephi and his brothers Laman and Lemuel. This power struggle sets the tone for the entire book. Almost from beginning to end, *The Book of Mormon* is an account of wars and battles between the Nephites and the Lamnites. This power struggle eventually ends in a great battle where the Nephites are exterminated.

In the middle of Smith's book is an account of the Jaredites and their continual struggle for power. Their struggle ended with the extermination of every person in the entire civilization except for one man, Coriantumur.

Smith's accounts of these great battles and struggles for power are truly sickening. His graphic description of bloody hand-to-hand combat and the millions of men, women, and children who were killed gives the reader an insight into the dark side of Smith's imagination.

John C. Kunich has pointed out that Smith's account of how many men were killed in these great battles is ridiculous even with a very high rate of population growth.[29] For example, in one battle Smith has two million men on each side killed along with their wives and children.[30] This could have amounted to a total of ten or fifteen million people! Once again, Smith is expecting us to believe his tall tales and fantastic stories.

The Lust for Power

I would like to end this chapter with some quotations about the use and abuse of power:

> Lust for power is the most flagrant of all passions.
>
> Tacitus

> Power tends to corrupt, and absolute power corrupts absolutely.
>
> Lord Acton

> In order to obtain and hold power a man must love it. Thus the effort to get it is not likely to be coupled with goodness, but with the opposite qualities of pride, craft, and cruelty.
>
> Leo N. Tolstoy

> There is a lure in power. It can get into a man's blood just as gambling and lust for money have been known to do.
>
> Harry S. Truman

> There is no more contemptible poison than power over one's fellow man.
>
> Maxim Gorky

> The truth is that all men having power ought to be mistrusted.
>
> James Madison

> Power is sweet; it is a drug, the desire for which increases with a habit.
>
> Bertrand Russell

> Think in this battered earth whose portals alternate night and day, how sultan after sultan with his pomp, abode his destined hour, and went his way.
>
> Omar Khayyam

This last quotation does not exactly apply to Joseph Smith. Even though he was a sultan with many wives and great power, and although he "abode his appointed hour," he did **not** go his way. He continues to dominate the lives of millions of men and women even from his grave.

Chapter 16

MORMONISM VS. TRADITIONAL CHRISTIANITY

> Rather than love, than money, than fame, give me truth.
> -Henry David Thoreau

Joseph Smith claimed that when he was just a young man, he went into a grove of trees to ask God which church he should join. Smith said that he experienced a remarkable vision in which Jesus told him:

> I was to join none of them, for they were all wrong; . . . that all their creeds were an abomination in his sight; that those professors were all corrupt . . .[1].

Well, there we have it. According to Smith, Jesus told him that **all** Christian churches were wrong, had abominable creeds, and corrupt ministers. Latter-Day Saints who accuse critics and doubters with "Mormon bashing" should remember that their founding prophet was one of the original "bashers."

Smith's *Book of Mormon* informs us:

> Behold there are save two churches only; the one is the church of the Lamb of God and the other is the church of the devil . . . and when the day cometh that the

> wrath of God is poured out upon the mother of harlots, which is the great and abominable church of all the earth, whose foundation is the devil, then at that day, the work of the Father shall commence, in preparing the way for the fulfilling of his covenants, which he hath made to his people who are of the house of Israel.[2]

According to this "scripture," Mormonism is the Church of the Lamb of God (Jesus) and all other churches are founded upon the Devil. Smith's reference to "the mother of harlots" was his way of accusing the Catholic Church of first prostituting Christianity and then of giving birth to Protestant churches which are also "harlots."

These insulting claims made by Smith and similar statements by other L.D.S. Church leaders make it very clear that Mormonism considers itself the only church in the world that is truly Christian, and whose doctrine and priesthood ordinances are acceptable to God. No other church has any priesthood authority to perform baptisms or any other ordinances essential for salvation in the kingdom of God. The L.D.S. Church has never backed down from this dogmatic and offensive position despite the millions of dollars it has spent on public relations.

Even though L.D.S. Church leaders feel free to question the Christianity of all other churches, Mormons can become highly offended when anyone questions their own Christianity. After all, don't Mormons pray and perform all of their ordinances in the name of Jesus Christ? Isn't *The Book of Mormon* a second witness for the divinity of Christ and a record of His mission to the ancient Americans? Don't Mormons believe in the divine birth, life, atonement, and resurrection of Jesus? Doesn't even the name, The Church of Jesus Christ of Latter-Day Saints, indicate that its members are Christians? How could anyone possibly question the Christianity of Mormonism? And yet, there are some fundamental theological differences between traditional or mainstream Christianity and Mormonism that make this a relevant question.

Different Gods

One very important difference is the Mormon concept of God (Gods). Although both the Bible and *The Book of Mormon* teach monotheism, a few years after publication of his *Book of Mormon*, Smith rejected the traditional Christian trinity and said that the Father, Son, and Holy Ghost were three separate personages, three Gods acting together as one. Then about ten years later, in April of 1844, just two months before he died, Smith told a conference of about twenty thousand saints in Nauvoo:

> There are but few beings in the world who understand rightly the character of God. The great majority of mankind do not comprehend anything, either that which is past or that which is to come, as it respects their relationship to God. . . . What kind of a being is God? . . . I will go back to the beginning before the world was, to show what kind of a being God is. . . . God himself was once as we are now, and is an exalted man, and sits enthroned in yonder heavens. That is the great secret. . . . I am going to tell you how God came to be God. We have imagined and supposed that God was God from all eternity. I will refute that idea, and take away the veil, so that you may see. . . . He was once a man like us; yea, that God himself, the father of us all, dwelt on an earth. . . . The head God called together the Gods and sat in grand council to bring forth the world. The grand councilors sat at the head in yonder heavens and contemplated the creation of the worlds which were created at the time. . . . We say that God Himself is a self-existing being. . . . Man does exist upon the same principles. . . . The mind or intelligence which man possesses is co-equal (co-eternal) with God himself. The intelligence of spirits had no beginning, neither will it have an end. That is good logic. That which has a beginning will have an end. . . . I take my ring from my finger and liken it unto the mind of man - the immortal part, because it has no beginning. . . . God never had the power to create the spirit of man at all. . . . Would to God that I had forty days and nights in which to tell you

> all! I would let you know that I am not a "fallen prophet." . . . You don't know me; you never knew my heart. No man knows my history. I cannot tell it; I shall never undertake it. I don't blame anyone for not believing my history. If I had not experienced what I have, I would not have believed it myself. I never did any harm to any man since I was born in the world. My voice is always for peace.[3]

Smith's new polytheistic, progressive, eternal generation of gods doctrine was quickly accepted by most Church leaders and members even though it clearly contradicted many scriptures in the Bible and *The Book of Mormon.* For example, in the Bible we read:

> Ye are my witnesses, saith the Lord . . . I am he: before me there was no God formed, neither shall there be after me. I, even I, am the Lord; and beside me there is no saviour.[4]

And in *The Book of Mormon* we read:

> I would that you should understand that God himself shall come down among the children of men, and shall redeem his people. And because he dwelleth in the flesh he shall be called the Son of God and having subjected the flesh to the will of the Father, being the Father and the Son. The Father, because he was conceived by the power of God; and the Son because of the flesh; thus becoming the Father and the Son and they are one God, yea, the very Eternal Father of heaven and earth.[5]

> Zeezrom said: "Is there more than one God"? And he answered, "No." . . . Now Zeezrom saith again unto him: "Is the Son of God the very Eternal Father?" Amulek saith unto him: "Yea, he is the very Eternal Father of Heaven and Earth, and all things which in them are, he is the beginning and the end, the first and the last."[6]

And yet, even today, most Church members believe that God once lived upon an earth like this, that there are many gods, and that Church members can become gods and goddesses themselves through eternal progression and obedience to Church leaders.

Adam Is The God Of This Earth.

In April of 1852, Brigham Young added greatly to the confusion about the identity of the Mormon God when he told members attending general conference in Salt Lake City:

> Now hear it, O inhabitants of the earth, Jew, Gentile, Saint and sinner! When our father Adam came into the Garden of Eden, He came into it with a celestial body, and brought Eve, one of his wives, with him. . . . He is our Father and our God, and the only god with whom we have to do. . . . When the Virgin Mary conceived the child, Jesus, the Father had begotten him in his own likeness. He was not begotten by the Holy Ghost. And who is the father? He is the first of the human family. . . . Jesus, our elder brother, was begotten in the flesh by that same character that was in the Garden of Eden, and who is our Father in Heaven. . . . If the Son was begotten by the Holy Ghost, it would be very dangerous to baptize and confirm females, and give the Holy Ghost to them, lest he should beget children to be palmed upon the Elders by the people, bringing the Elders into great difficulties. [7]

Statements like this about God, Jesus, Mary, and the Holy Ghost, made by Smith, Young, and other Church leaders are considered blasphemous and sacrilegious by most Christians and Christian clergy. Jesus said:

> Wherefore I say unto you, all manner of sin and blasphemy shall be forgiven unto men: but blasphemy against the Holy Ghost shall not be forgiven. And whosoever speaketh a word against the Son of man, it shall be forgiven him: but whosoever speaketh against the Holy Ghost, it shall not be forgiven him, neither in this world, neither in the world to come.[8]

If we accept the definition of blasphemy as "speaking about God in an irreverent and disrespectful manner or claiming for oneself the attributes of God," then Joseph Smith and Brigham Young are in serious trouble. It is not easy to think of anything more disrespectful of the Holy Ghost than Young's comment that if Mary was impregnated by the Holy Ghost, Mormon Elders had better not bestow the Holy Ghost upon young females lest the Holy Ghost impregnate them and then palm these illegitimate children off upon the Elders to support! All of this nonsense is highly offensive to traditional Christians.

Young's statement about the conception of Jesus clearly contradicts the New Testament:

> Now the birth of Jesus Christ was on this wise: When as his mother Mary was espoused to Joseph, before they came together, she was found with child of the Holy Ghost. . . . But while he thought on these things, behold the angel of the Lord appeared unto him in a dream, saying, Joseph, thou son of David, fear not to take unto thee Mary thy wife: for that which is conceived in her is of the Holy Ghost.[9]

Well, was it Adam or was it the Holy Ghost who was responsible for the virgin birth? And isn't it about time that Smith, Young, and other L.D.S. Church leaders were held responsible for having other gods and for blasphemy?

Heaven And Hell Vs. Three Degrees Of Glory

Another important difference between Mormonism and traditional Christianity relates to salvation. Even though many *Book of Mormon* scriptures are similar to those in the Bible, only two years after publication of his book, Smith announced a new revelation about three degrees of glory, the celestial (the kingdom of God), the terrestrial (the middle kingdom), and the telestial (hell).

Smith said that the lowest kingdom of glory (telestial) is where murderers, whoremongers, and other serious sinners go. He said, "These are they who are thrust down to hell." Then Smith described the "glory" of the telestial kingdom: "And thus we saw, in heavenly vision, the glory of the telestial which surpasses all understanding . . . "[10].

There is nothing like this in the New Testament nor in mainstream Christianity. Where in all of the scriptures do we read that hell is a kingdom of "glory" beyond all understanding? Neither Jesus nor any of his apostles taught such a thing. This is still Mormon doctrine, but it is not Christianity.

Grace Vs. Works

Also, related to salvation, Mormonism presents a different way of how a person gains entrance into the kingdom of God. The New Testament and mainstream Christianity emphasize the **grace** of God in gaining salvation. There are about fifty scriptures about grace in the New Testament alone. For example, The Apostle Paul said:

> For by grace are ye saved through faith; and that not of yourselves: it is the gift of God: Not of works, lest any man should boast.[11]

And yet, a person can attend L.D.S. Church meetings for years and never hear a lesson or a sermon on grace. Although everyone, even serious sinners, are resurrected and rewarded with some kingdom of glory, the only ones who can have “eternal life” in the celestial kingdom are those who attend their meetings, pay their tithing, go on missions, teach their children to believe in Mormonism, perform temple ordinances, do their genealogy, teach classes in Sunday School, Relief Society, or priesthood quorums, keep the word of wisdom, accept Church callings, and obey those in Church leadership positions. On judgment day, every person is rewarded with what he or she has **earned**, no more and no less.

This doctrine creates a strong work ethic and generates an amazing amount of energy and money dedicated toward the growth of Mormonism, but it does not agree with the teachings of the Bible and traditional Christianity. It also results in a considerable amount of stress, guilt, and depression for men and women struggling to earn exaltation in the celestial kingdom of God.

Polygamy

Another important difference between Mormonism and traditional Christianity concerns marriage and family relationships. Although a few Old Testament prophets apparently had more than one wife, there is no record of Jesus or any of his apostles teaching or practicing polygamy. And yet Smith, Young, and other Church leaders had as many as fifty wives. They also married sisters, and sometimes even a woman and also her daughter![12]

Young girls were indoctrinated that it was God's will that they give themselves to men old enough to be their fathers or even grandfathers. In his general conference sermon given in the Salt Lake City Tabernacle in April of 1861, Brigham Young Said:

> **I am now almost daily sealing young girls to men of age and experience.**[13]

Well, Brother Brigham, mainstream Christianity considers most of what you did to be very immoral, and most state laws consider it statutory rape!

It was also quite common for Mormon missionaries to convert married women. Many of these women left their non-believing husbands and then took their children thousands of miles away to Nauvoo or Salt Lake City. These women often became a polygamous wife of a Church leader. They were told they did not need a legal divorce from their first husband since their marriage had not been performed by L.D.S. priesthood authority and that Church authority superseded civil law. **Most Christians would call this adultery**.

An example of this Church sanctioned adultery was when Apostle Parley P. Pratt went on a mission to San Francisco, California and met Eleanore McLean, the wife of Hector McLean. Eleanore, a new convert to Mormonism, apparently fell in love with the charismatic Pratt. When Hector found out that his wife was planning to take their three children to Salt Lake City and teach them Mormonism, he became very angry and secretly sent them on a ship to their grandparents' home in New Orleans, Louisiana.

In 1855, Brigham Young married Eleanore and Parley without a legal divorce from Hector. But Eleanore (Pratt's twelfth wife) missed her children so much that Parley went with her to get them. When Eleanore and Parley tried to leave with the children, an angry Hector McLean killed Pratt in Arkansas.

When the news of Pratt's death reached Utah, he became a Mormon martyr. This incident created a climate of anger and revenge that helped to cause the massacre of the wealthy Fancher wagon train (from Arkansas) at Mountain Meadows in the southern part of the Utah Territory in 1857. However, greed also seemed to be a major motive for this atrocity at Mountain Meadows.

Pre-emptive Wives

Another little known aspect of early Mormon marriage that goes against traditional Christianity was the secret doctrine of pre-emptive wives. This secret doctrine created a pecking order in which any man in a position of higher authority could take the wife of any other man below him in the Church!

On October 8, 1861, Brigham Young preached a sermon in the Salt Lake City Tabernacle which included the following statement:

> The second way in which a wife can be separated from her husband, while he continues to be faithful to his God and his priesthood, I have not revealed, except to a few persons in this Church; and a few have received it from Joseph the prophet - as well as myself. If a woman can find a man holding the keys of the priesthood with a higher power and authority than her husband, and he is disposed to take her, he can do so, otherwise she has to remain where she is.[14]

On June 28, 1874, Young taught this same principle to Church members in the Brigham City, Utah, Bowery:

> It takes a higher power than a bill of divorce to take a woman away from a man who is a good man and honors his priesthood. It must be a man who possesses

> a higher power in the priesthood or else a woman is bound to her husband forever and ever.[15]

In my own family history, my Great Aunt Phoebe went to an L.D.S. Stake conference in Cedar City, Utah, married to one man and then went home that same day married to another man who held a higher position in the Church than her husband. This change was made by a visiting apostle from Salt Lake City.

When Brigham Young finally announced the principle of plural marriage in 1852, after lying about it for more than ten years, he said, "now we have let the cat out of the bag, but there are still other cats in the bag." The principle of pre-emptive wives, apparently, was one of those cats still in the bag.

It may be argued that polygamy and pre-emptive wives are no longer practiced in the L.D.S. Church and should no longer be used to judge Mormonism. But even though the L.D.S. Church has given up the **practice** of polygamy, it is still official Church **doctrine**. Section 132 of *The Doctrine and Covenants* is still an important part of the L.D.S. canon of scripture.

Eternal Marriage

Another part of the Mormon marriage system that is **not** found in the Bible nor accepted by mainstream Christianity is marriage for time and all eternity. Although ridiculed by Smith as "spiritual wifeism," and apostate doctrine,[16] eternal marriage in a Mormon temple has become the most sacred of all ordinances in the L.D.S. Church today.

But why doesn't traditional Christianity believe in eternal marriage? It is probably because Jesus pointedly denied this doctrine. When asked by the Sadducees about marriage in an afterlife in heaven, the book of Luke records the following comments of Jesus:

> The children of this world marry, and are given in marriage: But they which shall be accounted worthy to obtain that world and the resurrection from the dead, neither marry or are given in marriage.[17]

The book of Matthew records this same incident and says that Jesus chided the Sadducees for not knowing the scriptures:

> Ye do err, not knowing the scriptures nor the power of God. For in the resurrection they neither marry, nor are given in marriage, but are as the angels of God in heaven.[18]

Those who teach eternal marriage **do** err in not knowing the scriptures. There is not a single scripture teaching eternal marriage in the entire Bible, nor for that matter in *The Book of Mormon* which supposedly contains the "fullness of the everlasting gospel." Eternal marriage is **not** Christian doctrine.

The Word Of Wisdom

Another difference between Mormonism and mainstream Christianity relates to "the word of wisdom." L.D.S. Church members are not considered worthy to serve in leadership positions nor are they worthy to go into an L.D.S. temple if they use tobacco, drink alcoholic beverages, drink coffee or tea, or take non prescription drugs. The word of wisdom is considered a serious moral issue.

And yet, the New Testament says that one of the first miracles that Jesus performed was turning water into wine at a wedding in Cana.[19] Jesus also drank wine with his apostles at the last supper and said that he would not drink with them again until they were together in his Father's kingdom.[20] This may be an embarrassing time for those Latter-Day Saints who refuse to drink wine with Jesus because it is against their word of wisdom.

After the crucifixion, on the Day Of Pentecost, when Peter and the other apostles and disciples were speaking in tongues and prophesying, disbelievers accused them of being drunk. But Peter said:

> Ye men of Judaea, and all ye that dwell in Jerusalem, be this known unto you, and harken unto my words:

> For these are not drunken as ye suppose, seeing it is but the third hour of the day. But this is that which was spoken by the prophet Joel . . . [21].

Peter did not defend his noisy friends by saying that he, the other apostles, and all good Christians did not drink. He simply said that it was too early in the day to be drunk. And who can deny that The Apostle Paul was a Christian? And yet, Paul advised his close friend Timothy:

> Drink no longer water, but use a little wine for thy stomach's sake and thine oft infirmities.[22]

Mormon Tithing Vs. Biblical Tithing

Another distinguishing aspect of Mormonism that is different from mainstream Christianity is their payment of tithing. Church members who do **not** pay ten percent of their **income** to the Church each year are not considered worthy to serve in leadership positions nor are they worthy to enter an L.D.S. temple.

Even though tithing is mentioned several times in the Bible, Mormon tithing is not Biblical nor is it Christian. Jesus condemned the Scribes and Pharisees for paying their tithing while omitting the "weightier matters of the law."[23] He accused them of being blind guides who strained at gnats and swallowed camels.

Jesus also made reference to the prayer of a self righteous Pharisee who claimed special favor with God for paying his tithing:

> The Pharisee stood and prayed thus with himself, God, I thank thee, that I am not as other men are. . . . I fast twice in the week, I give tithes of all that I possess.[24]

Jesus did not praise this man for paying his tithing but rather condemned him for his self righteousness. It is also very significant that the Pharisee claimed that he paid tithing on all of his **possessions**. This was the Jewish law. The scriptures say that Abraham gave Melchizedek, King of Salem, and Priest Of The Most

High God, tithes of all his **possessions.**[25] Jacob (Israel) also made a promise to pay ten percent of his **possessions** unto the Lord.[26]

It is very important to note that every time tithing is mentioned in the Bible, it is based upon property **not** income. When based upon property, it becomes progressive (falling more heavily upon the wealthy). When based upon income, as in the L.D.S. Church today, it becomes regressive (a relatively much greater burden upon the poor).

Although, it would seem that if everyone paid ten percent of their income, tithing would be a flat or proportional assessment. In reality, it is very regressive in terms of relative sacrifice. For example, a person with an annual income of $200,000 can pay $20,000 tithing without sacrificing necessities such as food, clothing, housing, and medical care for his family. But the person who receives an income of only $20,000 a year will probably need to sacrifice important necessities in order to pay his $2,000 tithing. Jesus did **not** teach this soak-the-poor perversion of tithing. This is **not** Christianity.

In order to further illustrate the important difference between tithing based upon property as taught in the Bible, and tithing based upon income as taught by the L.D.S. Church, let's consider a situation where a person owns $10,000,000 worth of property. If he follows Abraham's example and pays ten percent of his **possessions**, he would pay $1,000,000 tithing.

However, when based upon the distorted Mormon version of tithing based upon **income**, this person is considered a full tithe payer if he pays only $100,000 (if we assume that his income was $1,000,000 during the year). Thus, he would have to pay ten times as much if based upon the true principle of tithing as contained in the Bible! It is no wonder that country-club Mormons prefer the distorted Mormon version of tithing.

Mormon tithing requires poor people and even beggars to pay tithing since they all have at least some income. Tithing, as taught in the Bible, does not require the poor to pay anything since they don't own anything.

L.D.S. tithing brings in millions of dollars every day. It has made Mormonism one of the wealthiest institutions in the world. The L.D.S. Church owns over one hundred temples, thousands of chapels, many businesses, and a vast amount of real estate and commercial property all over the world.[27] It is a multi-billion dollar corporation.

But Mormon tithing is also a form of **extortion**. A person cannot be married in an L.D.S. temple nor receive other ordinances necessary for exaltation in the celestial kingdom of God unless he or she pays tithing. Also, an L..D. S. man or woman is not allowed to see their own son or daughter get married in an L.D.S. temple unless they pay their tithing. **This ticket to the temple can cost thousands of dollars**. But Mormon tithing's burden upon the poor and its extortionary nature are **not** traditional Christian policies.

Missionary Work

Another important difference between Mormonism and traditional Christianity is its missionary work. The L.D.S. Church has thousands of missionaries all over the world (currently about 60,000). Most of these missionaries spend two years of their lives, mostly at their own expense, trying to convert the world to Mormonism. The Church also spends millions of tithing dollars on missionary work.

A person may ask, "Didn't Jesus send his apostles and disciples out to spread the gospel?" Or they may ask, "Don't traditional Christian churches do missionary work?" Of course, the answer to both of these questions is yes. But L.D.S. missionary work is different. Mormon missionaries spend very little time trying to convert Moslems, Hindus, Jews, and atheists to Christianity. At least ninety percent of their time is spent trying to convert Catholics, Methodists, Baptists, Lutherans, and other Christians to Mormonism. Mormon missionaries spend almost all of their time and energy teaching people about Joseph Smith and *The Book of Mormon*, **not** about Jesus and the Bible.

Adam In America

Still another difference between Mormonism and mainstream Christianity relates to the location of the Garden of Eden. While in Missouri, Smith made the startling claim that Adam-ondi-Ahaman, (the place where Adam and Eve lived upon the earth), was located on the north side of the Grand River, in Daviess County, Missouri, about twenty five miles north of Far West.[28] Smith made this claim despite the fact that traditional Christianity believes that the Garden of Eden was in the Old World, probably near ancient Babylonia.

No Cross In Mormonism

And still another difference between Mormonism and traditional Christian churches is that almost all Christian churches use the symbol of the cross in their architecture, worship services, their homes, and even in their jewelry. Mormons do **not** use the symbol of the cross.

Masonic Mormonism

One of the most controversial aspects of Mormonism pertains to the rituals and ordinances that take place in L.D.S. temples. These include baptisms for the dead, eternal marriages, endowments, and other ceremonies and ordinances that cannot be found in the New Testament.

Perhaps the L.D.S. temple ritual that is most foreign to traditional Christianity is the "endowment," a ceremony very similar to the secret rituals performed by the Masons. The endowment teaches a person secret signs, tokens, handclasps, and passwords that will enable him or her to pass by the angels and enter into the celestial kingdom of God. Participants in the endowment are also required to make a number of sacred covenants or promises.

The endowment ceremony has changed a great deal during the many years of Church history. The original endowment that Smith promised his followers at the dedication of his Kirtland, Ohio, Temple was to be an outpouring of the pentecostal spirit such as speaking in tongues, prophesying, and healing. It had nothing to do with Masonry.

But, about ten years later, on March 15th and 16th of 1842, Joseph Smith received the first three degrees of Masonry in Nauvoo. Less than two months later, on May 4th he announced his new "endowment" ceremony.[29] Smith's signs, tokens, penalties, handclasps, secret words, and five points of fellowship were almost identical to the Masonic ritual. Smith explained all of this by saying that the Masonic ritual was part of God's ancient priesthood and that it had become corrupted over the centuries just as Christianity had been changed during the great apostasy. Smith claimed that he had been commanded by the Lord to restore both pure Christianity and true Masonry.

Historians deny Smith's claim about the ancient origin of Masonry. Freemasonry evolved from the guilds of stonemasons and Gothic cathedral builders of the middle ages.[30] The original Masons borrowed from the Isis-Osiris myth, Rosicrucianism, Gnosticism, Hinduism, Theosophy, and traditional notions from the occult.[31]

Scotland and England became the centers of Masonry. Gradually, men who had nothing to do with the building trades joined this secret order and took over control of the Grand Lodge as well as local lodges. They did this in order to gain the social, political, and economic advantages that came from being part of a strong, secret brotherhood pledged to help and protect each other.

Despite wishful thinking, Masonry cannot be traced farther back than the cults and guilds of the 1500s. This is thousands of years later than the origin of Masonry according to Smith. Adam, Abraham, and King Solomon had absolutely nothing to do with Masonry. Again, Smith used his imagination and deception to explain his way out of a bad situation.

The Roman Catholics, Orthodox Catholics, Lutherans, Methodists, and many other Christian churches have declared Masonry to be incompatible with Christianity.[32] The Presbyterian Church condemned Masonry because "it constitutes a mystagogical system which reminds us of the ancient heathen mystery-religions and cults from which it descends and is their continuation and regeneration."[33]

First time L.D.S. Temple attendees who are shocked by the temple rituals and consider them offensive and unchristian should not feel guilty. They are only rebelling against the occult origins of Masonry despite claims to the contrary perpetrated by Smith, Young, and a long succession of other Church leaders.

Some of the most offensive parts of Smith's endowment were removed in 1990. These included demonstrating different ways a person can be killed for divulging the secrets of the ritual, the oath of obedience of a woman to her husband, depiction of non L.D.S. clergy as servants of Satan, and the physical contact required by the five points of fellowship through the veil. But this alteration did not make L.D.S. temple endowments Christian and approved of God. The simple truth is that God did **not** tell Joseph Smith how to patch up Christianity nor Masonry.

Unlike traditional Christians, Mormons spend millions of dollars and millions of hours building temples, searching genealogical records, and doing baptisms for the dead. And yet, this doctrine isn't taught anywhere in the Bible nor in *The Book of Mormon* for that matter. The Apostle Paul's letter to Titus calls genealogy "unprofitable and vain." (Titus 3:9)

Jesus Vs Joseph

I would like to end this chapter by presenting a contrast between the life and personality of Jesus Christ and that of Joseph Smith. As far as anyone knows, Jesus lived a celibate life dedicated to His divine mission. Joseph, on the other hand, had many women in his personal life.

Jesus was a man of peace who said to Peter, "Put up again thy sword into his place: for all they that take the sword shall perish by the sword."[34] Joseph was a military man with a private army and a secret band of terrorists (Danites). He lived a life of confrontation and violence and at one time in Nauvoo had about forty bodyguards. Smith died in a hail of bullets after he had shot two or three of the men who came after him. He shot these men with a pistol that had been smuggled into the Carthage Jail by one of his visitors.[35] Smith did not go "like a lamb to the slaughter."

Jesus told his disciples and apostles to obey the law:

> The Scribes and the Pharisees sit in Moses' seat: All therefore whatsoever they bid you observe, that observe and do . . .[36].

> Agree with thine adversary quickly, whiles thou art in the way with him; lest at any time the adversary deliver thee to the Judge, and the judge deliver thee to the officer, and thou be cast into prison. Verily I say unto thee, thou shalt by no means come out thence, till thou hast paid the uttermost farthing.[37]

Joseph was an outlaw and a fugitive from justice for most of his life. He broke state laws in New York, Ohio, Missouri, and Illinois. The President of the United States and the Governors of Missouri and Illinois all issued warrants for Smith's arrest, charging him with treason and a number of other serious crimes. Smith openly considered himself to be above the laws of the land.

Jesus said, "Lay not up for yourselves treasures upon earth . . . For where your treasure is, there will your heart be also.[38] He also said, ". . . A rich man shall hardly enter into the kingdom of heaven," and "Ye cannot serve God and mammon."[39] When Jesus died, apparently all he had were his clothes which were divided by the Roman soldiers.

Joseph died owning half of a riverboat, a hotel, and a large amount of other property. Brigham Young, who also claimed to be a Christian, died a millionaire. And today, the L.D.S. Church is a multi-billion dollar corporation, very much of this world.[40] Priesthood holders who are "successful" in their businesses or professions are much more likely to be called to Church leadership positions than working-class men and women.

Jesus never wrote any books or even his own biography. Joseph wrote *The Book of Mormon, The Doctrine and Covenants, The Pearl of Great Price,* seven volumes of his personal history, and a large number of other publications.

Jesus was humble and meek; Joseph was an arrogant and dominating personality. Smith loved to get all dressed up in his general's uniform, mount his white stallion, and review his private army. He claimed that he had more to boast about than any man who had ever lived including Adam, Paul, Peter, and even Jesus.[41]

Jesus spoke the truth. Joseph boldly lied about his ability to see underground treasures in his seer-stone, his gold plates, his ability to translate languages, his revelations, the Danites, polygamy, and a long list of other things.

Jesus was kind and loving. Joseph was quick tempered, vengeful, and physically violent. Jesus reached out to include everyone and never excommunicated or ostracized anyone. Smith turned against anyone who crossed him in any way including old friends such as Oliver Cowdery, Martin Harris, the Whitmers, John C. Bennett, William Law, and a long list of other benefactors who had made great sacrifices for him. Smith not only excommunicated these people, he burned their property and gave some of them only a few days to get out of town or else face the wrath of the Danites.[42] Who can imagine Jesus doing anything like that? This is not loving your enemies. **This is not Christianity**.

The list of differences between Jesus and Joseph goes on and on and on. It is not easy to find two men who represent a greater contrast.

Who Is A True Christian?

Jesus provided a simple way of identifying a true Christian when he said, "A new commandment I give unto you, that ye love one another; as I have loved you, that ye also love one another. By this shall all men know that ye are my disciples, if ye have love one to another."[43]

Jesus used the parable of the Good Samaritan to explain what it meant to love one's neighbor and thus become a good Christian. I think He deliberately used a Samaritan in His parable because the Samaritans did not know or believe true doctrine. But the Good Samaritan demonstrated great love and compassion even for a wounded stranger.

Using The Lord's criteria, I believe that many traditional Christians and many Latter-Day Saints **are** true Christians despite differences in their creeds and doctrine. Almost all denominations include many good men and good women who, like the Good Samaritan, have great love and compassion for all of God's children.

However, using the Lord's criteria of love for other people, I do not believe that Brigham Young nor his mentor, Joseph Smith were Christians. These men were users who did not show much kindness and love for others.

Ann Eliza, one of Brigham Young's wives claimed that Young was an atheist, a cynical and clever man who simply used religion and Mormonism in order to gain power, wealth, and a variety of women in his life because when life was over, it was over.[44] Some of Young's actions and teachings make this astonishing claim by Ann Eliza believable.

And what about Joseph Smith? If he had really believed in God would he have dared pretend to have gold plates, publish his "thus saith the Lord" revelations, take other men's wives and young girls in the name of God, and order men and young boys into battles that resulted in many casualties in order to promote Mormonism? Would he have sent Mormon missionaries all over the world teaching his false claims and campaigning for his political ambitions? If Smith had really believed in a judgment day where he would have to answer to the Lord for his actions and receive God's severest eternal punishments, I don't believe he would have dared to do these things. But then we must remember that, according to Smith, hell is "a kingdom of glory" beyond human comprehension!

A good case can be made that Smith and Young were both atheists who were only into religion for the ride, as long as it lasted! Both of these men were successful in gaining power, wealth, fame, women, and all of the other things that other worldly men have always striven for and dreamed about. And they were able to accomplish this by using religion. But a true Christian does not use religion for self serving, worldly purposes but to love and serve others.

In 1960, Hugh Nibley, a prominent L.D.S. author and intellectual, told Sterling M. McMurrin and a large assembly of students at the University of Utah that his extensive writings defending Mormonism were "nothing but a game." When McMurrin replied, "The people who read your articles do not regard your writings as a game," Nibley repeated himself and again said, "As far as I am concerned, it is nothing but a game."[45]

Is it possible that Joseph Smith, Brigham Young, Hugh Nibley, and a number of other Church leaders **have been playing games** with the lives, families, and souls of the little people, the "grasshoppers," as Sidney Rigdon called ordinary Church members? This is a frightening thought, and yet in light of considerable evidence, it seems to be a possibilty. But real Christians would not be capable of such astonishing deception, hypocrisy, and immorality.

Chapter 17

NEW SCRIPTURES

> The people have a right to the truth as they have a right to life, liberty, and the pursuit of happiness.
> -Frank Norris

Joseph Smith claimed that his *Book of Mormon* was a sacred book of new scriptures coming directly from God. His eighth article of faith states:

> We believe the Bible to be the word of God as far as it is translated correctly; we also believe *The Book of Mormon* to be the word of God.[1]

Church members were entitled to have some doubts about the Bible, but they were expected to accept *The Book of Mormon* as holy scripture without any stipulations or qualifications.

The Book of Mormon was only the beginning of Smith's new scriptures. In 1831, Joseph Smith claimed to receive a revelation from God giving him and a few others the power and authority to create new scriptures whenever they were moved upon by the Holy Ghost. This revelation, is in section 68 of his *Doctrine and Covenants*:

> **And whatsoever they shall speak when moved upon by the Holy Ghost shall be scripture, shall be the**

> **will of the Lord, shall be the mind of the Lord, shall be the word of the Lord, shall be the voice of the Lord, and the power of God unto salvation.**

Joseph Smith eventually presented the world with three new books of scripture, *The Book of Mormon, The Doctrine and Covenants* (a compilation of his many revelations), and *The Pearl of Great Price* (his translation of Chandler's Egyptian papyrus).

Brigham Young also claimed the power and authority to create new scripture. In 1870, Young told a congregation of Latter-Day Saints assembled in the Mormon Tabernacle in Salt Lake City:

> **I have never yet preached a sermon and sent it out to the children of men, that they may not call scripture. . . . Let this go to the people with "Thus saith the Lord," and if they do not obey it, you will see the chastening hand of the Lord upon them.**[2]

Early Church leaders had a strong sense of mission and destiny. They kept very careful records of their meetings and conferences. A professional stenographer, George D. Watt, was called to record the sermons of Church leaders and to submit his work back to them for editing and publication in the *Journal of Discourses,* twenty six volumes of holy scriptures coming from Salt Lake City after the death of Joseph Smith. In 1857, Brigham Young said:

> Our sermons are read by tens of thousands outside of Utah. Members of the British Parliament have those *Journals of Discourses,* (sic) published by Brother Watt. . . . In printing my remarks, I often omit the sharp words, though they are perfectly understood and applicable here; for I do not wish to spoil the good I desire to do. Let my remarks go to the world in a way the prejudices of the people can bear, that they may read them, and ponder them, and ask God whether they are true.[3]

Brigham Young and other Church leaders carefully edited their sermons removing the most offensive parts before they were published and distributed throughout the Church, the United States, and also in foreign countries.

A person may ask, "What does it matter what Church leaders said or did way back then? That was a long time ago; the Church is different today; it has changed." But it **does matter** because the most important aspect of Mormonism is its claim to exclusive priesthood power, and its claim to be the only true Church.

If Joseph Smith, Brigham Young, and other Church leaders were impostors who, in reality, had no divine priesthood and were only pretending to create new scriptures, then all of those who trace their priesthood back to these men are living with illusions and passing these illusions on to their children and grandchildren. Therefore, it is of great importance what early leaders did and said.

Let's take Brigham Young up on his challenge. Let's study and pray about his sermons and those of other Church leaders recorded in the *Journal of Discourses* to see if they are, in fact, holy scriptures.

A few years ago, a prominent L.D.S. Church leader, a man who has written several Church books, gave a talk in which he said that Church members need not concern themselves about the sermons published in the *Journal of Discourses* because he had read them all and found nothing that caused him any doubts about the divine inspiration of early Church leaders and nothing that caused him to question his own testimony of Mormonism.

I decided to find out if this man was telling the truth by reading the *Journal of Discourses* for myself. Contrary to the claims of this man, I found a great deal of meanness, bigotry, deception, false doctrine, and nonsense in these sermons given by men holding themselves up to be prophets of God.

I have selected only a few topics out of the twenty six volumes for the reader's consideration. I believe that each person should decide for himself or herself whether these quotations are inspired words of sacred new scripture coming from true prophets of God or whether they are arrogant pretensions coming from ignorant impostors intoxicated with delusions of priesthood power.

All of the following references are from the *Journal of Discourses*. The volume, page, and person giving the sermon is given after each quotation. B.Y. is Brigham Young; H.C.K. is Heber C. Kimball (first counselor to Brigham Young); W.R. is Willard Richards (second counselor to Brigham Young); O.P. is Apostle Orson Pratt; P.P.P. is Apostle Parley P. Pratt; O.H. is Apostle Orson Hyde; J.T. is Apostle and third Church President John Taylor; W.W. is Apostle and fourth Church President Wilford Woodruff; L.S. is Apostle and fifth Church president, Lorenzo Snow; G.A.S. is Apostle George A. Smith who also became first counselor to Brigham Young after the death of Heber C. Kimball; E.T.B. is Apostle Ezra Taft Benson; J.M.G. is Apostle Jedediah M. Grant who later became second counselor to Brigham Young; D.H.W. is Danniel H. Wells, counselor to Brigham Young and commander of the Nauvoo Legion; and E.S. is Apostle Erastus Snow.

These Church leaders boldly gave their sermons (mostly in the tabernacle at Salt Lake City) and then expected not only Church members but the entire world to accept their words as holy scripture!

Women

> Some of the questions propounded by Brother Clements, in his remarks produced in me rather a humorsome feeling, especially the inquiry of the lady as to why she was not a man. . . . Who the lady is I know not, and I have seen a great many like her, and I think there would be much more sound judgement and true, sound philosophy exhibited, if persons would inquire why about three-fourths or seven-eighths of the men are not women. Why so? Because of the imbecility of the brains of men. . . . Hundreds of thousands, yes millions of men, do not exhibit the mental ability one might suppose women should possess and exhibit. (B.Y. 7:160-161)

Do not be frightened because a few rotten, corrupt scoundrels in our midst cry out, "O the troops are coming, and that will be the end of Mormonism," in order to deceive the weak-minded females. (B.Y. 3:278)

True there is a curse upon the woman that is not upon the man, namely, that "her whole affections shall be toward her husband," and what is next? "He shall rule over you." . . . I will not hear any more of this whining. (B.Y. 4:57)

There are probably but few men in the world who care about the private society of women less than I do. (B.Y. 5:99)

Do you think that I am an old man? I could prove to this congregation that I am young; for I could find more girls who would choose me for a husband than can any of the young men. (B.Y. 5:210)

Women are made to be led, and counseled, and directed . . . and if I am not a good man, I have no just right in this Church to a wife or wives, or the power to propagate my species. What then should be done with me? Make a eunuch of me, and stop my propagation. (H.C.K. 5:29)

I am fully aware that many people have been raised in poor-pussyism all their days, both in America and in Europe, and when they hear doctrines and principles taught by men who speak as freedom permits them, and as freemen have a right to speak, those who are clothed with the garments of poor-pusseyism get the grunts; well grunt on until you grunt it all out. . . . If a man has fifty wives and the fiftieth is the best, does the most good, she will get the greatest reward, in spite of all the grunting on the part of the first one. (J.M.G. 3:126)

I do not consider that one of my wives, or one of my children, has a right to partake of these emblems, until they make full and proper restitution to me, if they have offended me. Why is this? Because I am their dictator, their revelator, their prophet, and their priest, and if they rebel against me they at once raise a mutiny in my family. (H.C.K. 4:81)

It requires a great exertion on the parts of wives to keep pace with their husbands. . . . It is much more difficult for wives to learn than it is for husbands, because women have not the degree of light and knowledge that their husbands have; they have not the power over their passions that their husband have; therefor they have to suffer one for another until they get power over themselves like unto those that have advanced more fully in the knowledge of our God. (L.S. 5:315-316)

And we have women here who like anything but the celestial law of God; and if they could break asunder the cable of the Church of Christ, there is hardly a mother in Israel but would do it this day. And they talk to their husbands, to their daughters, and to their neighbors, and say they have not seen a week's happiness since they became acquainted with that law, or since their husband took a second wife. . . . Then, again there are men that are used as tools by their wives, and they are just a little better in appearance and in their habits than a little black boy. They live in filth and nastiness, they eat it, they drink it, they are filthy all over. (J.M.G. 4:50)

Dear Brothers and sisters, it is with feelings not a little peculiar that I arise to address you this morning. . . . Had I copied the style of address adopted by the fashionable world, I might have said, "Ladies and gentlemen." . . . The order of heaven places man in the front rank; hence he is first to be addressed. Woman follows under the protection of his counsels, and the superior strength of his arm. Her desire should be unto her husband, and he should rule over her. (O.H. 4:257-258)

We read on a certain occasion the sister of Moses, Miriam, and certain others in the great congregation of Israel, got very jealous. What were they jealous about? About the Ethiopian woman that Moses had taken to wife, in addition to the daughter of Jethro, whom he had taken before in the land of Midian. . . . Are there any Miriams in our congregation today, any of those who professing to belong to Israel of the latter-days, sometimes find fault with the man of God standing at their head, because he not only believes in but practices this divine institution of the ancients? If there be such in our midst, I say, remember Miriam the very next time you begin to talk with your neighboring women, or anybody else against this holy principle. Remember the awful curse and judgment that fell on the sister of Moses when she did the same thing, and then fear and tremble before God, lest He, in His wrath, may swear that you shall not enjoy the blessings ordained for those who inherit the highest degree of glory.(O.P. 13:189)

Joseph says all covenants are done away, and none are binding but the new covenants; now suppose Joseph should come and say he wanted your wife, what would you say to that? . . . What would a man of God say, who felt aright, when Joseph asked him for his money? He would say, "Yes, I wish I had more to help to build up the kingdom of God." Or if he came and said, "I want your wife?" "Oh yes, . . . here she is, there are plenty more." . . . Did the Prophet Joseph want every man's wife he asked for? He did not, but in that thing was the grand thread of the priesthood developed. . . . A man who has got the Spirit of God, and the light of eternity in him has no trouble about such matters. (J.M.G. 2:13-14)

> . . . in the sight of heaven these marriages are illegal and the children illegitimate. . . . is there any way to make their marriage legitimate, in the sight of heaven? Yes. How? By having them re-married by a man who has the authority from God to do it. . . . and it is the same with baptism. (O.P., 16:176)

The Word Of Wisdom

> Young men, take this advice from me, and practice it in your future life, and it will be more valuable to you than the riches of this world. "Why," you say, "I see the older brethren chew tobacco, why should I not do likewise?" . . . Take a course that you can know more than your parents.(B.Y. 2:18)

> . . . Let us suffer our fathers and mothers to drink the tea and the coffee, and chew all the tobacco they want, as long as we can get it for them, because they have imbibed this practice years ago, and now to deprive them of these things altogether might endanger their lives. (G.A.S. 2:364)

> I consider it a disgrace to any young man under thirty five years of age to use tobacco.(G.A.S. 5:111)

> In the name of the Lord Jesus Christ, I command the Elders of Israel - those who have been in the habit of getting drunk - to cease drinking strong drink from this time henceforth, until you really need it.(B.Y. 7:337)

> Here this ye Bishops and Elders, for I will tell you of it. Why do you not do your duty? "Why," some of you, perhaps, can say in great truthfulness, "I was drunk last week, and dare not, for fear of being told of it." (H.C.K. 7:350)

> If every woman in this Church will cease drinking tea, coffee, liquor, and all other powerful stimulants, and live upon vegetables, not many generations will pass before the days of man will again return.(B.Y. 8:64)

I delight in seeing my children temperate, and it would please me even more if they would not touch liquor at all. (H.C.K. 8:257)

You know that we all profess to believe the "Word of Wisdom." There has been a great deal said about it, more in former times than in latter years. . . . How much do you suppose annually goes out of this territory, and has for ten or twelve years past, in gold and silver, to supply the people with tobacco? . . . I say that $60,000 annually is the smallest figure I can estimate sales at. Tobacco can be raised here as well as it can be raised in any other place. . . . Some of the brethren are very strenuous upon the "Word of Wisdom," and would like to have me preach upon it and urge it upon the brethren, and make it a test of fellowship. I do not think I shall do so. I have never done so. . . . Some would ask brother Brigham whether he keeps the "Word of Wisdom," No. (B.Y. 9:35)

We found that the brethren in Washington County had again raised, last year, a good quality of cotton, which would be highly creditable in any other country. We have also soil and climate that will produce tobacco as fine as is grown in Virginia: it only needs to be cultivated. . . . Many of us choose to use tobacco, and we could save $60,000 from going out of the Territory every year, if we raise these articles within ourselves. (G.A.S. 9:67-68)

It is our duty to strive to raise every thing we need for our own consumption. The tea, the coffee, the tobacco, and the whisky, (if we must have such articles) can all be produced and manufactured here. (D.H.W. 9:183)

I recollect being at a trial not long since where quite a number of Bishops had been called in as witnesses, but I could not learn that there was one who did not drink whisky, and I think that most of them drank tea and coffee. I think that we have some Bishops in this city who do not chew tobacco, nor drink liquor nor tea nor coffee to excess. . . . Well, Brother Brigham, have you not done it? Yes, for many years, but I ceased its habitual practice. I used it for toothache; now I am free from that pain, and my mouth is never stained with tobacco. . . . I am naturally a great lover of tea. (B.Y. 12:402-404)

During our Conference we shall require the people to pay attention and to preserve good order. . . . There is another subject I wish to refer to. Last Sabbath this front gallery, the gentleman's gallery, was very full. After meeting was dismissed, I took a walk through it. . . . there were great quids of tobacco, and places of one or two feet square smeared with tobacco juice. . . . We do not want to have our new Tabernacle defiled. It is an imposition for gentlemen to spit tobacco juice around or leave quids of tobacco on the floor; they dirty the house, and if a lady happens to besmear the bottom of her dress, which can hardly be avoided, it is highly offensive. We therefore request all gentlemen attending Conference to omit tobacco chewing while here. To the Elders of Israel who cannot or will not keep the Word of Wisdom, I say omit tobacco chewing while here. (B.Y. 13:343)

Many of the brethren chew tobacco, and I have advised them to be modest about it. Do not take out as whole plug of tobacco in meeting before the eyes of the congregation, and cut off a long slice and put it in your mouth, to the annoyance of everybody around. Do not glory in this disgraceful practice. If you must use tobacco, put a small portion in your mouth when no one sees you, and be careful that no one sees you chew it. I do not charge you with sin. (B.Y. 8:361)

Blind Obedience To Church Authorities

I do not know of any religion except doing what I am told; and if you do, you have learned something that I have never learned. (H.C.K. 5:163)

We want you to go where you are sent, for you cannot get your endowments until you have proved yourselves, that is what we intend: it is the mind of brother Brigham, the President of the Church of Jesus Christ of Latter-day Saints, and the Prophet of God, who holds the keys of life and salvation pertaining to you, and me and all the world - not a soul is excepted, neither man, woman, nor child; they all belong to him. . . . (H.C.K. 1:296)

Probably there are but few men in the United States but what know that we look up to President Brigham Young as our leader, Prophet, and dictator. (H.C.K. 2:222)

If it is necessary for me to be subject to my file leaders, I wish to know whether it is not equally for you, and every High Priest, Elder, Seventy, Apostle, and all others to be obedient to the priesthood of those who are appointed to direct them? Is it not right for all men to be obedient to their superiors? (H.C.K. 3:270)

Nothing but obedience to his law, obedience in families, obedience to Bishops, and to the Priesthood in all its ramifications, and especially to President Brigham Young as the head, to carry out his law to the whole people, can accomplish the purposes of God or our salvation as a people. . . . What does this obedience imply? Obedience in all things, - that the twelve should be obedient to the Presidency, the Seventies to the Twelve, and so on through all of the ramifications of the priesthood, - obedience of wives to husbands, children to parents, - and that a general order of this kind should be established in every neighborhood, in every house, and in every heart. (J.T. 5:265)

If a person with an honest heart, a broken, contrite and pure spirit . . . says that he wishes to be baptized for the remission of his sins, and the ordinance is administered by one having authority, is that man saved? Yes, to that period of time. . . . But after he is baptized and hands have been laid upon his head for the reception of the Holy Ghost, suppose that on the next day he is commanded to go forth and preach the gospel, or to teach his family, or to assist in building up the kingdom of God, or take all his substance and give it for the sustenance of the poor, and he says, "I will not do it," his baptism and confirmation would depart from him, and he would be left as a son of perdition. (B.Y. 8:124)

It is not with us as it is with democracy. We do not believe that any people are capable of governing themselves. (J.T. 9:9)

. . . no other people are controlled so easily as the people in this territory. . . . And where is another people that is controlled as easily as this people? (B.Y. 11:324)

Whenever there is a disposition manifested in any of the members of this church to question the right of the President of the whole church to direct in all things, you see manifested the evidences of apostasy. (B.Y. 11:136)

These were the first revelations given to the Church; yet there are men today who are Bishops and presidents of settlements, who express their willingness to labor for the welfare of the people and the building up of the kingdom, but feel that no person holding the priesthood has a right to dictate them with regard to their property. They are very willing that Brother Brigham should dictate in spiritual matters, and trust their eternal salvation to the principles he teaches, but the property they may have acquired or the manner in which their labor should be directed, or who they should trade with . . . are things with which, they think, he has no business. I think it would be well to cleanse the inside of the platter. (B.Y. 11:285)

We have heard considerable about "down with one man power!" All right, down with it! What is it and how are you going to get it down? When you get down the power of God, that which is called one man power in the midst of the Latter-day Saints will fall, but not before! (B.Y. 13:266)

. . . every government lays the foundation of its own downfall when it permits what are called democratic elections. (B.Y. 14:93)

When we entered into the fullness of the gospel - into a sacred and holy covenant with God, we virtually agreed to surrender our will to Him; we agreed to place ourselves under his direction, guidance, dictation, and counsel, that our will should be merged with His. Hence we are duty bound, and it is for our best interest to strive to attain to that state of mind and feeling that we shall have no will of our own, independent of the will of our Father in Heaven. (E.S. 7:352)

The United States Government

Will the President (Buchanan) that sits in the chair of state be tipped from his seat? Yes, he will die an untimely death, and God Almighty will curse him: and He will also curse his successor. (H.C.K. 5:133)

What is the priesthood? I answer, "It is the legitimate rule of God, whether in the heavens or on the Earth;" and it is the only legitimate power that has a right to rule upon the earth. (J.T. 5:187)

The Church and kingdom to which we belong will become the kingdom of our God and his Christ, and brother Brigham will become President of the United States. . . . he is foreordained to take that station, and he has got it: and I am Vice President and Brother Wells is Secretary of the Interior - Yes and of all the armies in the flesh. . . . You may think that I am joking; but I am perfectly willing that brother Long should write every word of it. (H.C.K. 5:219)

We used to have a difference between Church and State, but it is all one now. Thank God, we have no more temporal and spiritual. We have got Church and State together. (J.T. 5:266)

. . . the United States or united hell, for the terms are synonymous as the Government is now conducted. (B.Y. 5:331)

. . . the Almighty saw fit to bring forth His work under this Constitution. It has served and fulfilled its purpose. (O.H. 6:153)

From what has been said, we begin to understand something about the kingdom of God. It is to originate in the mountains and roll down out of them, like a stone; and as it rolls it will gather force and greatness until it shall become in due time like a great mountain, and fill the whole earth. . . . Before that great day the saints will have great dominion and rule on the earth. Zion will send forth her laws and her institutions. (O.P. 7:226)

. . . there is no true government on earth but the Government of God, or the holy priesthood. . . . There is no other true government in heaven or upon the earth. (B.Y. 7:142)

Would not we, as a people, be willing to let the Lord dictate our affairs temporally and spiritually? . . . Has He not the right to rule on this earth? . . . The prophets have intimated that the kingdoms of this world should be broken in pieces, and become the kingdom of our Lord and Christ. This is what we are expecting in this our day and generation. The work has commenced, we have become participants in it - citizens of the kingdom of God. This is what makes the people of God so enthusiastic in regard to their religion. (D.H.W. 7:292)

What will King Abraham do? . . . if Mr. Lincoln takes the oath of office, and enters into the administration of the Government with as great pleasure as he resigns his official duties, he will be a happy man. . . . God has come out of His hiding place, and has commenced to vex the nation that has rejected us, and He will vex it with a sore vexation. It will not be patched up - but it will be sifted with a sieve of vanity, and in a short time it will be like water spilt upon the ground. (B.Y. 8:323-324)

That Government known as the United States has become like water spilled upon the ground, and other governments will follow. (B.Y. 8:336)

The South and the North are at war with each other - are slaying each other. . . . the wicked are slaying the wicked. . . . they will whip each other, first one and then the other. Let the saints acknowledge the hand of God in it all. War and bloodshed will follow until it has spread over every nation tongue and people who reject the gospel after it has been proffered to them. (H.C.K. 10:46)

We do believe it, and we honestly acknowledge that this is the kingdom which the Lord has commenced to establish upon the earth, and that it will not only govern all people in a religious capacity, but also in a political capacity. "Well," some say "is not that treason?". . . I do not know that it is treason against the government of the United States, or any other government. (J.T. 11:53)

It startles men when they hear the Elders of Israel tell about the kingdoms of this world becoming the kingdom of our God and His Christ. They say it is treason for men to teach that the kingdom Daniel saw is going to be set up and bear rule over the whole earth. (W.W. 13:164)

Jesus

The man, Joseph, the husband of Mary, did not, that we know of have more than one wife, but Mary, the wife of Joseph had another husband. . . . That very babe that was cradled in the manger, was begotten, not by Joseph, the husband of Mary, but by another Being. Do you inquire by whom? He was begotten by our heavenly Father. This answer may suffice you - you need never inquire more upon that point. (B.Y. 11:268)

The grand reason why the Gentiles and philosophers of his school persecuted Jesus Christ, was because he had so many wives; there were Elizabeth, and Mary, and a host of others that followed him . . . The grand reason of the burst of public sentiment in anathemas upon Christ and his disciples, causing his crucifixion, was evidently based upon polygamy. . . . A belief in the doctrine of a plurality of wives caused the persecution of Jesus and his followers. We might almost think they were "Mormons." (J.M.G. 1:345-346)

There is one revelation that this people are not generally acquainted with. I think it has never been published, but probably it will be in the Church History. It is given in questions and answers. The first question is "What is the name of God in pure language?" The answer says. "Aman." "What is the name of the Son of God?" answer, "Son Aman." (O.P. 2:342)

Jesus was the Bridegroom at the marriage of Cana of Galilee, and he told them what to do. . . . I shall say here that before the Savior died, he looked upon his own natural children, as we look upon ours. (O.H. 2:82)

It will be borne in mind that once on a time, there was a marriage in Cana of Galilee; and on a careful reading of

> that transaction, it will be discovered that no less a person than Jesus Christ was married on that occasion. . . . At this doctrine, the long faced hypocrite and the sanctimonious bigot will probably cry, blasphemy! . . . How much soever of holy horror this doctrine may excite in persons not impregnated with the blood of Christ, and whose minds are consequently dark and benighted, it may excite still more when they are told that if none of the natural blood of Christ flows in their veins, they are not of the chosen or elect of God. (O.H. 4:259-260)

Some Other New "Scriptures" By Brigham Young, Prophet And Church President For Thirty Years.

> "Did you not go to school?" Yes; I went eleven days, that was the extent of my schooling. (B.Y. 13:176)

> Who can tell us of the inhabitants of this little planet that shines of an evening, called the moon? . . . When you inquire about the inhabitants of that sphere you find that the most learned are as ignorant in regard to them as the most ignorant of their fellows. So it is with regard to the inhabitants of the sun. Do you think it is inhabited? I rather think it is. Do you think there is any life there? No question, of it; it was not made in vain. (B.Y. 13:271)

> . . . you will find that temple which is built of mud or adobies, as some call them, still remains in better condition than at the first day it was built . . . it will petrify in the wall and become solid rock in five hundred years, so as to be fit to cut into millstones to grind flour while the other materials I have mentioned (marble and stone), will have decomposed and gone back into their native elements. . . . The elements of which this tera firma is composed, are every moment either composing or decomposing. . . . Go into Egypt, for instance and you will find the . . . pyramids . . . were built of what we call adobies . . . but you cannot find a

stone column that was reared in those times, for they are all decayed. (B.Y. 1:219)

When our father Adam came into the Garden of Eden, he came into it with a celestial body, and brought Eve, one of his wives, with him. . . . He is our Father and our God, and the only God with whom we have to do. Every man upon the earth, professing Christians or non-professing, must hear it, and will know it sooner or later. . . . Jesus, our elder brother, was begotten in the flesh by the same character that was in the Garden of Eden, and who is our Father in Heaven. (B.Y. 1:50-51)

I do know that there are sins committed, of such a nature that if the people did understand the doctrine of salvation, they would tremble because of their situation. And furthermore, I know that there are transgressors, who, if they knew themselves, and the only condition upon which they can obtain forgiveness would beg of their brethren to shed their blood, that the smoke thereof might ascend to God as an offering to appease the wrath that is kindled against them, and that the law might have its course. I will say further; I have had men come to me and offer their lives to atone for their sins. It is true that the blood of the Son of God was shed for sins through the fall and those committed by men, yet men can commit sins which it can never remit. . . . What a delight it was to hear brother Joseph talk upon the great principles of eternity; he would bring them down to the capacity of a child, he would unite heaven with earth, this is the beauty of our religion. (B.Y. 4:53-54)

When will we love our neighbors as ourselves?. . . Suppose that he is overtaken in a fault, that he has committed a sin that he knows will deprive him of the exaltation which he desires, and he cannot attain it without the shedding of his blood, and also knows that by having his blood shed he will atone for that sin, and be saved and exalted with the Gods, is there a man or woman in this house but what would say, "Shed my blood that I may be saved and exalted with the Gods?" . . . Will you love your brothers or sisters likewise, when they have committed a sin that cannot be atoned for without shedding of their blood? Will you love that man or woman well enough to shed their blood? That is what Jesus Christ meant. . . . I could refer you to plenty of cases where men have been righteously slain, in order to atone for their sins. . . . I have known a great many men who have left this Church for whom there is no chance whatever for exaltation, but if their blood had been spilt, it would have been better for them. . . . This is loving our neighbor as ourselves; if he needs help, help him; and if he wants salvation and it is necessary to spill his blood on the earth in order that he may be saved, spill it. (B.Y. 4:219-220)

(After putting the motion for himself to be sustained as "Prophet, Seer, and Revelator,") Brigham Young remarked: I will say that I never dictated the latter part of that sentence. I make this remark because the words in that connection always made me feel as though I am called more than I am deserving of. I am Brigham Young, an Apostle of Joseph Smith, and also of Jesus Christ. If I have been profitable to this people, I am glad of it. The brethren call me so; and if it be so, I am glad. (B.Y. 5:296) (Being sustained as a prophet, seer, and revelator probably made Young uncomfortable because he knew that he was none of these things).

. . . have I yet lived to the state of perfection that I can commune with the Father and the Son at my will and pleasure? No. . . . If I am faithful, until I am eighty years of age, perhaps the Lord will appear to me and personally dictate me in the management of his Church and people. (B.Y. 7:243) (Brigham died at age 76).

We have not seen the person of the Father, neither have we seen that of the Son. (B.Y. 11:42)

> If the question is asked, "Brother Brigham, do you pay your tithing?" I can answer with all propriety in the negative. I have never paid my tithing.(B.Y. 16:111-112)

> **. . . I can say truly and honestly that the thought never came into my mind, in all my labors, what my reward will be, or whether my crown would be large or small. . . . I do not know that I shall have a wife or child in the resurrection. I have never had any thoughts of reflections upon this, or cared the first thing about it. (B.Y. 16:70)**

These quotations are but a small sample of the Salt Lake City Tabernacle sermons that faithful Church members are expected to accept as new scriptures.

Rationalization

It is not easy to understand how so many people can believe that early Church leaders were true prophets of God despite the fact that they insulted and humiliated women, ignored their own "word of wisdom," demanded blind obedience to Church leaders, denied freedom and democracy, hated the United States Government, taught false doctrine about Adam and Jesus, claimed that the sun and the moon were inhabited, and even taught that since the atoning power of Christ was limited to minor sins, many people would need to atone for major sins by having their own blood shed! How can Church leaders and members today rationalize away all of this evil and nonsense?

The answer has to be that most Latter-Day Saints know very little about Church history except for the sanitized propaganda they read in lesson manuals and faith promoting magazines. Those who also read books tend to restrict their reading to the publications of Church leaders. And many Latter-Day Saint intellectuals and free thinkers, who know the truth about Church history, are reluctant to bring up serious questions and doubts for reasons of their own.

Chapter 18

OTHER DOUBTERS

> The men the American people admire most extravagantly are the most daring liars; the men they detest most violently are those who try to tell them the truth.
>
> -H.L. Mencken

This chapter is more for L.D.S Church members who are struggling to overcome childhood indoctrination than for readers who have never believed in Mormonism in the first place. Leaving one's comfort zone of familiar illusions can become very frightening. It isn't easy to be the only one in a person's family who says, "The Emperor has no clothes." Sometimes a person can even begin to question his or her own sanity and ask, "Why don't my family members and my friends seem to see things the same way I do?"

When this happens, it can be good for a person's mental health to realize that many other honest and intelligent people share their doubts. It is somehow comforting for a person to know that he or she is not the only one who has unorthodox ideas and feelings of disillusionment, betrayal, and entrapment.

This chapter includes only a few examples of the thousands of men and women of who have carefully and even prayerfully studied Joseph Smith and then come to the sad conclusion that his level of dishonesty and hypocrisy is almost beyond human comprehension.

Oliver Cowdery

Oliver Cowdery was a very close associate of Joseph Smith. He wrote most of *The Book of Mormon* with his own hand as dictated by Smith. And yet as time went on, Cowdery began to have grave doubts about Smith. First he charged Smith with demanding absolute power over every aspect of a person's life including marriage, family, money, property, and politics. Then in 1838, Cowdery was excommunicated when he also accused Smith of adultery.[1]

Martin Harris

Martin Harris was another close associate of Smith. He was the man who sold his farm to pay for publication of *The Book of Mormon*. Harris got into trouble when he accused Smith of drinking too much liquor while writing *The Book of Mormon*.[2] Smith turned against his old friend and benefactor saying that Harris was "full of wickedness and hypocrisy."[3] Harris left Smith and his Church but later came west to Utah.

David, John, Peter, Jacob, And Christian Whitmer

The Whitmer family were very close friends of Joseph Smith. Smith organized his Church in their home on April 6, 1830. All five of these men were "witnesses" to the gold plates and *The Book of Mormon*. After holding high offices in the Church, they all came to doubt Smith's honesty and integrity. They accused him of changing previous revelations from God to suit himself, instigating polygamy and spiritual wifeism, organizing the secret terroristic Danites, banking fraud at Kirtland, teaching false doctrine, and trying to be a king.

In 1887, David Whitmer wrote a book, *An Address to all believers in Christ* in which he said:

> If you believe my testimony of *The Book of Mormon*; if you believe that God spake to us three witnesses by his own voice, then I tell you that in June, 1838, God spake to me again by his own voice from the heavens, and told me to separate myself from among the Latter-Day Saints. . . . In June, 1838, at Far West, Missouri, a

> secret organization was formed. . . . A certain oath was to be administered to all the brethren to bind them to support the heads of the church in everything they should teach. All who refused to take this oath were considered dissenters from the church, and certain things were to be done to these dissenters. . . . About the same time that I came out, the spirit moved upon quite a number of brethren who came out with their families . . . I will now proceed to show you how the heads of the church went into one error after another. . . . I was the third person baptized into the church. . . . Sidney Rigdon was the cause of almost all the errors which were introduced while he was in the church. I believe Rigdon to have been the instigator of the secret organization known as the "Danites" which was formed in Far West Missouri in June, 1838. . . . Some of the revelations as they are now in the book of *Doctrine and Covenants* have been changed and added to. Some of the changes are of the greatest importance as the meaning is entirely changed on some very important matters. . . . This I know and will prove it to you. These revelations were arranged for publication by Brothers Joseph Smith, Sydney Rigdon, Orson Hyde, and others at Hyram, Ohio, while I was there and sent to Independence, to be published. In the winter of 1834 they saw that some of the revelations in *The Book of Commandments* had to be changed. . . . So the book of *Doctrine and Covenants* was printed in 1835. . . . I was present when nearly all the early revelations were received. There are several of the old *Books of Commandments* yet in the land; bring them to light and see for yourselves that these revelations were changed just as I tell you.

David Whitmer goes on to explain many other contradictions and reversals in Church doctrine including the name of the Church which was supposedly given in 1830 by direct revelation from God. The original name, "The Church of Christ" was changed to "The Church of Latter-Day Saints" in 1834, and then again to "The Church of Jesus Christ of Latter-Day Saints in 1838.[4]

Whitmer's book explains that he was a personal witness when Smith received most of his revelations and that Smith received them by placing his seer stone in his hat and then dictating the words that he saw, the same way Smith dictated his *Book of Mormon.* Whitmer wrote:

> Brother Joseph did not write a word of *The Book of Mormon*; it was already written by holy men of God who dwelt upon this land. God gave to Brother Joseph the gift to see the sentences in English, when he looked into the hat in which was placed the stone.[5]

One of the major themes in Whitmer's book is that some of Smith's revelations were **not** from God. After recalling the incident of Smith's failed revelation that he would be able to pay off his debts by selling the copyright to *The Book of Mormon* in Canada, Whitmer heard Smith admit that some of his revelations were from his own imagination and that some were from Satan![6]

Whitmer quotes this startling admission from Smith about five or six times in his book. He then makes a list of Smith's false revelations including the one on polygamy, creation of the Danites, ordination of high priests, gathering of Israel into one place (The New Jerusalem), secret oaths, covenants, and marriages, baptism for the dead, changing the name of the Church, and setting himself up as a one man dictator.[7]

Whitmer's book claims that Smith's revelation making him the prophet, seer, and revelator to the Church and that the Church should receive his words as if from God's own mouth, was not from God but from Smith's own lust for power. This revelation, (D. & C. 21:4-5) made Smith godlike unto Church members, created spiritual slavery, gave rise to absolute obedience, and all kinds of other extreme doctrine and behavior.

Emma Smith

Apparently, Emma Smith agreed with Whitmer that not all of Joseph's revelations were from God. For example, when Smith showed her his written revelation on polygamy, she became very angry and insisted that he burn it.[8] Emma would not have done this if she actually believed Joseph's new revelation had come from God.

Smith pretended to admit his error and repent of the entire incident. He even burned his revelation in front of Emma to appease her.[9] But once again, Smith was deceiving his wife. He had already instructed William Clayton to make a copy which was then secretly circulated and taught as sacred doctrine by Smith and other Church leaders.[10] In 1876, one year before Brigham Young died, Clayton's copy of this infamous revelation was finally published as section 132 of the *Doctrine and Covenants* of The Church of Jesus Christ of Latter-Day Saints.[11] It remains in this book of sacred Mormon scripture even to this day.

Dr. John C. Bennett

Dr. John C. Bennett was a close associate and special assistant to Joseph Smith. Bennett, a medical doctor and abortionist, came to Nauvoo in 1840 and helped save Church members from malaria. He then went to the Illinois Legislature and obtained a charter for the City of Nauvoo and the Nauvoo Legion. He was the first Mayor of Nauvoo and second only to Smith in command of the Nauvoo Legion.[12] Bennett also used his political influence to obtain Illinois state owned armaments for Smith's private army, the Nauvoo Legion.

In May of 1842, Bennett suddenly resigned as Mayor and left town. He then wrote a book, *The History of The Saints or an Exposure of Joseph Smith and Mormonism.* Bennett's book claims that the reason he left town suddenly was because Smith threatened to kill him. His book also accuses Smith of lying, adultery, polygamy, secret oaths and rituals, and having at his command "destroying angels" (Danites) who would kill anyone when ordered to by Smith.[13]

Bennett also listed a number of women that Smith had secretly married including several women with living husbands. He listed these women by the first initial of their first and last names followed by an asterisk for each of the letters in their name. For example, Louisa Beeman was L***** B*****, and Eliza R. Snow was E**** R. S***.

Bennett, once a very close friend of Smith's, proved to be quite accurate with his information. A few years later, when two of Smith's sons came to Utah to claim their right to lead the Church, Brigham Young listed many of these same women as wives of Joseph Smith.

Bennett was a womanizer almost the equal of his mentor. Even after Hyrum Smith and William Law told Joseph that they had talked with Bennett's secret wife in Pittsburgh, Pennsylvania, and that Bennett had been kicked out of a Masonic lodge for adultery, Smith kept him on as his special assistant.[14] And even after Bennett, who presented himself as a single man, admitted having sex with a number of married women in Nauvoo, Smith defended Bennett in his Church trial and kept him on as special assistant![15] Bennett knew too many of Smith's secrets.

It seems that the falling out came when both men went after the favors of Nancy Rigdon and when the public confessions of several women turned Bennett's secret adultery into a public scandal. But the opportunistic Smith immediately saw a new use for Bennett. By making a scapegoat of Bennett, Joseph could divert anger and trouble away from himself. Smith accused his old friend and benefactor of apostasy, adultery, and inventing lies about Smith's secretly teaching and practicing polygamy and "spiritual wifeism."[16] This same polygamy and "spiritual wifeism" publicly condemned by Smith and blamed upon the apostate lies of Bennett, later became known in the Church as the sacred doctrine of celestial or eternal marriage.

William Law

William Law became first counselor to Smith in the Church at Nauvoo. Law was very loyal to Smith even at the risk of his own life when many others were turning away. But after Smith tried to add William's wife, Jane, to his harem, William and also his brother Wilson turned against Smith and, with the help of a few friends, ordered a printing press and started a newspaper, the *Nauvoo Expositor.*[17] (See Appendix A for Law's interesting editorials from the first and only edition of his newspaper.)

After their printing press and some of their other property in Nauvoo had been destroyed by Smith's "destroying angels," Law and some of his friends escaped from Nauvoo to save their lives. They went to Carthage and filed the charges against Smith that eventually ended in his arrest, imprisonment, and death.

Other Prominent Nauvoo Doubters

About this same time, a number of other men in prominent Church positions also came to the sad conclusion that Smith was a liar, adulterer, and a false prophet. These men included Nauvoo Stake President, William Marks, Dr. Robert D. Foster, James Foster, Chancey L. Higbee, and Francis M. Higbee.[18]

Brigham Young and many others who did not turn against Smith at this time were out of town campaigning in every state of the union for his presidential campaign. But Joseph Smith's widow, Emma, his brother William, and many other relatives and close friends considered Brigham Young and those loyal to him to be power-hungry renegades and usurpers. They refused to recognize Young's priesthood authority or follow him west to his Great Basin Kingdom.[19]

We may ask why so many of Smith's closest friends and counselors, who knew him on a personal and intimate basis, came to the sad conclusion that he was a liar and a fraud? It doesn't make sense that after sacrificing so much for Smith and his Church, that they all decided to self-destruct at the jeopardy of their immortal souls.

The traditional answer by Church leaders, is that all of these people were apostates who became possessed by Satan in a vain attempt to destroy Smith and the kingdom of God. But history has proven that nearly all of the charges against Smith made by these apostates were true.

In addition to the men and women who knew Smith on a very personal, day to day basis, a number of other honest and intelligent

Church members have come to the same sad conclusion about Smith's dishonesty and immorality. Some of the most candid, intelligent, and courageous of these Mormon dissenters have been women.

Fanny Stenhouse

Fanny Stenhouse was a well educated, high class convert from England who migrated to Utah to join the saints in Zion. She soon became disillusioned by the great difference that she saw between what she had been told by Mormon missionaries and what she experienced in Salt Lake City. For one thing the missionaries had not told her about polygamy and about the crude and threatening tabernacle sermons by Brigham Young and other uneducated, low class Church leaders. She saw the authoritarian dictatorship of Young and his loyal friends as a theocratic slave empire.

Fanny was shocked and frightened by the blood oaths of the Mormon endowment ceremony that she experienced. She was offended by threats of blood atonement and other things which were taught in the Mormon Tabernacle. Fanny was well aware of a number of crimes that took place including the Mountain Meadows Massacre. In 1869, Fanny, her husband, and a few other prominent men and women left the Church and got out of the Utah Territory.

Fanny wrote a book, *Tell It All,* in which she explained the degradation and fear that most people, and especially women, experienced in Mormonism. Harriet Beacher Stowe, of *Uncle Tom's Cabin* fame, wrote the preface for Fanny's book.

Ann Eliza Webb Young

One of last women married to Brigham Young, Ann Eliza sued Young for divorce and a substantial monetary settlement. Young defended himself in court claiming that he was not legally married to Ann Eliza since she was never divorced from her first husband. This, of course, was an admission by Young that he had been living in adultery with another man's wife.

Ann Eliza won her divorce and a monetary settlement but upon appeal, this decision was overturned. The appeals court said that by granting a divorce and a monetary settlement the judge had declared all plural marriages in the Utah Territory legal despite federal and state laws declaring them illegal.

Ann Eliza left Utah in 1873, went on an extended lecture tour lasting about ten years, and wrote a book, *Wife No. 19.* Her book and over 2,000 speeches in front of audiences which included U.S. Congressmen and Senators, helped create a public outrage resulting in the Edmunds Act of 1882 and the Edmunds-Tucker Act of 1887 which forced the L.D.S. Church to give up polygamy. All of the women in the L.D.S. Church today who hate polygamy owe a large debt of gratitude to this "evil apostate."

Maurine Whipple

In 1941, Maurine Whipple published her historical novel, *The Giant Joshua.* This book was based upon diaries and journals of pioneers in Southern Utah. Whipple's narrative depicted the painful realities of human degradation and the great suffering that was caused by the authoritarian, patriarchal, and polygamous Mormon theocracy in Utah.

Families were publicly "called" to the Cotton Mission, the Iron Mission, and other missions by Brigham Young from the pulpit in the Salt Lake Tabernacle. They had little choice but to follow Young's counsel (orders) or else be disfellowshipped or even excommunicated as apostates.

Church members were not free to leave proselytizing nor colonizing missions until "released" by Young. Supreme power has always been held by Church leaders, never by the individual. The physical, social, and spiritual slavery endured by early pioneers and even by Church members today who honestly believe that they must always obey Church leaders and that all of their sacrifices are for the kingdom of God, is heartbreaking to those of us who do not share this point of view.

In 1976, a second edition of Maurine Whipple's book was published. Maurine told me on several occasions about the serious trouble that her book had caused her. Church leaders threatened her and former friends and neighbors turned against her.

Fawn McKay Brodie

In 1945, Fawn McKay Brodie, a niece of Church President David O. McKay, published her definitive biography of Joseph Smith, *No Man Knows My History.* A second edition was published in 1976.

Mrs. Brodie had access to many Church records that are no longer available to researchers. Her book reflects a high level of scholarship and also remarkable communication skills. It includes detailed accounts of Smith's criminal behavior, his dishonesty, his political ambitions, and his secret polygamous activities. Brodie's courageous book cost her some very important family relationships and her Church membership.

Juanita Brooks

In 1951, Juanita Leavitt Brooks, another gifted and courageous Mormon mother and college professor published *The Mountain Meadows Massacre,* a detailed account of the tragic murders that took place in 1857 near her home in Southern Utah.

In 1961, Juanita published *John D. Lee, Zealot, Pioneer Builder, & Scapegoat.* This book detailed the conversion of Lee to Mormonism, his absolute loyalty to Joseph Smith and Brigham Young, his participation in the Mountain Meadows Massacre, and an account of how Young used Lee for a scapegoat in order to protect himself and other Church leaders. Juanita's books have been revised and expanded with subsequent editions.

Brooks also wrote several other publications. Most of her research and writing took place in the middle of the night at her kitchen table. The energy, honesty, courage, and candor demonstrated by Juanita are very rare indeed. Juanita also told me about the trouble her books had caused her with Church leaders and with her family and neighbors. She was a person of rare courage who was more highly honored outside of Southern Utah than in St. George, her home town. The content and tone of her books reflect her serious doubts about the honesty and morality of early Church leaders.

Linda Newell and Valeen Avery

In 1984, Linda Newell and Valeen Avery published their well researched and well written book, *Mormon Enigma: Emma Hale Smith, Prophet's Wife, "Elect Lady," Polygamy's Foe.* This book explains how Joseph and Emma were secretly married despite serious opposition from Emma's parents, Isaac and Elizabeth Hale. It traces their turbulent lives in New York, Ohio, Missouri, and Illinois.

A major portion of Newell and Avery's book is about Joseph's many wives and Emma's strong objections to polygamy. It also details some of Smith's duplicity. For example, when Smith organized the Relief Society and set Emma apart as president, Emma didn't even know that several women in that organization, including one of her own counselors, were secretly married to her husband and having intimate relations with him![20]

I have had some personal conversations with Linda and Valeen. One of them told me that some of her research actually made her physically ill. I can empathize with this reaction. I have had this same experience.

Both of these courageous Mormon women have paid a high price for their honesty and courage. I believe that Linda and Valeen's book reflects some serious doubts about the honesty and morality of Joseph Smith.

Anna Jean Backus

Anna Jean Backus is another couragous Mormon woman. She may or may not consider herself a doubter but her 1996 book, *Mountain Meadows Witness, The Life And Times of Bishop Philip Klingensmith,* resonates doubts. Klingensmith was the Mormon Bishop of Cedar City, in the southern part of the Utah Territory at the time of the Mountain Meadows Massacre. In 1872, some fifteen years after the massacre, Klingensmith violated his oath of secrecy. While living in Pioche, Nevada, he made and signed an affidavit detailing the entire episode including his own participation in the murders. Klingensmith also implicated a number of other Church leaders including Brigham Young, George A. Smith, Colonel Dame, Lieutenant Colonel Haight, and Major John D. Lee. A large number of other Church members living in the Utah Territory were also involved, according to Klingensmith's affidavit.[21]

Klingensmith said that he was told by his military and Church superiors that the order to destroy the wagon train and take their property had come from "Church headquarters."[22] This, of course, would have meant Brigham Young. He also said that although he was entirely opposed to the treacherous plan to disarm the Fancher train and then kill everyone except little children, he went along because he was afraid that if he were to disobey orders, it would have cost him not only his Church membership but also his own life.[23]Klingensmith's affidavit said:

> I have made the foregoing statements before the above entitled Court for the reason that I believe that I would be assassinated should I attempt to make the same before any Court in the Territory of Utah[24]

After making this affidavit, Klingensmith suffered extreme hardships including the loss of his wives and children. He became a fugitive hiding out in some of the most desolate and remote regions of Nevada, Arizona and Mexico. He was eventually found dead by some Native Americans.[25]

Juanita Brooks explained the terrible blood oath of secrecy that was taken by those who participated in the Mountain Meadows Massacre, the oath that was violated by Klingensmith:

> Now the most important thing was that they should not talk of what happened here yesterday, not to anyone, not even their wives. Nor should they discuss it among themselves. They should blot it from their minds and from their memories and leave God to accept of their actions in the light of their loyalty to His Cause and the establishment of His Kingdom upon the earth. Then they closed in the circle, so that each man placed his

> left hand on the shoulder of the man nearest him and raised his right arm to the square. In the center stood Dame, Haight, Higbee, and Lee, facing them at the four points of the compass. Haight led the pledge, as the highest in ecclesiastical authority, and they repeated it after him. It was to the effect that each of them promised before God, angels, and their companions in this circle, that they would never under any conditions speak of this action to anyone else or to each other, and if any did so, he would suffer his life to be taken. This was done in the name of God and for His glory.[26]

Where did these men learn such things? Where did they learn about secrecy and blood oaths? Unfortunately, many Church members will recognize immediately where the wording for this oath of secrecy came from. But aren't murders and secret oaths the very things that Smith condemned the Gadianton Robbers for doing in his *Book of Mormon*? He called them the works of darkness and of Satan. How could anyone believe that these same things were now the will of God and necessary to establish His kingdom?

B.H.Roberts

B.H.Roberts was another person who studied *The Book of Mormon* and Church history for many years and then in the last part of his distinguished life came to have serious doubts about Joseph Smith and Mormonism. In 1985, his unpublished manuscripts were edited by Brigham D. Madsen and published by the University of Illinois Press under the title, *Studies of The Book of Mormon*. These manuscripts contain almost nothing in support of *The Book of Mormon* and a large amount of information expressing questions and doubts about its authenticity.

Dale Morgan

Dale Morgan was born in 1914 into a Mormon family. He was brought up as a child with stories about angels, gold plates, prophets, and pioneers. When he was five years old, his father died, leaving his mother, Emily, with four small children. When Dale was thirteen, he contracted meningitis which left him totally and permanently deaf. From this time on, Morgan's life was a world of silence. Despite this handicap, Morgan graduated from The University of Utah and went on to become a famous author and historian. His work is widely known in academic circles for its honesty, accuracy, and originality. Morgan traveled all over America in order to gain access to original documentation.

Although Morgan wrote several books on the history of the American West, Mormonism held a fascination that occupied much of his thirty years of research and writing. He never married and died of cancer in 1971.

Dale Morgan on Early Mormonism, a book edited by John Philip Walker, was published in 1986. This book includes some of Morgan's unpublished manuscripts and also some of his correspondence with others doing Mormon history research.

Morgan's major conclusion is that *The Book of Mormon* is not history but fiction. In reference to Smith, Morgan said:

> He was a mythmaker of prodigious talents. The moving power of Mormonism was a fable - one that few converts stopped to question, for its meaning seemed profound and its inspiration was contagious. And after a hundred years the myths he created are still an energizing force in the lives of millions of followers.[27]

Sterling M. McMurrin

Sterling M. McMurrin came from an old Mormon pioneer family and even taught at an L.D.S. seminary. Sterling went on to become a distinguished scholar and philosophy professor at The University of Utah. In 1961 he was appointed United States Commissioner of Education by President John F. Kennedy. It has been one of the highlights of my life to have the rare privilege of knowing Sterling M. McMurrin.

McMurrin had an amazing mind. It was almost like an encyclopedia. He was able to quote effortlessly from a large number of important writers and philosophers and even make their ideas understandable. One of his favorite philosophers was Bertrand Russell.

Sterling also took a keen interest in ordinary people. He was perhaps the most kind, humble, and gracious person that I have ever known. McMurrin seemed to have no concept of status. He treated a student, a custodian, a waitress, or any other person with the same respect and dignity that he treated the President of the Church or even the President of The United States.

I had several personal conversations with Sterling. He told me that after very serious consideration, he had come to the conclusion that there never were any gold plates or angels except in the imagination of Joseph Smith. McMurrin said that although he didn't believe that Mormonism was true, it was his cultural home. He considered himself a "heretic" but not an apostate because he didn't believe that it was his mission to discredit Mormonism. As an agnostic, McMurrin considered Mormonism just as good as any other religion for those who need to believe in God and an afterlife.

Thomas Stewart Ferguson

Thomas Stewart Ferguson was a brilliant man from Idaho who became a lawyer but whose first love was to prove the authenticity of *The Book of Mormon* through the study of Mesoamerican archaeology. Ferguson talked B.Y.U. President Howard S. McDonald into establishing a new department of Archaeology and Anthropology at B.Y.U in order to help with this important mission. Ferguson also persuaded Church President David O. McKay into investing $250,000 of Church funds toward establishment of the "New World Archaeology Foundation," an organization dedicated to the discovery of archaeological evidence to support *The Book of Mormon.*

After twenty years of tireless dedication to his perceived life's mission, Ferguson sadly came to the heartbreaking conclusion that *The Book of Mormon* was not history or scripture but fiction. After spending all those years and a great deal of money, he was not able to discover any historical or archeological evidence in support of *The Book of Mormon.*

Furguson confided his doubts to several of his close friends but never openly published his findings.[28] He became a "closet doubter" because he said, "Several of my dearly loved family members want desperately to believe and do believe it and they each need it."[29] Stan Larson's 1996 book, *Quest for The Gold Plates, Thomas Stuart Ferguson's Archeological Search for The Book of Mormon,* details Ferguson's energetic but ultimately futile struggle.

Jerold And Sandra Tanner

Jerold and Sandra Tanner were both members of old Mormon families with deep roots in the soil of L.D.S myths and illusions. As they began a more serious study of Church history and doctrine, they started to have some doubts. This painful ambivalence led to still more study in order to regain their faith. But instead of regaining their testimonies, they found even more reasons to seriously doubt the authenticity of *The Book of Mormon* and the divine mission of the L.D.S. Church. Finally they had to choose whether to remain closet doubters or to openly express themselves, come what may.

The Tanners made the courageous decision to publish some of their findings. This was not easy since they had no publisher, no money, no printing press, and no distribution network. They started the Modern Microfilm Company (later the Utah Lighthouse Ministry) with little more than a typewriter and a duplicating machine. Despite threats and lawsuits the Tanners have published a number of well researched books exposing Mormonism.

Thousands Of Other Honest And Intelligent Doubters

The list of doubters contained in this chapter is but the tip of the iceberg. There are thousands of others. Most doubters, for reasons of their own, do not openly admit that they no longer believe in Mormonism. Some would lose important family relationships. Others would lose friends and business contacts. Those who work for the Church, such as B.Y.U. professors, would lose their jobs.

As a matter of fact, I know a number of B.Y.U. professors who no longer believe in Mormonism. They have become closet doubters who keep their opinions to themselves in order to maintain their employment and stay out of serious family trouble. Most of them continue to pay tithing, go to the temple, hold high Church positions, and even send their children on missions. But it has been my experience that this kind of duplicity can be quite stressful and sooner or later takes its physical and emotional toll.

This chapter is dedicated to the mental health and happiness of L.D.S. doubters. I think it is important for doubters to know that they are not alone, mentally ill, or filled with the Devil. We doubters are part of a large number of intelligent men and women who have studied Mormonism and Church history very carefully (as if our salvation depended on it), and then come to the painful and sad conclusion that *The Book of Mormon* is a fraud, that Joseph Smith was dishonest and immoral, and that much of Mormonism is **not** true.

EPILOGUE

> God offers to every mind its choice between truth and repose. Take which you please; you can never have both.
>
> -Ralph Waldo Emerson

Even from his grave, Joseph Smith has dominated my life. During my first twenty years, my parents, Sunday School teachers, priesthood quorum advisors, seminary teachers, and others did their very best to program me with Mormonism. I went to hundreds of meetings where I was told over and over and over again about Joseph Smith's visions, gold plates, revelations, divine calling, and martyrdom. I was very well indoctrinated.

I spent the next twenty years of my life going on a full time mission, teaching Sunday School classes and priesthood quorums, building chapels, working on welfare farms, doing temple work, paying tithing, serving in bishoprics, and doing my very best to indoctrinate other people, including my own children, with Mormonism.

Starting at about the age of forty, after some serious research into Church history, I began to question my early programming. I spent the next twenty years of my life reading almost everything I could get my hands on, writing down my questions and doubts, searching for the truth, and writing this book.

My Search For Truth

Deprogramming is not easy. Dreams die hard. I am not sure that a person can ever entirely overcome his or her childhood indoctrination. It seems to be woven into a person's brain, nervous system, and emotional structure. Even though I no longer believe in Mormonism, I can still become emotional when I hear the old Mormon hymns, "Oh My Father" or "Come, Come, Ye Saints."

However, my search for truth has, to a large degree, set me free. **It feels wonderful to know that Church leaders have no power or influence with God, and that their ordinances, promises, threats, and even excommunication are meaningless**. It feels great to no longer find it necessary to explain and rationalize away many of the contradictory teachings and immoral actions of Joseph Smith, Brigham Young and other Church leaders.

I believe that freedom from spiritual slavery is one of the greatest freedoms a person can ever experience. But I am still part of a family and a community. I feel pain and heartbreak when friends and relatives see me as a troublemaker, apostate, or child of the Devil. This is a high price to pay. Freedom, including spiritual freedom, is never free.

Another price I (and other doubters like me) pay for spiritual freedom, is giving up comfortable illusions, the great luxury of feeling special in the eyes of God, and the warm security of certainty. Perhaps Emerson was right when he said, "God gives to every mind its choice between truth and repose. Take which you please; you can never have both."

I do not believe anyone in this life has absolute truth. All of us, at one level or another, live by myths and illusions. As the Apostle Paul wrote, "For now we see through a glass darkly . . ."[1] If Paul is correct, then anyone who pretends to have absolute truth and spiritual certainty is engaged in self-deception and in the deception of others. About the best a person can do in this world is to maintain an open mind and seek for as much truth as possible. Truth is a quest and a journey that is never completed. An open minded person never "arrives."

Speaking The Truth Can Be Dangerous.

Many people who claim to reverence truth, in reality, go to great lengths to escape from the truth in order to protect their sacred illusions. They reward those who reassure them that what they believe is true and punish those who question their assumptions and opinions.

Just as a family may try to protect itself from the outside world by hiding the truth about an alcoholic mother or an abusive father, organizations also go to great lengths in order to maintain their illusions and shared reality. Whistle-blowers and truth-tellers are **not** popular people. Telling the truth can cost a person his church membership, his job, his marriage, his property, and in some cases, even his life.

In his classic distopian novel, *Brave New world*, Aldous Huxley explains why heretics, whistleblowers, and apostates are even more dangerous than murderers. The Director of Hatcheries makes the following comment to Henry Foster:

> It is better that one man should suffer than that many should be corrupted. Consider the matter dispassionately, Mr. Foster, and you will see that no offense is so heinous as unorthodoxy of behavior. Murder kills only the individual -- and, after all, what is an individual? . . . Unorthodoxy threatens more than the life of a mere individual; it strikes at society itself. Yes, at society itself.[2]

Joseph Smith says about the same thing in justification for Nehi's killing of Laban in his *Book of Mormon*:

> And it came to pass that I was constrained by the Spirit that I should kill Laban. . . . Behold the Lord slayeth the wicked to bring forth his righteous purposes. It is better that one man should perish than a nation should dwindle in unbelief.[3]

Sadly, world history suggests that many powerful men and women agree with this notion. For every person executed for murder, there have been hundreds killed for political dissent or religious heresy. Ideology is very, very important. On the other hand, the individual who dissents is expendable. Thus, a person should be willing to die or kill for an ideology. But what a sad legacy this kind of thinking has created.

When Joseph Smith and Brigham Young threatened to kill apostates, they were only doing what men in positions of power have always done. But shouldn't we expect better things from men claiming to be prophets of God? When did Jesus ever command one of his followers to kill someone, even an apostate?

Jesus said, "And ye shall know the truth, and the truth shall make you free?"[4] Maybe knowing the truth and speaking the truth are two different things. After all, it was speaking the truth that got Jesus killed.

Speaking the truth has resulted in the imprisonment and death of millions of religious heretics and apostates throughout world history. Speaking the truth has also cost the lives of millions of political dissenters in Hitler's Germany, Stalin's Soviet Union, Mao's China, Hussein's Iraq, and in many other countries all over the world. Speaking and writing the truth has also cost many Latter-Day Saints their Church memberships, their marriages and property, their jobs, their friends, and in some cases, even their lives.

***The Book Of Mormon* Is The Keystone Of Mormonism.**

I agree with Joseph Smith, Ezra Taft Benson, B.H. Roberts, and a large number of other L.D.S. Church leaders that *The Book of Mormon* **is** the keystone of Mormonism. If there were no angels or gold plates and Smith wrote this book using his own remarkable imagination along with other resources available, then Smith is a bold liar, a fraud, and a false prophet. I also agree with the archaeologists, anthropologists, historians, and geographers who say that *The Book of Mormon* is not authentic history but fiction.

A Womanizer And A False Prophet

I agree with Oliver Cowdery, William Law, John C. Bennett, Nancy Rigdon, Sarah Pratt, Martha Brotherton, Jane Law, and a large number of other men and women closely associated with Joseph Smith who say that he was a womanizer, an adulterer, and a polygamist. His pretensions of integrity and virtue were ludicrous. I also agree with William Smith that his brother, Joseph, was an impostor and a false prophet.

"No Man Knows My History."

Joseph Smith had two different personalities, one for public consumption and another for his private life. In public Smith was an honest, virtuous, law abiding, innocent, misunderstood, and often persecuted prophet of God. He was a "seer" who could translate dead languages, a faithful husband with only one wife, and a true disciple of Christ.

In private, Smith was a womanizer, a bold liar, an outlaw, an arrogant man with great military ambitions, a false prophet, and a person who didn't know how to translate Egyptian or any other foreign language. Smith was a world class myth-maker and myth-salesman.

When Joseph Smith said, "No man knows my history," he was probably telling the truth even though he had already dictated seven volumes of personal history. The reason that no one knew his history was because of his deception, different personalities, and his public facade.

Smith was a charismatic actor and a convincing storyteller. He could keep an audience spellbound for hours, even outside in bad weather. Even now, his stories are being told and retold by thousands of missionaries and by millions of Latter-Day Saints all over the world who are dedicating not only their own lives but the lives of their children and grandchildren for generations to come to Smith's illusions, visions, revelations, and fantastic stories.

Painful Disillusionment

It has been a heartbreaking and a frightening experience for me to write this book. **Disillusionment with Mormonism has been**

the most painful experience of my life. It has made me unbearably sad to realize how many men and women have sacrificed so much, even their very lives, for Smith's fraud. And even after I decided to dedicate an important part of my life to writing this book, I made no serious attempts to publish it for several years because I didn't want to break the hearts of my aged parents and embarrass my family. I have also been afraid of a number of other things that could happen to me.

I am not proud of this long delay. But after prayerful consideration, I have become more concerned with how my excuses will sound when I am brought before the judgment bar of God. What does the Lord say to a person who prays for discernment and then is afraid to publish what he has learned? It seems that I "must speak now or forever hold my peace." I am almost seventy years old and have had two kinds of cancer.

The Challenge Revisited

In the introduction to this book, I quoted the following challenge from L.D.S. Apostle Orson Pratt:

> **The nature of *The Book of Mormon* is such, that if true, no one can possibly be saved and reject it; if false, no one can possibly be saved and receive it. Therefore, every soul in all the world is equally interested in ascertaining its truth or falsity. . . . If after a rigid examination, it be found an imposition, it should be extensively published as such; the evidence and arguments on which the imposture was detected, should be clearly and logically stated, that those who have been sincerely yet unfortunately deceived may perceive the nature of the deception and be reclaimed, and that those who continue to publish the delusion, may be silenced.**

I believe that I have met this challenge and that my arguments have been "clearly and logically stated." I also believe, as Apostle Pratt has suggested, that my work should be "extensively published."

I am well aware that publication of this book will make me an apostate and could result in my excommunication from the Church. I am not afraid of excommunication except for the embarrassment that it may cause my family. But I believe in a God who loves truth and who expects every one of His children to search for truth.

Since many of the doctrines of Mormonism are not true, Mormonism may stand in the way of salvation for many people including some of my own family and friends. This makes it my painful duty to share what I have learned with others.

Although I am not as sure about anything related to religion as I used to be, one thing that I **am** quite sure about is that I can no longer believe in many L.D.S. doctrines nor the God or Gods of Mormonism. However, I do believe that the gospel of Jesus Christ (as contained in the New Testament) along with science could solve most of the problems in our world.

New Pathways

After becoming disillusioned with Mormonism, I have had to decide what to do with my life. One possibility was to remain a member of the Church but stop making sacrifices of time or money. I would attend Church meetings with my family, perhaps once a month, but just sit on the back row, so to speak, and try to pick and choose only those things which were edifying from the Mormon menu and reject all of the other things. This option was not easy because of great pressure to participate in everything. Many relatives, friends, and neighbors just didn't understand this kind of behavior. For example, I was pressured by well meaning bishops, elders' quorum presidents, and home teachers to become active again. Some of them even told me that I could regain my testimony of Mormonism if I would just read *The Book of Mormon*!

This first option was also difficult because many Church meetings were so stressful. For example, I found it quite painful to attend testimony meetings, missionary farewells, funerals, and meetings dedicated to tithing and temple work. Church attendance also seemed to leave the false impression with friends and relatives that, deep down, I still believed in Mormonism.

A second option for me after leaving Mormonism was to join another church. Over a period of years, I have attended a number of other churches and have always been welcomed. I have found friendly people and dedicated clergy almost everywhere. This choice is not an easy one for me or for most other people leaving Mormonism. Once a person has been deceived and betrayed, it is not easy to be trusting again. Joining another church can also be difficult if strongly resisted by other family members.

And still a third possibility is to give up on organized religion and cultivate a more private relationship with God. This third option is easier for a person who is, by nature, a strong, independent, and confident personality and also for those who come from families who consider religion to be a personal decision rather than a family matter. Also, a person who does not have a strong need for fellowship and community may find this third option a good choice.

A fourth option, one chosen by some of my friends, is to become an agnostic or even an atheist. But I don't want to give up my faith in God and my hope in an afterlife. Giving up on Joseph Smith and Mormonism has been painful enough; I just can't give up on Jesus Christ and Christianity.

The End Of Our Journey

And now, as I write the last page of this book, I would like to congratulate those of you who have come this far with me on this truth-seeking adventure. Perhaps it has been almost as difficult for some of you to read this book as it has been for me to write it. I have experienced some very deep feelings of betrayal, entrapment, alienation, sadness, fear, and anger. But strangely, I have also found great happiness, freedom, and exhilaration. It is my sincere hope that my readers have also experienced these same positive feelings and rewards. It has been quite a struggle, but **freedom feels great!**

A major concern of mine has always been that this book, if taken to heart, may cause serious personal or family problems for some readers. This has been another reason for my long delay in publishing this book. But my experience has been that most of those who are thoroughly indoctrinated with Mormonism will not read anything that may call into question their assumptions and opinions. Also, it is doubtful that most true believers will even get through my introduction, nor will they take the trouble to check any of my references or consider the possibility that they may be wrong about Joseph Smith and his "keystone." They will reject my research outright.

Readers who already have some serious questions and doubts about Mormonism may welcome my logical analysis and also the valuable resources contained in my references. Such readers, if they are open about their doubts, are probably already having problems with family members who are **not seeking for truth** because they sincerely believe that they already have it.

I dedicate my work to all of you open minded men and women who have the courage to seek truth wherever it may be found, even from an unknown author who is also continuing his search for truth. **Thank you for allowing me to be a part of your life**.

Appendix A

QUOTATIONS FROM THE *NAUVOO EXPOSITOR*

The *Nauvoo Expositor* was a very important document in L.D.S. Church history. In spite of that, very few Church members have any idea what it contained or why Joseph Smith found it necessary to destroy this newspaper and its printing press, thus leading to a chain of events resulting in Smith's arrest, imprisonment, and death at Carthage.

The *Nauvoo Expositor* was published by Smith's former first counselor, William Law, and six other prominent men who had served in positions of Church and civic leadership. These men were Wilson Law, Charles Ivins, Francis M. Higbee, Chauncey L. Higbee, Robert D. Foster, and Charles A. Foster.

William Law had made great sacrifices and worked very hard to promote Mormonism. He had always been loyal to Smith even at the peril of his own life. It took a large amount of evidence to convince Law that Smith had at least two personalities and that one of these personalities was a man of secrets, deception, and immorality.

The first and only edition of the *Nauvoo Expositor* was published in Nauvoo, Illinois on June 7, 1844. This paper had local news items, stories, recipes, and other folksy things usually found in small-town newspapers, but the really important parts of this paper were the editorials which exposed the secret polygamy, adultery, duplicity, meanness, criminal activity, and abuse of power, of Joseph Smith and other Church leaders. Some excerpts from these editorials are as follows:

PROSPECTUS OF THE *NAUVOO EXPOSITOR*

The undersigned propose publishing a Journal of the above title, which will appear on Friday of each week, on an Imperial sheet, with a new press, and materials of the best quality, and rendered worthy of the patronage of a discerning and enlightened public. . . . The publishers therefore deem it a sacred duty they owe to their country and their fellow citizens to advocate through these columns of the Expositor the UNCONDITIONAL REPEAL OF THE NAUVOO CHARTER. . . . to advocate unmitigated disobedience to political revelations, . . . and to oppose with uncompromising hostility, any union of Church and state. . . . The publishers bind themselves to issue the paper weekly for one year, and forward fifty two copies to each subscriber during the year. . . . Terms two dollars in advance, two dollars and fifty cents at the expiration of six months, three dollars at the end of the year.

William Law
Wilson Law
Charles Ivins
Francis M. Higbee
Chauncey L. Higbee
Robert D. Foster
Charles A Foster

AFFIDAVITS

I hereby certify that Hyrum Smith did,(in his office) read to me a certain written document, which he said was a revelation from God, he said that he was with Joseph when it was received. He afterwards gave me the document to read, and I took it to my house and read it, and showed it to my wife, and returned it next day. The revelation (so called) authorized certain men to have more wives than one at a time, in this world and in the world to come.

Signed: William Law

State of Illinois, Hancock County,
I Robert D. Foster, Certify that
the above certificate was sworn
to before me, as true in substance,
this fourth day of May, A.D. 1844.

Robert D. Foster, J.P.

I certify that I read the revelation referred to in the above affidavit of my husband, it sustained in strong terms the doctrine of more wives than one at a time, in this world, and in the next, it authorized some to have the number of ten, and set forth that those women who would not allow their husbands to have more that one should be under condemnation before God.

Jane Law

Sworn and subscribed before me
this fourth day of May, A.D. 1844.

Robert D. Foster, J.P.

In the latter part of the Summer, 1843, the Patriarch, Hyrum Smith did in the High Council, of which I was a member, introduce what he said was a revelation given through the Prophet; that the said Hyrum Smith did essay to read the said revelation in the said Council, that according to his reading there was contained the following doctrines; 1st, the sealing up of persons to eternal life, against all sins, save that of shedding of innocent blood or consenting thereto; 2nd, the doctrine of plurality of wives, or marrying virgins. . . . This revelation with other evidence, that the aforesaid heresies were taught and practiced in the Church;

determined me to leave . . . the Church at Nauvoo, inasmuch as I dared not teach or administer such laws. And further deponent said not.

Austin Cowles

State of Illinois, Hancock County,
To Whom it may concern, I
hereby certify that the above
certificate was sworn and
subscribed before me, this fourth
day of May 1844.

Robert D. Foster, J. P.

PREAMBLE

. . . We believe that all men, professing to be ministers of God, should keep steadily in view, the honor and glory of God, the salvation of souls, and the amelioration of man's condition: and among their cardinal virtues ought to be found faith, virtue, and charity; but with Joseph Smith and many other official characters in the Church, they are words without meaning. . . . We most solemnly and sincerely declare, God this day being witness of the truth and sincerity of our designs and statements, that happy will it be with those who examine and scan Joseph Smith's pretensions to righteousness; and take counsel of human affairs, and of the experience of times gone by. Do not yield up tranquilly, a superiority to that man which the reasonableness of past events, and the laws of our country declare to be pernicious and diabolical. We hope many items of doctrine, as now taught, some of which, however, are taught secretly and denied openly, (which we know positively to be the case,) and others publicly, considerate men will treat with contempt; for we declare them heretical and damnable in their influence, though they find many devotees. . . . We are aware, however, that we are hazarding every earthly blessing, particularly property, and probably life itself, in striking this blow at tyranny and oppression. . . . Many of us have sought a reformation in the Church, without a public exposition of the enormity of crimes practiced by its leaders . . . but our petitions were treated with contempt. . . . We would ask him on the other hand if the overthrow of the Church was not inevitable; to which he often replied, that we would all go to hell together, and convert it into heaven, by thrusting the devil out; and says he, "Hell is by no means the place this world of fools suppose it to be, but on the contrary, it is quite an agreeable place."

It is a notorious fact, that many females in foreign climes, and in countries unknown to us . . . have been induced, by the sound of the gospel, to forsake friends, and embark upon a voyage across waters, . . . as they supposed, to glorify God. . . . But what is taught them on their arrival at this place? They are notified that brother Joseph will see them soon, and reveal the mysteries of Heaven to their full understanding. . . . The harmless, inoffensive, and unsuspecting creatures are so devoted to the Prophet, and the cause of Jesus Christ, that they do not dream of the deep laid and fatal scheme which prostrates happiness and renders death itself desirable. . . . They are told, after having been sworn in one of the most solemn manners to never divulge what is revealed to them, with a penalty of death attached, that God Almighty has revealed that she should be his (Joseph's Spiritual wife; for it was right anciently and God will tolerate it again; but we must keep those pleasures and blessings from the world, for until their is a change in government, we will endanger ourselves by practicing it. . . . She is thunder-struck, faints, recovers and refuses. The Prophet damns her if she rejects him. She thinks of the great sacrifice, and of the many thousands of miles she has traveled over sea and land, that she might save her soul from pending ruin, and replies, "God's will be done and not mine." The prophet and his devotees in this way are gratified.

The next important item which presents itself for our consideration is the attempt at political power and influence which we verily believe to be preposterous and absurd. We believe it is inconsistent, and not in accordance with Christian religion. We do not believe that God ever raised up a Prophet to Christianize a world by political schemes and intrigue. It is not the way God captivates the heart of the unbeliever; but on the contrary by preaching truth in its own native simplicity, and in its own original purity, unadorned with anything except its own indigenous beauties. . . . Among the many items of false doctrine that are taught in the Church, is the doctrine of <u>many Gods</u>. . . . We do not know what to call it other than blasphemy, for it is most unquestionably speaking of God in an impious and irreverent manner.

. . . Joseph Smith has started an inquisition. . . . On Thursday evening, the 18th of April, there was a council called, unknown to the Church, which tried, condemned, and cut off brothers William Law, Wilson Law, and sister Law (William's wife), and Brother R.D. Foster, . . . which we contend is contrary to the book of <u>Doctrine and Covenants</u>, for our law condemns no man until he is heard. . . . Why should Joseph, with others, refuse to hear individuals in their own defense? We will answer, it is because the court fears the atrocity of its crime will be exposed to public gaze. . . . On Monday, the 15th of April, Brother R.D. Foster had a notice served on him to appear before the High Council the Saturday following, the 20th, to answer charges preferred against him by Joseph Smith. On Saturday, while Mr. Foster was preparing to take his witnesses, 41 in number, to the council room, that he might make good his charges against Joseph, President Marks notified him that the trial had been on Thursday evening, . . . and that he had been cut off from the Church, and that same council cut off brother Laws' and sister law . . . all without their knowledge. They were not notified, neither did they dream of such a thing being done. . . . Brigham Young, one of the twelve, presided, whose duty it was not, but the President of the High Council.- See book of *Doctrine and Covenants.*

RESOLUTIONS

. . . inasmuch as they have introduced false and damnable doctrines into the Church, such as plurality of Gods above the God of this universe, and his liability to fall with all of his creatures; the plurality of wives, for time and eternity; the doctrine of unconditional sealing up to eternal life, against all crimes except that of shedding innocent blood . . . we therefore are constrained to denounce them as apostates from the pure and holy doctrines of Jesus Christ.

We disapprobate and discountenance every attempt to unite church and state; and we further believe the effort now being made by Joseph Smith for political power and influence is not commendable in the sight of God.

We consider the religious influence exercised in financial concerns by Joseph Smith as unjust and unwarranted. . . .

We discountenance and disapprobate the attendance at houses of reveling and dancing; dram shops and theaters; verily believing they have a tendency to lead from paths of virtue and holiness to those of vice and debauchery.

We consider the gathering in haste, and by sacrifice, to be contrary to the will of God; and that it has been taught by Joseph Smith and others for the purpose of enabling them to sell property at most exorbitant prices not regarding the welfare of the Church. . . . thus the wealth that is brought into this place is swallowed up by one great throat, from whence there is no return, which if it had been economically disbursed amongst the whole would have rendered all comfortable.

Notwithstanding our extensive acquaintance with the financial affairs of the Church, we do not know of any property which in reality belongs to the Church (except the temple) and we therefore consider the injunction laid upon the saints compelling them to purchase property of the Trustee in Trust for the Church, is a deception practiced upon them; and that we look upon the sending of special agents abroad to collect funds for the Temple and other purposes as a humbug practiced upon the saints by Joseph and others, to aggrandize themselves, as we do not believe the moneys and property so collected, have been applied as the donors expected, but have been used for speculative purposes by Joseph. . . .

We consider all secret societies, and combinations under penal oaths and obligations (professing to be organized for religious purposes) to be anti-Christian, hypocritical, and corrupt.

We will not acknowledge any man as king or law-giver to the Church; for Christ is our only king and law-giver.

We hereby notify all those holding licenses to preach the gospel, who know they are guilty of teaching the doctrine of other Gods above the God of this creation; the plurality of wives; the unconditional sealing up against all crimes, save the shedding of innocent blood, the spoiling of the gentiles, and all other doctrines, (so called) which are contrary to the laws of God, or the laws of our country, to cease preaching . . . .

CIRCUIT COURT

The May term of the Circuit court of this county closed on the 30th, after a session of ten days. . . . The Grand Jury found two bills against Smith, one for perjury, and another for fornication and adultery; on the first of which Smith delivered himself up for trial. but the State, not being ready, material witnesses being absent, the case was deferred to the October term.

Appendix B

WHO HAS BEEN HURT BY MORMONISM?

The Church of Jesus Christ of Latter-Day Saints spends millions of dollars every year on advertising and public relations in order to present an image of a patriotic, Christian, altruistic, and family oriented organization trying to bring salvation, truth, happiness, and good will to the world.

As a young, well indoctrinated person I strongly believed this propaganda. I never thought about all of those who have been hurt by Mormonism. And it wouldn't have mattered much anyway since converting the world to the Lord's only true religion was such an important cause. The end seemed to justify almost any means necessary. But now, overwhelmed by scientific evidence against the honesty of Joseph Smith and the authenticity of his *Book of Mormon,* I see all of this from a different perspective. I now realize that a large number of people have been hurt in the past and continue to be hurt by Mormonism today, and that expanding Mormonism by almost any means is not justified. The end does **not** justify the means.

Non-Members

When one person in a family becomes converted to Mormonism and leaves his or her parents, husband or wife, brothers and sisters, and friends for what they now believe to be the "truth," this can break many hearts, cause divorces, and result in all kinds of stress, anger, and bitterness. As a young missionary in the Chicago area during the 1950s, I helped convert many people to Mormonism. I also helped break up a number of families when only the husband or wife (usually the wife) became converted. **I am truly sorry. I wish I could go back and undo all of the damage that I have done.** But at the time, I thought no sacrifice was too great for me or anyone else to make for such an important cause.

Another example of the pain caused by Mormonism is when the son or daughter of a non-member is converted and then decides to get married in a Mormon temple. The new convert's parents and other family members are not permitted to attend the temple wedding. This has saddened and angered many non-members. It has also caused great anxiety and stress for the convert who doesn't really want to exclude his or her loved ones but is forced to do so.

Also among the non-members who are hurt by Mormonism are the many Christian priests and ministers who lose parishioners from their congregations when these people are converted by Mormon missionaries. These same clergy are also insulted by the missionaries who claim that God told Joseph Smith that their creeds were an "abomination" and that they were "all corrupt."

Also insulted by Joseph Smith and his *Book of Mormon* are 90 percent of the people on this Earth who are not "white and delightsome." Smith's *Book of Mormon* God is a racist. How can the L.D.S. Church expect to convert the world while their *Book of Mormon* insults the vast majority of its people.

Other non-Mormons who have been hurt by the mindless authoritarianism of early Mormonism include the men, women, and children who were killed in the Mountain Meadows Massacre and also those non-members who were killed in other violent altercations in Missouri, Illinois, and in Brigham Young's Great Basin Kingdom.

Early Converts

Early converts who died in the religious conflicts in Missouri or Illinois, and also those who died following their leaders West to establish Zion, the mythical Mormon utopia were certainly hurt by Mormonism. The suffering endured by the frozen handcart companies in Wyoming, those who died of cholera or scurvy in Nebraska, and the many others who died of starvation and exposure along the trail is almost incomprehensible. But no price was too high for these early converts to pay in order to please God and gain exaltation in His celestial kingdom. One of their favorite hymns included the words, "And should we die before our journey's through, all is well, all is well."[1]

Also hurt, were those who didn't die tragic deaths but lived to dedicate their lives and the lives of their descendants for many generations to the Church. Great sacrifices of time and money to perpetuate Smith's illusions and deceptions have caused stress and hardships for millions of people.

Many early converts were coerced by Church leaders into living outside of the law in polygamous relationships. These women and men suffered great hardships. Some went to jail, others hid from the law, others lied and taught their children to lie in order to protect their loved ones and the Church. Many women lived lives of humiliation and loneliness and were forced to support themselves and their children while their shared husbands were away on Church missions or else in jail. Young girls were married to men old enough to be their fathers or even grandfathers. Sadly, some of these painful practices are still happening among fundamentalist Mormon communities today such as the one in Colorado City, Arizona.

Early converts who were coerced by their leaders into violent outlaw activity at Mountain Meadows and in other parts of the Utah Territory must also be listed among those hurt by authoritarian obedience as taught by early Mormonism. In 1857, many of these men were ordered to burn government property and steal livestock from the Federal Government in the mountains and plains east of Salt Lake City. Those men who were turned into treasonous outlaws by their leaders are certainly among those hurt by Mormonism.

Church Members Today

One group of believers in our day who are hurt by Mormonism are young Church members who are excluded from temple weddings. For example, a fifteen year old girl is not allowed to see her older sister get married in a Mormon temple regardless of how dedicated and innocent she may be because she doesn't yet have her own endowments. Also excluded are parents, grandparents, uncles, aunts, and other relatives who do not pay tithing and otherwise live lives "worthy" to obtain a temple recommend. What other church excludes loving family members from weddings? I have experienced this painful and humiliating ostracism. And yet, Mormonism claims to be a loving and kind family oriented religion.

Another large group of people hurt by Mormonism are the thousands of "closet doubters" who no longer believe in the Church but find it necessary to keep up appearances and pretend to believe in order to prevent serious family trouble. For several years, I was one of these closet doubters. But living a double life can result in all kinds of stress and depression along with a number of physical and emotional problems.

Many active and believing Latter-Day Saints also experience anxiety, guilt, and depression simply because they cannot live up to the many commandments, rules, expectations, and sacrifices expected of Church members. Utah (about 70 percent L.D.S.) leads the nation in prescriptions for anti-depressant drugs at about twice the national average![2] Utah also has one of the highest suicide rates in America.[3] It also leads the nation in bankruptcies.[4] Payment of tithing along with supporting a missionary can easily cost one-third of a family's income. Having a large family can also add considerably to these overwhelming financial pressures.

Salt Lake County's divorce rate has been about twice the national average.[5] Financial problems along with arguments about payment of tithing and about other Church doctrine and activity can result in high levels of stress and anger within a Mormon family. An L.D.S. woman recently said to me, "Nearly all of my friends who have gotten a divorce have split up over the Church. I thought that religion was supposed to help people get along and love each other."

Although many true believers have apparently found great satisfaction and happiness from their Church membership and activity, there have also been, and still continue to be, many casualties caused by Smith's religion. It is time for everyone to recognize that there are two sides to this coin.

Appendix C

OUR CAST OF CHARACTERS

JOSEPH SMITH, JR.
(1805-1844)

Charismatic, larger than life, creative genius, story teller, myth maker, illusion creator, our main character and leading man.

EMMA SMITH
(1804-1879)

Daughter of Isaac and Elizabeth Hale, first and only legal wife of Joseph Smith, mother to eleven children, "elect lady," first L.D.S. Relief Society president, first Mormon hymnbook organizer, temperance advocate, polygamy foe, adversary of Brigham Young, widowed at age 40, died in Nauvoo at age 75. [1]

HYRUM SMITH
(1800-1844)

Joseph Smith"s older brother, loyal companion, counselor, Church Patriarch, polygamist, Master Mason, General in the Nauvoo Legion, Vice Mayor of Nauvoo, member Council of Fifty. Stood by Joseph whether right or wrong in life and in death. Fellow martyr.

DR. JOHN C. BENNETT
(1804-1867)
(From John C. Bennett, *History of the Saints*)

Close friend and special assistant of Joseph Smith. Medical doctor who helped save Nauvoo from malaria. Abortionist, city planner, first mayor of Nauvoo. Major-General in the Nauvoo Legion, womanizer, author of *History of The Saints*, a book exposing Smith's secret life, notorious apostate. Secretary of Nauvoo Masonic lodge. A very important person in early Mormon history.[2]

BRIGHAM YOUNG
(1801-1877)

Apostle, missionary, Mason, loyal to Joseph Smith. Nauvoo City Council, Council of Fifty, second president of the L.D.S. Church for thirty years. Governor of the Utah Territory, colonizer, commander of The Nauvoo Legion in the Utah Territory, husband to many women, outlaw, authoritarian dictator, businessman and millionaire. Only a few days of formal education, but very clever and cunning in the art of gaining and using power.

DAVID WHITMER
(1805-1888)

An original Church member, Apostle, witness to gold plates, missionary, close friend of Joseph Smith. Excommunicated in 1838 for opposing radical new doctrine. Opposed the Danites, a secret Mormon terrorist organization. Ordered out of town at the peril of his life. Wrote *An address to All believers in Christ.*

OLIVER COWDERY
(1806-1850)

Second Elder in the Church, Counselor, Apostle, Church Historian, witness to gold plates. Wrote most of *The Book of Mormon* as dictated by Smith. Objected to Smith's claim that he had a right to dictate Church members in temporal affairs as well as in spiritual matters. Accused Smith of adultery, excommunicated, forced to flee Far West, Missouri, with David Whitmer and other dissenters under a death threat from Smith, Rigdon, Avard, and other Danites.

SIDNEY RIGDON
(1793-1876)

Charismatic, hot tempered, counselor and close friend of Joseph Smith. Religious and civic leader in Kirtland, Ohio, who brought many of his congregation into Smith's new Church. Danite leader in Missouri, Nauvoo City Councilman and postmaster. Nauvoo Legion Judge Advocate, member Council of Fifty. Refused to go along with Smith's secret and illegal polygamy. Became outraged when Smith tried to add his daughter, Nancy, to his harem. Left Nauvoo but came back and tried to claim leadership of the Church in opposition to Brigham Young, William Smith, and a number of others.

PARLEY P. PRATT
(1807-1857)

An original member of Smith's new Church. Perhaps Mormonism's greatest missionary and salesman. Brought hundreds of people into Mormonism. Apostle, Danite, polygamist, Nauvoo City Council member, Council of Fifty. Close friend of Joseph Smith and Brigham Young. Murdered in Arkansas by Hector McLean, the undivorced husband of Pratt's last plural wife, Eleanore.[3]

ORSON PRATT
(1811-1881)

Younger brother of Parley. Missionary, Apostle, polygamist, Nauvoo City Council, Nauvoo Legion, Council of Fifty. Mason, mathematician, astronomer. Excommunicated for believing his wife, Sarah, when she told him that Smith had tried to seduce her while Pratt was away on a mission. Left a suicide note and left Nauvoo. Changed his mind, apologized to Smith. Was reinstated as an Apostle but lost his seniority to Brigham Young. Publicly announced the doctrine of polygamy to Church Members and to the world in a conference sermon in Salt Lake City in 1852 at the request of Brigham Young. Had a difficult time accepting some of Young's doctrine including Adam-God, and blood-atonement.[4]

ORRIN PORTER ROCKWELL
(1813-1878)

One of Joseph Smith's oldest and closest friends going all the way back to his boyhood in Palmyra, New York. Trusted bodyguard. Polygamist, Danite, outlaw, "destroying angel" at the disposal of Smith and later Brigham Young. Arrested for attempted murder of Lilburn W. Boggs, Governor of Missouri, but released for lack of evidence. Friend of infamous Danite and destroying angel, Bill Hickman. Accused of killing at least one hundred enemies of Joseph Smith and Brigham Young.[5]

JOHN TAYLOR
(1808-1887)

Apostle, missionary, polygamist, loyal friend of Joseph Smith and Brigham Young, wounded at Carthage Jail when Smith was killed. Third President of the L.D.S. Church. Refused to give up polygamy even under great pressure from the U.S. Government. Taylor was a firm believer that the Mormon Priesthood was the only legitimate government on Earth. He said, "The kingdom or nothing."[6]

WILFORD WOODRUFF
(1807-1898)

Apostle, missionary, polygamist, loyal friend of Joseph Smith and Brigham Young. Fourth L.D.S. Church President. **Woodruff tried to Americanize the L.D.S. Church**. He issued a manifesto giving up polygamy. He renounced the doctrine that the Mormon Priesthood was the only legitimate government on earth. He disbanded The Nauvoo Legion. He gave up the idea that the saints would go back to a gathering place in Zion, Missouri. He declared that a priesthood holder should be sealed to his own father and then to his own progenitors instead of to a missionary or Church leader. Woodruff was a very significant and courageous Church leader, but **Mormon fundamentalists consider him the apostate president and false prophet who betrayed many of the basic ideas and doctrines that were taught by Smith, Young, and Taylor.**

DANIEL H. WELLS
(1814-1891)

Loyal friend and armed bodyguard for Smith and then Young. Nauvoo Associate Justice, Deseret Attorney General, Deseret (Utah Territory) Secretary of State, Deseret Supreme Court Judge, Nauvoo Legion Major-General (second in command only to Brigham Young), Commander in charge of the attack upon the U.S. Army east of Salt Lake City in 1857. Manti Temple President, polygamist. Brigham Young rewarded Wells' absolute loyalty with high positions of power and also with some of the wives and children of other Mormon men who refused or even hesitated to follow Young's "counsel."

HEBER C. KIMBALL
(1801-1868)

Missionary, Apostle, Captain in Zion's Camp, Nauvoo City Council, Officer Nauvoo Legion, Council of Fifty, husband to about forty women, close and loyal friend of Joseph Smith and Brigham Young, first counselor to Brigham Young. Deseret Lieutenant-governor, Utah Territory legislature President, alter-ego to Brigham Young and major conference speaker as recorded in the *Journal of Discourses.* Strong advocate of the Mormon reformation and "blood atonement." A very powerful but crude and uneducated man.

JOHN D. LEE
(1812-1877)

A loyal soldier for Smith and Young, doing whatever he was commanded to do, whether right or wrong. Lee was a member of the infamous Danites and second sergeant in the Nauvoo City Police. Lee was an adopted son of Young (sealed to Brigham Young). Young betrayed Lee and used him for a scapegoat in order to save himself from prosecution for The Mountain Meadows Massacre. Although Young and other high ranking officers were in command of the Nauvoo Legion that killed over 100 innocent and unarmed men, women, and children in Southern Utah in 1857, Lee was the only one ever tried and executed for this unthinkable atrocity.

ANN ELIZA WEBB YOUNG

1844- Unknown

One of last women married to Brigham Young, Ann Eliza sued Young for divorce and a substantial monetary settlement. Ann Eliza left Utah in 1873, went on an extended lecture tour lasting about ten years, and wrote a book, *Wife No. 19*. Her book and over 2,000 speeches in front of audiences which included U.S. Congressmen and Senators, helped create a public outrage resulting in the Edmunds Act of 1882 and the Edmunds-Tucker Act of 1887 which forced the Church to give up polygamy. All of the women in the L.D.S. Church today who hate polygamy, owe a debt of gratitude to this "evil apostate." Actually, Ann Eliza was much closer to wife number fifty! She eventually became a recluse and probably died alone. She was last seen in New York City by a close relative.[7]

B. H. ROBERTS
(1857-1933)

Missionary, Church leader, theologian, historian, polygamist, author, and political leader. Many L.D.S. scholars (including Sterling M. McMurrin) considered Roberts to be to be the greatest historian, theologian, and author ever produced by Mormonism. Toward the end of his distinguished life, Roberts had many serious questions and doubts about the authenticity of *The Book of Mormon*, the claims of Joseph Smith, and the divine mission of Mormonism.

REFERENCES

These references represent many years of research. I hope they will become a valuable source of information for serious readers. I invite those who read this book to carefully examine any or all of my references, especially those that seem to be astonishing or unbelievable. I have tried to make my references as straightforward and accurate as possible.

It is not necessary to seek out non-Mormon or anti-Mormon sources in order find overwhelming evidence against the authenticity of *The Book of Mormon* and the honesty of Joseph Smith. About eighty percent of my over 600 references are from *The Book of Mormon*, the Bible, the *Doctrine and Covenants*, the *Pearl of Great Price*, and the writings and sermons of Joseph Smith, Brigham Young, B.H. Roberts, and other Church leaders.

References in this book are listed by chapter and number. Those that are used quite often may be abbreviated after the first usage. For example, *A Comprehensive History of The Church of Jesus Christ of Latter-Day Saints, Century I* will simply be referred to as C. H. C. The *Journal of Discourses* will be J. D. The *Doctrine and Covenants* will be D. & C. and *The Pearl of Great Price* will be P. of G. P. The *History of The Church of Jesus Christ of Latter-Day Saints* will be referred to as H. C. The Bible and *The Book of Mormon* will be referred to by book, chapter, and verse. References containing several volumes such as the *Journal of Discourses* will be referred to by volume and page. For example, a reference from the *Journal of Discourses*, Volume Three, page fifty two, will be J. D. 3:52.

INTRODUCTION

1. Joseph Smith, *Doctrine and Covenants*, (Salt Lake City: The Church of Jesus Christ of Latter-Day Saints, 1953), Section 84, Verse 41. This book will be referred to hereafter as D. & C.
2. Joseph Smith, *History of the Church of Jesus Christ of Latter-Day Saints*, Seven Volumes, (Salt Lake City: Deseret Book Company, 1978), Volume 4, p.461. This reference will be referred to hereafter as H. C.
3. H. C. 2:52
4. Ezra Taft Benson, "The Book of Mormon-Keystone of Our Religion," *Ensign*, November, 1986, pp.4-6.
5. B. H. Roberts, *New Witness For God*, 2 Volumes (Salt Lake City: The *Deseret News* Press, 1909), Vol. 2, pp. III, IV.
6. Linda King Newell and Valeen Tippetts Avery, *Mormon Enigma: Emma Hale Smith, Prophet's Wife "Elect Lady," Polygamy's Foe*, (Garden City, New York: Doubleday & Company, Inc. 1984), pp. 98, 137-147. Also, Fawn M. Brodie, *No Man Knows My History, The Life of Joseph Smith*, (New York: Alfred A. Knopf, Second Edition Revised and Enlarged 1976), pp. xi, 334, append. C.
7. Newell and Avery, *Mormon Enigma*, p. 146.
8. Newell and Avery, *Mormon Enigma*, p. 146.
9. Brodie, *No Man Knows My History*, p. 310.
10. Brodie, *No man Knows my History, p.310.*
11. Joseph Smith, *The Book of Mormon*, (Salt Lake City: Deseret Book Company, 1953), Jacob 2:23,24. This reference will hereafter be quoted by book, chapter and verse.
12. Dean C. Jessee, "The Early Accounts of Joseph Smith's First Vision," *Brigham Young University Studies*, IX, No. 3, 1969. Also, see, Brodie, *No Man Knows My History*, pp. 405-409.
13. Brodie, *No Man Knows My History*, pp. 310-311. Also, Newell and Avery, *Mormon Enigma*, pp. 111-112.
14. H. C. 2:181-182.
15. Brodie, *No Man Knows My History*, P. 316.
16. Holy Bible, King James Translation, (Cambridge: University Press. 1954), Matthew 5:28. This reference will hereafter be quoted by book, chapter and verse.
17. H.C. 5:255-256.

18. Brodie, *No Man Knows My History*, pp. 306-307.
19. *St. Louis Bulletin*, July 15, 1842, p. 2.
20. Brodie, *No Man Knows My History*, p. 307.
21. *Millenial Star*, August, 1842.
22. Newell and Avery, *Mormon Enigma*, p. 98.

Chapter 1

THE LAW OF MOSES AND CHRISTIANITY

1. 1 Nephi 4:15-16, 1 Nephi 3:19-20, 1 Nephi 5:10-20.
2. 1 Nephi 4:10-13.
3. 1 Nephi 4:14-18.
4. 2 Nephi 5:10, 2 Nephi 25:24, Jacob 4:5, Jerom:5, Alma 30:3.
5. 1 Nephi 5:14.
6. Deuteronomy 25:5-10.
7. Exodus 2:21, Numbers 12:1.
8. Jacob 1:15, 2:23-28, 3:5, Mosiah 11:1-2, Ether 10:5.
9. 2 Nephi 5:10.
10. 3 Nephi Chapters 9-28.
11. Richard E. W. Adams, *Mysteries of The Ancient Americas*, (New York: Reader's Digest Association Inc., 1986), pp. 284-305. Also, see Richard E. W. Adams, "Rio Azul", *National Geographic*, April 1986, pp. 420-465. Also, see William R. Coe, *Tikal*, (Philadelphia: The University Museum, University of Pennsylvania, 1967), pp. 36, 57, 65.
12. Adams, "Rio Azul" p. 464.
13. Adams,*Mysteries of The Ancient Americas*,pp.284-295.
14. 3 Nephi 2:8.

Chapter 2

TALL TALES, A FANTASY WORLD

1. 1 Nephi 1:2.
2. 1 Nephi 3:19.
3. Mormon 9:32.
4. 1 Nephi 2:4-9.
5. 1 Nephi 4:6-38.

6. 1 Nephi 4:18.
7. 1 Nephi 17:4.
8. 1 Nephi 17:2.
9. 1 Nephi 16:10, 27-30.
10. John Phillip Walker, Editor, *Dale Morgan on Early Mormonism*, (Salt Lake City: Signature Books ,1986), pp. 321-339. Also, Brodie, *No Man Knows My History*, pp. 427-429.
11. 1 Nephi 16:18-19.
12. *The New Encyclopedia Britannica, Macropedia, Knowledge In Depth*, 15th Edition, (Chicago: University of Chicago, 1986), Vol. 21, p. 350.
13. 1 Nephi 17:5.
14. 1 Nephi 17:8-16.
15. 2 Nephi 5:16
16. 2 Nephi 5:28.
17. 2 Nephi 5:1-16.
18. I Kings 5:1-16, I Kings 6:38.
19. Mosiah 22:7-16.
20. Mosiah 20:1-5, Mosiah 23:33-39, Mosiah 24: 1-4.
21. Alma, Chapters 17, 18, and 19.
22. Alma 53:18, Alma 56:55-56.
23. Ether 1:33-43, Ether 2:16-17, Ether 6:4.
24. Ether 2:23.
25. *The New Encyclopedia Britannica, Macropedia, Knowledge in Depth*, 15th Edition, (Chicago: University of Chicago, 1986), Vol. 21, pp. 236-238.
26. Ether 2:16-17.
27. Ether 2:1-2.
28. Ether 9:19.
29. Ether 2:19-20, Ether 6:6-16.
30. Ether 7:8-9.
31. *The New Encyclopedia Britannica, Macropedia, Knowledge in Depth*, 15th Edition, (Chicago: University of Chicago, 1986), Vol. 21, p. 350.
32. 3 Nephi 8:17-25, Also, 3 Nephi 9:1-12.
33. 2 Nephi 1:5-6.
34. 2 Nephi 1:9,20, 2 Nephi 4:4, Jarom 9, Omni 6, Mosiah 1:7, Mosiah 2:41.

35. Lucy Smith, *Biographical Sketches of Joseph Smith, The Prophet and His_Progenitors for Many Generations*, (Liverpool: S. W. Richards, 1853), p. 85.

Chapter 3

BEWARE OF FALSE PROPHETS

1. Matthew 24:11.
2. Deuteronomy 18:20-22.
3. H. C. 1:373.
4. 1 Nephi 13:39.
5. 2 Nephi 27: 7-11.
6. 2 Nephi 29:12-14, also see Ether 13:11 and D. & C. 133:26.
7. 1 Nephi 14:13-17, 1 Nephi 22:14, 2 Nephi 30:10, 2 Nephi 6:14-15.
8. 2 Nephi 27:1-3.
9. 2 Nephi 29:14.
10. 2 Nephi 30:5-6.
11. B. H. Roberts, *A Comprehensive History of The Church of Jesus Christ of Latter-Day Saints, Century I*, Seven Volumes, (Provo: Brigham Young University press, 1965), Vol. 3, p.484. This reference will hereafter be referred to as C. H. C.
12. 3 Nephi 16:14-15, 3 Nephi 20:16, 3 Nephi 21:12, 3 Nephi 25:3, Mormon 5:20-24.
13. 3 Nephi 21:14-21.
14. H. C. 1:315-316.
15. H. C. 2:37-38, Also D. & C., 103:15-28.
16. H. C. 1:315-316, H. C. 3:67, H. C. 6:58.
17. D. & C. Section 111.
18. H. C. 2:182.
19. H. C. 5:336.
20. D. & C. 87:1-6.
21. H. C. 1:301.
22. J. D. 9:142-143.

Chapter 4

CONTRADICTORY DOCTRINE

1. Mosiah 15:1-4.
2. Alma 11:28-29, 38-39.
3. Ether 3:14-15.
4. Joseph Smith, *The Pearl of Great Price*, (Salt Lake City: The Church of Jesus Christ of Latter-Day Saints, 1953), Moses 6:3, Moses 7:4. This reference will hereafter be referred to as P. of G. P. and then book, chapter and verse. Also, see D. & C. 107:53-54.
5. 1 Nephi 14:3, 2 Nephi 9:19, Jacob 3:11, Mosiah 2:38-41, Mosiah 3:25-27.
6. 2 Nephi 9:16,19, Jacob 3:11.
7. 1 Nephi 14:3, 2 Nephi 9:19, 2 Nephi 28:22,23.
8. 1 Nephi 14:3.
9. D. & C. 76:84-89.
10. 1 Nephi 15:35, 2 Nephi 28:22-23.
11. Alma 40:16-19. Also, see Mosiah 15:24.
12. D. & C. 76:50-64.
13. Jacob 2:24.
14. D. & C. 132:38.
15. Brigham Young, et al., *Journal of Discourses*, Twenty Six Volumes, (Liverpool: F.D. Richards, 1855), Vol. 9, p. 322, Vol. 11, p. 269. This will hereafter be referred to as J. D.
16. D. & C. 132:38, I Kings 11:1-3.
17. Jacob 2:24.
18. Joseph Smith, P of G. P. Abraham 1:21-26. Also, Moses 7:22. Also, see J. D. 2:184 for Brigham Young's comments about blacks and the priesthood.
19. 1 Nephi 11:13-15.
20. 1 Nephi 13:15.
21. 2 Nephi 5:21.
22. 3 Nephi 2:14-15.
23. 2 Nephi 30:5-6.
24. Jacob 3:8.
25. J. D. 10:110.
26. Ether 8:14-21.
27. Ether 8:14-25.

28. David Persuitte, *Joseph Smith and The Origins of The Book of Mormon*, (Jefferson, North Carolina: McFarland & Company, 1985), p. 175.
29. David Persuitte, *Joseph Smith and The Origins of The Book of Mormon*, pp. 179-80.
30. Brodie, *No Man Knows My History*, p. 459.
31. William Morgan, *Illustrations of Masonry*. 3d ed. (New York: 1827), p.26.
32. 3 Nephi 4:7.
33. David Persuitte, *Joseph Smith and The Origins of The Book of Mormon*, p.177.
34. 3 Nephi 3:9.
35. P. of G. P., Moses 5:31.
36. D. & C. 20:9, D. & C. 42:12. Also see "Origin of *The Book of Mormon*" in the introductory pages of *The Book of Mormon*. (In later editions this is called "Testimony of the Prophet Joseph Smith").
37. H. C. 6:58, 217, 333, 410.
38. H. C. 6:311-312. Also see J. D. 6:238.
39. J. D. 16:70.
40. Matthew 22:29.
41. Luke 20:34-35.
42. Matthew 3:9.
43. Titus 3:9.
44. 1 Timothy 1:4.
45. 1 Corinthians 15:29.

Chapter 5

FICTITIOUS TRANSLATIONS

1. Edward Stevenson, "One of The Three Witnesses", *Deseret News*, (Salt Lake City: November 30, 1881), Also, *Millenial Star*, (Liverpool: Febuary 6, 1882), pp. 86-87.
2. David Whitmer, *An Address to all Believers in Christ*, (Richmond, Missouri: 1887), pp. 31-32.
3. David Whitmer, *An Address to all Believers in Christ*, pp. 31-32. Also, see C.H.C. I:162-165.

4. Oliver Cowdery, *Defense of My Grounds For Separating Myself From The Latter-Day Saints*, (Morton, Ohio: 1839).
5. *The Susquehanna Register*, (New York: May 1, 1834).
6. Eber D. Howe, *Mormonism Unveiled*, (Painsville, Ohio: 1834), pp.242-245. Also, Richard Van Wagoner, Steve Walker, "Joseph Smith: The Gift of Seeing", *Dialogue*, Summer, 1982, p.54.
7. C. H. C., VI:230.
8. P. of G. P., p.28.
9. F.S. Spalding,D.D., *Joseph Smith as a Translator*, (Salt Lake City: The Arrow Press, 1912), pp. 26-30.
10. P. of G. P., p. 42.
11. Spalding, *Joseph Smith as a Translator*, pp. 22-30.
12. Spalding, *Joseph Smith as a Translator*, p. 23.
13. H. C., 5:372.
14. H. C., 5:378. Also, Stanley P. Kimball, "Kinderhook Plates Brought to Joseph Smith Appear to Be a Nineteenth Century Hoax", *Ensign*, (Salt Lake City: August 1981), pp. 66-74. Also, Ernest H. Taves, *Trouble Enough*, (Buffalo, New York: Prometheus Books, 1984), pp. 108-109.
15. David Persuitte, *Joseph Smith and the Origins of The Book of Mormon*, (Jefferson, North Carolina: McFarland & Company, 1985), p. 216.
16. P. of G. P., Abraham 1:23.
17. P. of G. P., Abraham 1:26.
18. Persuitte, *Joseph Smith and the Origins of The Book of Mormon*, pp. 257-258.
19. Ernest H. Taves, *Trouble Enough, Joseph Smith and The Book of Mormon*, (Buffalo, New York: Prometheus Books, 1984), p. 110.
20. Spaulding, *Joseph Smith as a Translator*, p. 23.

Chapter 6

ANACHRONISMS EVERYWHERE

1. H. Michael Marquardt, *The Use of the Bible in The Book of Mormon*, (Salt Lake City: Modern Microfilm Co., 1979), p. 107. Also, see Marquardt's appendices I,II, and III. Compare Alma

5:52 with Matthew 3:10; Alma 3:5 with Hebrews 7:1-2; Alma 40:13 with Matthew 8:12; Alma 58:40 with Galations 5:1; 1 Nephi 10:8-10 with John 1:27-29; 3 Nephi 20:23-26 with Acts 3:22-26; Mormon 9:22-24 with Mark 16:15-18; 3 Nephi 7:8 with 2 Peter 2:22. Also, see George D. Smith, Jr., "Defending The Keystone", *Sunstone*, (May/June, 1981), p. 48.
2. H. C. 4:537.
3. Isaac Asimov, *Asimov's Guide to the Bible*, (New York: Avenel Books, 1981), pp. 547-549. Also, see Butrick et al., *The Interpreter's Bible*, Twelve Volumes, (Nashville: Abingdon Press, 1980), Vol. 5, p. 397. Also, George D. Smith Jr., "Isaiah Updated", *Sunstone*, (Summer 1983), p.38.
4. 1 Nephi Chapters 13, 14, Mosiah 3:8. Also, 2 Nephi 29:3-10, 26:26, Alma 7:15.
5. William D. Russell, "A Further Inquiry Into The Historicity of *The Book of Mormon*", *Sunstone*, (September-October 1082), p.23.
6. Jerom:8.
7. 1 Nephi 2:4-9.

Chapter 7

CONFLICTS WITH SCIENTIFIC FACTS

1. Marquardt, *The Use of The Bible in The Book of Mormon*, p.130.
2. "A New Wave to The New World", *Science*, (December, 1983), p.7.
3. "A New Wave to The New World", *Science*, (December, 1983), p.8.
4. Michael D. Coe, "Mormons and Archeology, an Outsiders View", *Dialogue, A Journal of Mormon Thought*, Vol. VIII, No. 2, 1973), p.46.
5. John L. Sorenson, *An Ancient American Setting For The Book of Mormon*, (Salt Lake City: Deseret Book Company, 1985), pp. 55, 83, 84, 87, 88, and 94. Also, see John L. Sorenson, "Digging Into The Book of Mormon", *Ensign*, September 1984, pp. 27-37.
6. 2 Nephi 1:9.

7. Joseph Smith, "Origin of *The Book of Mormon*", (Published as an introduction to *The Book of Mormon.*) In later editions this part of the introduction is called, "Testimony of the Prophet Joseph Smith."
8. *The World's Last Mysteries*, (Pleasantville, New York: The Reader's Digest Association, Inc., 1981), pp. 267-279. Also, "Unearthing the Oldest Known Maya", *National Geographic*, (July, 1982), pp. 126-140.
9. *Dialogue*, Summer 1969, p. 81.
10. *Times and Seasons*, September 15, 1842.
11. Alma 18:9-12.
12. Jacob Bronowski, *The Ascent of Man*, (Boston: Little, Brown and Company, 1973), pp. 80, 100, 101. Also, *Mysteries of The Ancient Americas*, pp. 25, 29, 100.
13. Alma 11:3-7.
14. George D. Smith, "Is There Any Way To Escape These Difficulties? *The Book of Mormon* Studies of B. H. Roberts", *Dialogue*, Summer, 1984, p. 105. Also, see *Mysteries of The Ancient Americas*, pp. 92-105.
15. Ether 10:24, Alma 4:6.
16. *Mysteries of The Ancient Americas*, pp. 129, 161, 198-201, 248.
17. *The New Encyclopedia Britannica, Macropedia, Knowledge in Depth.* 15th Edition, (Chicago: University of Chicago, 1986) Vol. 21, p. 361.
18. Bronowski, pp. 100-104. Also, *Mysteries of The Ancient Americas*, p. 31.

Chapter 8

PLAGIARISM FROM OTHER BOOKS

1. Ethan Smith, *View of the Hebrews* (Poultney, Vermont: Smith, 1825), pp. 2-46. This book will be referred to in the future as V. H.
2. V. H., pp. 48-49, 71-74, 79-81.
3. V. H., p. 56, P. of G. P., Joseph Smith 2:40.
4. V. H., pp. 78, 79, 152, 168, 169, 1 Nephi 18.
5. V. H., pp. 88, 152, 2 Nephi 5:21.

6. V. H., pp. 184, 195, 199, Mormon 6.
7. V. H., pp. 217-220, 223, Mormon 6, Moroni 10.
8. V. H., pp. 53, 2 Nephi 3:12, Ezekiel 37:15-17.
9. V. H., p. 184, Mormon 9:32.
10. V. H., pp. 150, 166, Origin of The Book of Mormon (part of the introduction of *The Book of Mormon*). This is called "Testimony of the Prophet Joseph Smith" in later editions.
11. V. H., pp. 125, 187, 204-206, 2 Nephi 5:10, 3 Nephi 11.
12. V. H., pp. 228, 229, 245, 256, 1 Nephi 13:37, 2 Nephi 6:12,13, 2 Nephi 10:13, 2 Nephi 27:3.
13. V. H., p. 256, p. 160, 2 Nephi 28:2, 2 Nephi 30:3-6, Alma 46:23-24.
14. V. H. pp. 189-191, Alma 48:8-10, Alma 50:1-6, Alma 55:25, 3 Nephi 3:14.
15. V. H., pp. 172, Jarom :8
16. V. H., p. 245.
17. Moroni 10:4.
18. V. H., pp. 217-223.
19. P. of G. P., Joseph Smith 2:63-65, H.C. 1:20, 2 Nephi 27:15-20.
20. Vernal Holley, *A Report on The Book of Mormon Spaulding Theory*, (Salt Lake City: Zenos publications, 1982), pp.1-12.
21. Marquardt, *The Use of the Bible in The Book of Mormon*, pp. 102-105.
22. Lucy Smith, *Biographical Sketches of Joseph Smith, The Prophet and His Progenitors For Many Generations*, (Liverpool: S. W. Richards, 1853), p. 54.
23. Lucy Smith, pp. 58-59.
24. 1 Nephi 8:4-33.

Chapter 9

THE MOST CORRECT BOOK ON EARTH

1. H. C. 4:461.
2. Mark Twain. *Roughing It*, (New York: Airmont Books, 1967), pp. 69-72.

3. Jerald Tanner, Sandra Tanner, *3913 Changes in The Book of Mormon,* (Salt Lake City: Utah Lighthouse Ministry, 1970).
4. Moroni 9:7-10.

Chapter 10

CREDIBILITY OF WITNESSES

1. H. C. 3:232.
2. H. C. 3:228.
3. H. C. 1:20, P. of G. P., Joseph Smith 2:63-65.
4. "Champollian, Jean-Francois," *Encyclopedia Americana,* Vol. 6, (Danbury, Connecticut: Grolier Inc., 1982), pp. 266-267. "Champollian, Jean-Francois," *Colliers Encyclopedia,* Vol. 5, (New York: Macmillan Educational Co., 1981), pp. 685-686. Also Fawn M. Brodie, *No Man Knows My History,* (New York: Alfred A. Knopf, 1976), p. 50.
5. Eber D. Howe, *Mormonism Unveiled,* pp. 270-272.
6. Isaiah 29:11-12, 14.
7. P.of G. P., Joseph Smith 2:63-65.
8. H. C. 3:16.

Chapter 11

REASON VS. TESTIMONY

1. Moroni 10:4.
2. B.H. Roberts, *Studies of The Book of Mormon,* (Chicago: University of Illinois Press, 1985),pp. 21-23.
3. 1 Nephi 17:36-37, 1 Nephi 22:16, 2 Nephi 4:4, Jarom :9, Omni :6, Mosiah 1:7, Mosiah 2:41, Alma 9:13.
4. 2 Nephi 9:30, Mosiah 4:16-23, Mosiah 18:7-10, Alma 1:26-30, Alma 34:27-29, Moroni 7:41-48.
5. 1 Nephi 1:5-15, 20.
6. 1 Nephi 8:2.
7. 1 Nephi 5:2-3, 1 Nephi 16:37-38.
8. 1 Nephi 16:10, Ether 3:3-6, Ether 6:2-3, Alma 18:40-43, Alma 19:1-36, Alma 22:17-23, Mosiah 5:1-5, 3 Nephi 28:19-22.

9. 1 Nephi 11:1-34, 2 Nephi 25:11-19.
10. 3 Nephi Chapters 11-28.
11. 1 Nephi 13:1-29.
12. 1 Nephi 2:20, 2 Nephi 1:5-6.
13. 1 Nephi 13:13-15,34.
14. 2 Nephi 30:3-6.
15. 2 Nephi 5:21, 1 Nephi 12:23.
16. Helaman 6:20-30, Ether 8:13-26.
17. Moroni 10:4.
18. Adolf Hitler, *The Twisted Cross*, (A classic McGraw-Hill W.W. II film).
19. Adolf Hitler, *The Twisted Cross.*

Chapter 12

SOCIAL PATHOLOGY

1. P. of G. P., Joseph Smith 2:19.
2. Juanita Brooks, *Quicksand And Cactus*, (Salt Lake City: Howe Brothers, 1984), pp. 161-169.
3. Eric Fromm, *Beyond The Chains of Illusion*, (New York:Simon & Schuster, Inc., 1962), pp. 126-127.
4. H. C. 5:23.
5. Matthew 9:12.
6. Eric Fromm, *Escape From Freedom*, (New York: Avon Books, 1965), pp. 208-209.
7. George Seldes, *The Great Quotations*, (New York: Pocket Books, 1972), p. 523.
8. Seldes, *The Great Quotations*, p. 589.
9. Bronowski, *The Assent of man*, pp. 367-374.
10. Seldes, *The Great Quotations*, pp. 657-658.
11. Fromm, *Escape From Freedom*, pp. 210-212.
12. Fromm, *Beyond The Chains of Illusion*, p. 100.
13. J.D. 1:83, J.D. 4:165, D. & C. 104:5.
14. Matthew 10:35-37.

Chapter 13

A LEGACY OF DECEPTION

1. D. Michael Quinn, *Early Mormonism and the Magic World View*, (Salt Lake City: Signature Books, 1987), pp. 25-52. Also, see Brodie, *No Man Knows_My History*, pp. 16-20.
2. Persuitte, *Joseph Smith and The Origins of The Book of Mormon*, pp. 42-55. Also, see Brodie, *No Man Knows My History*, pp. 16, 491. Also, see John Phillip Walker, Editor, *Dale Morgan on Early Mormonism*, (Salt Lake City: Signature Books, 1986), pp. 326-327.
3. Persuitte, *Joseph Smith and The Origins of The Book of Mormon*, pp. 42-55.
4. Helaman, 13:33-37.
5. Marvin S. Hill, *Quest For Refuge*, (Salt Lake City: Signature Books, 1989), p. 12.
6. Rodger I. Anderson, *Joseph Smith's New York Reputation Re-examined*, (Salt Lake City: Signature Books, 1990), pp. 57, 126-129,149. Also, Newell and Avery, *Mormon Enigma*, pp. 20, 24.
7. Anderson, *Joseph Smith's New York Reputation Re-examined*, pp. 57, 126-129, 149. Also, Newell and Avery, *Mormon Enigma*, pp. 20, 24.
8. D. & C. Section 20.
9. Orson F. Whitney, *Life of Heber C. Kimball*, (Salt Lake City: Bookcraft, 1888), pp. 323-327. Also, Newell and Avery, *Mormon Enigma*, pp. 125, 146-147.
10. Illinois State Laws, 1833, (Sections 121 and 122).
11. C. H. C., II:103.
12. John A. Widtsoe, *Evidences and Reconciliations*, (Salt Lake City: Bookcraft, 1943), p.213.
13. I Thessalonians 5:22.
14. C. H. C. I:431-432, H. C. 6:411, H. C. 3:16.
15. Titus 1:2, 2 Nephi 2:18.
16. *Elders Journal*, Vol. I No. 2, p. 28. Also H. C. 3:28.
17. Parley P. Pratt, *Millennial Star*, August 1842.
18. C. H. C. Vol. II:100-102.
19. H. C. 6:411.
20. H. C. 6:448-449.
21. John Taylor, *Times and Season*, May 1, 1845.

22. Kate B. Carter, *Brigham Young, His Wives and Family*, (Salt Lake City: Daughters of The Utah Pioneers, 1967), pp.11-12.
23. C. H. C. II:103. Also, J. D. 23:131.
24. J. D. 2:83.
25. C. H. C. VI:400.
26. H. C. 7:611-615. Also, see C.H.C. III pp. 67-84.
27. J. D. 5:231-232.
28. J. D. 8:335-336.
29. P. of G. P., The Articles of Faith, #13.
30. 2 Nephi 2:18, P.of G.P. Moses 4:4, 2 Nephi 9:34.

Chapter 14

THE OUTLAWS

1. P. of G. P., The Articles of Faith, #12.
2. Walker, *Dale Morgan on Early Mormonism*, pp. 326-327, Persuitte, *Joseph_Smith and The Origins of The Book of Mormon*, pp. 47-55.
3. D. & C. 103:15.
4. H. C. 2:467-473.
5. H. C. 3:1-2.
6. H. C. 3:108.
7. Hill, *Quest for Refuge*, pp. 75.
8. Hill, *Quest for Refuge*, pp. 77.
9. J. D. 6:125-126.
10. Hill, *Quest for Refuge*, P. 77
11. Hill, *Quest for Refuge*, pp. 80-81.
12. H. C. 3:209.
13. H. C. 3:167-168.
14. H. C. 3:327.
15. Hill, *Quest for Refuge*, p. 80.
16. H. C. 6:288-289.
17. H. C. 5:526.
18. Whitney, *Life of Heber C. Kimball*, pp. 323-324.
19. H. C. 6:408-409.
20. H. C. 5:3.
21. H. C. 5:363.
22. H. C. 6:277, 282.
23. H. C. 6:335-340.

24. H. C. 6:105, 124.
25. J. D. 1:187-188.
26. J. D. 2:13.
27. J. D. 5:187.
28. J. D. 5:266. Also, J. D. 7:292.
29. J. D. 9:37.
30. H. C. 4:483-484. Also, Wilford Woodruff, *Proclamation of the Twelve Apostles of The Church of Jesus Christ of Latter-Day Saints to All the Kings of The World, To The President of The United States of America; To The Governors of The Several States, And to The Rulers And People of All Nations,* (Liverpool: Church of Jesus Christ of Latter-Day Saints, 1945), pp. 1-16. Also, see Samuel W. Taylor, *The Kingdom of God or Nothing,* New York: Macmillan Publishing Company Inc., 1976), p. 39.
31. Juanita Brooks, *John D. Lee,* (Glendale, California: The Arthur H. Clark Company, 1973), pp.215,339. Also, Anna Jean Backus, *Mountain Meadows_Witness,* (Spokane, Washington: The Arthur H. Clark Company, 1996), pp.139-144.
32. Brooks, *John D. Lee,* p.372.
33. Brooks, *John D. Lee,* pp.372-376.
34. Robert Kent Fielding, *The Unsolicited Chronicler, An Account of The Gunnison Massacre, Its Causes and Consequences,* (Brookline Massachusetts, 1993), p.170.
35. Harold Schindler, *Orrin Porter Rockwell, Man of God, Son of Thunder.* Also, C.H.C. Vol. IV, p.176.
36. Harold Schindler, *Orrin Porter Rockwell, Man of God, Son of Thunder.* Also, see Charles Kelley and Hoffman Birney, *Holy Murder, The Story of Porter Rockwell,* (New York, Minton, Balch & Company 1934). Also, see William A. Hickman, *Brigham's Destroying Angel, Being The Life, Confession, and_Startling Disclosures of The Notorious Bill Hickman, The Danite Chief of Utah,* edited by J.H. Beadle, (New York, 1872).
37. C. H. C., Vol. IV, pp.273-287.
38. C. H. C., Vol. IV, pp.292-3.
39. J. D. Vol. 5, pp.132-136,226, J. D. Vol. 6, p.18, J. D. Vol. 9, p.42.
40. C. H. C. Vol. IV, pp.425-428.
41. Backus, *Mountain Meadows Witness,* p. 98.
42. C. H. C. Vol. V, p.7.
43. C. H. C. Vol. V, pp. 469-474.

44. C. H. C. Vol. VI, pp. 41-45.
45. C. H. C. Vol. VI, pp. 147-8, 193-4, 196-7.
46. D. & C. OFFICIAL DECLARATION, (D. & C. p. 256.)

CHAPTER 15

A LUST FOR POWER

1. P. of G. P., Moses 4:3.
2. D. & C., 121:36-39.
3. Orson F. Whitney, *Life of Heber C. Kimball*, pp. 323-324, Samuel W. Taylor, *The Kingdom or Nothing*, p. 88.
4. Juanita Brooks, *John D. Lee*, p. 274.
5. J. D. Vol. 2, p.8.
6. D.& C. 42:30-39, 49:20, 51:1-20, 70:7-14, 72:15. Also, J. D. 4:249-251.
7. Robert Kent Fielding, *An Unsolicited Chronicler*, p.56.
8. Robert Kent Fielding, *An Unsolicited Chronicler*, p.56.
9. J. D. 3:265.
10. J. D. 6:257.
11. Richard S. Van Wagoner, *Mormon Polygamy, A History*, (Salt Lake City: Signature Books, 1986), pp.42-43.
12. J. D. 6:154.
13. J. D. 3:242, J. D. 4:165:, J. D. 13:72.
14. D. & C., 104:5. Also, H. C. 3:167,180. Also, Elder David Whitmer, *An Address to All Believers in Christ*, Also, J. D. 1: 83,187.
15. Newell and Avery, *Mormon Enigma: Emma Hale Smith, Prophet's Wife, "Elect Lady," Polygamy's Foe*, p.101. Also, see C.H.C. II:101. Also, see Orson F. Whitney, *Life of Heber C. Kimball*, p.321.
16. Newell and Avery, *Mormon Enigma: Emma Hale Smith, Prophet's Wife, "Elect Lady," Polygamy's Foe*, p.146.
17. D. & C., 132:64.
18. H. C. 2:334-335,341-343.
19. H. C. 2:338.
20. H. C. 2:297.
21. H. C. 2:343.
22. H. C. 2:343.

23. H. C. 5:316.
24. H. C. 5:524.
25. H. C. 5:531.
26. H. C. 2:83, 6:238.
27. J. D. 8:317-318.
28. H. C. 5:466.
29. John C. Kunich, "Multiply Exceedingly: Book of Mormon Population Sizes", ed. Brent Lee Metcalf, *New Aproaches to The Book of Mormon* , (Salt Lake City: Signature Books, 1993), pp.231-265.
30. Ether 15:2, Also, see Mormon 6:8-15.

CHAPTER 16

MORMONISM VS. TRADITIONAL CHRISTIANITY

1. P. of G. P., Joseph Smith 2:19.
2. 1 Nephi, 14:10-17.
3. H. C. 6:302-317.
4. Isaiah 43:10-11.
5. Mosiah 15:1-4.
6. Alma 11: 28-29, 38-39.
7. J. D. 1:50-51.
8. Matthew 12:31-32.
9. Matthew 1:18-19.
10. D. & C., 76:84-89.
11. Ephesians 2:8-9.
12. Brodie, *No Man Knows My History*, pp.457-488. Also, Newell and Avery, *Mormon Enigma: Emma Hale Smith, Prophets Wife, "Elect Lady," Polygamy's_Foe*, pp.130-156. Also, see Brooks, *John D. Lee, Zealot, Pioneer Builder, Scapegoat*, p.378.
13. J. D. 9:37.
14. Dennis R. Short, *For Men Only*, (Salt Lake City: Dennis R. Short, 1957), p.85. This quotation is from a sermon given by Brigham Young on October 8, 1861.
15. J. D. 17:119.
16. H. C. 6:279-280.
17. Luke 20:34-35.
18. Matthew 22:23-30.

19. John 2:1-10.
20. Matthew 26:26-29.
21. Acts 2:13-16.
22. Timothy 5:23.
23. Matthew 23:23.
24. Luke 18:11-14.
25. Genesis 14:18-20.
26. Genesis 28:22.
27. John Heinerman, Anson Shupe, *The Mormon Corporate Empire*, (Boston: Beacon Press, 1985), pp.76-127.
28. H. C., 3:39.
29. H. C. 4:551-552, H. C. 5:1-2. Also, see Jerald and Sandra Tanner, *Evolution of The Temple Ceremony: 1842-1990*, (Salt Lake City: Utah Lighthouse Ministry, 1990). p.20.
30. *New Encyclopedia Britannica 15th Edition*, (Chicago: Encyclopedia Britannica, 1986), Vol. 4, p.966. Also see Steven Knight, *The Brotherhood, The Secret World of The Freemasons*, (U.S.A.: Dorset press, 1986), pp. 15-18.
31. Steven Knight, *The Brotherhood, The Secret World of The Freemasons*, p.16.
32. Steven Knight, *The Brotherhood, The Secret World of the Freemasons*, p.241.
33. Steven Knight, *The Brotherhood, The Secret World of The Freemasons*, p.241.
34. Matthew 26:51-52, also John 18:10-12.
35. Fawn M. Brodie, *No Man Knows My History*, p. 393, Also, Ernest H. Taves, *Trouble Enough*, pp.212-213.
36. Matthew 23: 2-3.
37. Matthew 5: 25-26.
38. Matthew 6:19-21.
39. Matthew 19:23, Matthew 6:24.
40. John Heinerman, Anson Shupe, *The Mormon Corporate Empire*, pp.76-127.
41. H. C. 6:408-409.
42. David Whitmer, *An Address to All Believers in Christ*, p.27, Marvin S. Hill, *Quest For Refuge*, pp. 75-77.
43. John 13:34-35.
44. Ann Eliza Young, *Wife No. 19*, (Hartford: Dustin, Gilman & Co., 1876), p.39.

45. Brigham D. Madsen, Sterling M. McMurrin, *Reply to John W. Welch and Truman G. Madsen*, (Salt Lake City: Brigham D. Madsen and Sterling M. McMurrin, 1986).

CHAPTER 17

NEW SCRIPTURES

1. P. of G. P. p.60. (Articles of Faith #8)
2. J. D. 13:95. Also, J. D. 13:264.
3. J. D. 5:99-100.

CHAPTER 18

OTHER DOUBTERS

1. H. C. 3:16.
2. H. C. 2:26.
3. H. C. 3:232.
4. D. & C. 20:1, H. C. 2:136,243. Also, see David Whitmer, *An Address to All Believers in Christ*, (Richmond Missouri, Elder David Whitmer, 1887), p.62. Also, D. & C. 115:3.
5. Whitmer, *An Address to All Believers in Christ*, p.37.
6. Whitmer, *An Address to All Believers in Christ*, p.35.
7. Whitmer, *An Address to All Believers in Christ*, pp.1-75.
8. Newell and Avery, *Mormon Enigma*, pp.151-4. Also, C.H.C. II: 107.
9. Newell and Avery, *Mormon Enigma*, pp.151-154.
10. C.H.C. II, 95-107.
11. Joseph Smith, *The Doctrine and Covenants*, Section 132. (This revelation was not added to this canon of L.D.S. scripture until 1876, one year before Brigham Young died.)
12. H. C. 4:248-9, 287,294, 309-10, 327, 341, Also, Brodie, *No Man Knows My History*, pp. 311-12.
13. John C. Bennett, *The History of The Saints or an Expose of Joe Smith* and *Mormonism*, (Boston, 1842), pp.387-392, Also see H. C. 5:364. Also, see Brodie, *No Man Knows My History*, p.312.

14. C.H.C. II:146-7. Also, see H. C. 5:22.
15. Brodie, *No Man Knows My History,* p.313. Also H. C. 5:18-21, 71.
16. H. C. 6:217, Also, see John Taylor, *Times and Seasons,* May 1, 1845, Also, C. H. C. II:104.
17. H. C. 6:432. Also, Brodie, *No Man Knows My History,* pp.370-380.
18. Brodie, *No Man Knows My History,* pp.370-380.
19. Newell and Avery, *Mormon Enigma,* pp. 281-285.
20. Newell and Avery, *Mormon Enigma,* pp.119-120.
21. Anna Jean Backus, *Mountain Meadows Witness,* pp.98, 95, 78, 100, 101.
22. Anna Jean Backus, *Mountain Meadows Witness,* pp.275-277, Also, pp. 147-8.
23. Anna Jean Backus, *Mountain Meadows Witness,* pp.118-119.
24. Anna Jean Backus, *Mountain Meadows Witness,* pp. 276-7.
25. Anna Jean Backus, *Mountain Meadows Witness,* p. 234.
26. Juanita Brooks, *John D. Lee,* p.221.
27. John Phillip Walker, *Dale Morgan on Early Mormonism,* (Salt Lake City, Signature Books, 1986), p. 80.
28. Jerald and Sandra Tanner, "Ferguson's Two Faces," *Salt Lake City Messenger, Utah Lighthouse Ministery,* September 1988, pp. 1-10. Also, see Stan Larson, *Quest for the Gold Plates: Thomas Stuart Ferguson's Archaeological Search for The Book of Mormon,* (Salt lake City, Freethinkers Press, 1996).
29. Jerald and Sandra Tanner, "Ferguson's Two Faces," p. 6.

EPILOGUE

1. I Corinthians 13:12.
2. Aldous Huxley, *Brave New World,* (New York: Harper and Row, 1969), p.99.
3. 1 Nephi 4:10-13.
4. John 8:32.

APPENDIX A

QUOTES FROM THE *NAUVOO EXPOSITOR*

(NO REFERENCES)

APPENDIX B

WHO HAS BEEN HURT BY MORMONISM?

1. Hymns, The Church of Jesus Christ of Latter-Day Saints, (Salt Lake City, Deseret Book Company, 1972), pp.13-14.
2. C.B.S. Evening News, "Unhappy in Utah," June 3, 2002.
3. C.B.S. Evening News, "Unhappy in Utah," June 3, 2002. Also, see K.S.L. Eyewitness News, June 9, 2000.
4. *Salt Lake Tribune* , January 11, 1990, p. 1-E. Also, see Associated Press, *The Spectrum* , August 25, 2002, p. A3. Also, see Associated Press, *The Spectrum*, September 10, 2002, p.6.
5. *Salt Lake Tribune* , January 11, 1990, p. 1-E.

APPENDIX C

OUR CAST OF CHARACTERS

1. Newell and Avery, *Mormon Enigma*, pp. 281 - 303.
2. Newell and Avery, *Mormon Enigma*, pp. 92, 111,112. Also, see D. Michael Quinn, *Origins of Power*, (Salt Lake City: Signature Books, 1994), pp. 536 - 538.
3. D. Michael Quinn, *Origins of Power*, pp. 571-573.
4. D. Michael Quinn, *Origins Of Power, pp. 569-570.*
5. Harold Schindler, *Orrin Porter Rockwell, Man of God Son of Thunder*, (Salt Lake City: University of Utah Press, 1966), p.9.
6. Samuel W. Taylor, *The Kingdom or Nothing*, (New York: Macmillan Publishing Co., Inc., 1976).
7. Ann Eliza Young, *Wife No.19, or The Story of a Life in Bondage, Being a Complete Expose of Mormonism, and Revealing The Sorrows, Sacrifices and Sufferings of Women in Polygamy*, (Hartford, Connecticut: Dustin, Gilman, and Co., 1876). Also, see Irving Wallace, *The Twenty-Seventh Wife*, (New York, Simon and Schuster, 1961).

INDEX

INDEX

A

B

C

D

E

F

I

J

K

L

M

N

O

P

R

S

U

V

W

Y

Z